The Politics of Environmental Concern

Walter A. Rosenbaum

PRAEGER PUBLISHERS
New York • Washington • London

6 00 163822 4
TELEPEN

The Politics of Environmental Concern

ic

PRAEGER PUBLISHERS
111 Fourth Avenue, New York, N.Y. 10003, U.S.A.
5, Cromwell Place, London SW7 2JL, England

Published in the United States of America in 1973
by Praeger Publishers, Inc.

Library of Congress Cataloging in Publication Data

Rosenbaum, Walter A
The politics of environmental concern.

Bibliography
1. Environmental policy—United States. 2. Environmental protection—United States. 3. Industry and state—United States. I. Title.
HC110.E5R67 301.31'0973 72-83007

Printed in the United States of America

For Jean

Contents

The Politics of Environmental Concern

1 *The New Environmental Politics*

The patron saint of Birmingham is not Robert E. Lee, as one might suppose, but Vulcan. Atop Red Mountain overlooking the city, the community has erected a 55-foot-high cast iron statue of the Roman god in a smithy's apron, a lofty reminder that for more than a century, since Birmingham fashioned the Confederacy's weapons, steel has been the sinew of the local economy. At night, according to a tourist guide, the steel industry illuminates the city: "Birmingham at night is a startlingly beautiful sight, a city punctuated by the rise and fall of flames from the many steel furnaces." Though tourist literature may rhapsodize about the nocturnal delights of the city's furnaces, they are often invisible by day, for a thick blanket of smog frequently envelops the area, the residue of 25,000 tons of waste poured into the atmosphere yearly by the city's mills. Still, over the years few complained because Vulcan was benevolent; the incessant furnaces fired a vigorous economy, and air pollution was the price of economic security.

Then something happened.[1] Early in the week of November 14, 1971, the U.S. Weather Bureau warned that a huge mass of stagnant air had settled over many eastern states, reaching from Massachusetts southwestward through New York, Pennsylvania, West Virginia, and Tennessee, then cutting sharply southward into parts of Georgia and Alabama. The air hung like a dead weight over such industrial centers as Pittsburgh, New York, Charleston, and Birmingham. No longer ambient, without strong winds to carry the waste away, it was heavily fouled, increasing in pollutants and potential toxicity. On Monday, November 15, the National Weather Service in Birmingham issued its first air stagnation alert. The air pollution index, a measure of the suspended particulate matter in the city's atmosphere, was approaching 700 micrograms per cubic meter of air (ug/m^3)—the federal government considered 260 ug/m^3 the maximum safe level. Only the extremely high level of suspended particulates was a novelty; air pollution had been common for decades. Although federal experts believe that the particulate concentration in cities should not exceed 260 ug/m^3 more than once a year, the *average* mean daily pollution count in Birmingham had been 275 during the previous year. In heavily industrialized North Birmingham, the air was technically "unsafe" almost every day; throughout the metropolitan area, the airborne particulates had exceeded safe margins during sixty-seven days in 1970. But the situation on Monday, November 15, was ominous. As the day progressed, the particulate count climbed above 700, and the effect, more than dangerous, might be lethal if the rise continued. As the level approached 1,000, warned a federal environmental official, "you might start finding bodies in the street."

The next day, Tuesday, November 16, the particulate count climbed to 771 ug/m^3, close to the level considered a disaster by federal officials. On Wednesday the particulate count still remained at a threatening 758 ug/m^3. The air was now stinging, inert, and hazardous; public officials acted. The director of the Jefferson County Health Department sent an urgent telegram to twenty-three major industries in the city urging them to curtail 60 per cent of their production in the hope that smoke emissions would be drastically abated. Five of the major polluters, including giant U.S. Steel, took no significant action. "No action was required, none was volunteered," commented a company official. Now convinced that an environmental disaster might be impending and angered by the intransigence of U.S. Steel, the director of the County Health Department appealed directly to Washington. Would the Environmental Protection Agency obtain an immediate court injunction halting further production in twenty-three major Birmingham industries—including U.S. Steel—until the emergency had passed? The Environmental Protection Agency acted immediately. Armed with new emergency powers from the recently enacted Clean Air Amendments of 1970, the agency aroused U.S. District Court Judge Sam C. Pointer from his sleep in Birmingham early Thursday morning and obtained a temporary injunction halting further production in the twenty-three Birmingham firms, the first injunction obtained under the new law. The spur to this unusually vigorous demonstration of federal muscle had clearly been U.S. Steel. "U.S. Steel did nothing," declared one federal official, "although they have the major plants involved and contribute 35 per cent of the particulate emissions."

For most of Birmingham's residents, November 17 must have been remarkable. For the first time within memory, the stacks of the city's mammoth steel complex belched no smoke skyward. U.S. Steel had banked its open hearth furnaces to only 35 per cent operating capacity, barely enough to prevent their shutdown. More than five thousand workers at U.S. Steel had been temporarily "furloughed" without pay and thousands more were idled elsewhere; if the injunction continued, many more would be home. But in the afternoon, the particulate count was down to 410, still above the 375 level customary for a pollution alert, yet apparently decreasing.

Then the crisis disappeared. On Friday, November 18, a brisk west wind accompanied by a cold drizzle rapidly blew the stagnant air from the city. The particulate count dropped to only 41, convincing federal officials that the emergency had passed; federal attorneys now confronted Judge Pointer with a request, quickly granted, to lift the injunction and permit the companies to resume operation. By evening, Birmingham's furnaces were again incandescent for the pleasure of tourists and the profit of the community.

The confrontation between steel and the federal government, short and virtually bloodless, left bitterness and recrimination. Steel spokesmen charged that public officials had been irresponsible in seeking the injunction and protested that the company had been made unfairly the villain in the incident. Some participants saw the incident differently, as an overdue lesson to Birmingham's industrial giants. A community activist predicted that the incident ended an era of industrial supremacy in local politics. "There was a time, until very recently, that industry could do as it pleased in Birmingham," he asserted. "Laws were written by industry. . . . We've been one of the last holdouts in the pollution fight, but now the message is going out that if industry wants to come to Alabama, we want them to be responsible citizens who can't pollute at will." Some citizens, apparently, were awakened to the seriousness of the city's air pollution problems. "As far as I'm concerned," said one local union leader, "if they have to shut this whole damned town down to clean it up, that's o.k. with me."

Despite all the drama, very little was accomplished in Birmingham. The city had survived one environmental crisis without solving a single major environmental problem. The mills rolled again, the familiar dull gray smoke returned to its accustomed habitat, and it was clear that a west wind and steady rain had spared the city the painful, difficult political complications that might have followed. Could the government have maintained its injunction in the face of a legal challenge from steel, and for how long? If smoke emission controls were necessary, would they, and could they, be enforced with the primitive available technology and the industry's influence in the community? Would steel voluntarily spend the $12 million it had promised for air emission controls to prevent future crises? Steel officials did not seem seized by contrition or spurred into action by the events, and the public's momentary apprehension about air pollution faded so quickly it seemed unlikely to spur environmental improvement.

Nonetheless, Birmingham was a singular event—not because U.S. Steel had been chastened by Washington's action but because such a direct public confrontation between industry and federal officials had occurred at all. Never before had Washington exercised emergency powers to order a total, immediate cessation of production within a major industrial complex in the name of pollution control. Such an event would have been impossible a few years ago and unthinkable earlier. When Richard Nixon took office, Washington possessed no such power and no Environmental Protection Agency to enforce it. Air pollution emergencies had occurred for decades prior to Birmingham's; the Donora, Pennsylvania, disaster of 1948 claimed forty lives, and residents of Los Angeles, Pittsburgh, and New York know smog alerts as a way of life. Still, the public seemed largely indifferent to the problem, and public officials, while admitting the problem's existence, were unable or unwilling to do much about it. In short, air pollution had not been a major political issue. But the events in Birmingham testify to the fact that times have changed.

The Environmental Decade

Birmingham marks the advent of the Environmental Era in American politics. Historians may prefer to mark the event by other episodes—there have been many—but Birmingham serves nicely. It is the most dramatic example to date of the awakened governmental concern with environmental pollution. It reveals the collision between public officials and private business that permeates most environmental issues. It had the suddenness and surprise that often accompanies the beginning of a new policy era.

Concern for environmental degradation is that rare political phenomenon, a genuinely new issue in American civic life. America has experienced two other periods of heightened governmental concern with ecological issues—the "conservation" years of the two Roosevelts—but neither era approached the current one in the breadth of environmental concern, sense of urgency, and mobilization of private and public resources involved. Nixon's publicists, anxious to advance the President's environmental legislation, began speaking of the 1970's as the environmental decade. Unlike many political clichés, this seems accurate.

Governmental Involvement. One hallmark of this era is the increasing involvement of government at all levels in environmental protection, especially the massive involvement of the federal government. The environmental issue is now thoroughly politicized. Ecological considerations are currently injected into debates over almost all public policies; a growing number of groups have mobilized and devote themselves largely to environmental protection through the governmental process, while public bodies almost routinely place ecological issues on their agendas for consideration. At local levels, for example, zoning policy has been given an added dimension by groups and individuals battling over the impact of zoning practices on "the ecology"; high-rise buildings, shopping centers, high-density housing, uncontrolled road construction, and careless land clearing outrage the sensibilities of many ecologists. State officials unaccustomed to public interest in the administration of state land have been confronted with mobilized, newly potent conservation groups demanding (and sometimes presenting) schemes to ensure greater protection of public land from lumber, petroleum, and grazing interests. Few policy matters before governmental bodies now seem immune from the searching attention of militant environmentalists. The scope of issues they now consider within the ambit of "ecology" can be gauged from a recent manual by Environmental Action, a national environmental pressure group. "Virtually every aspect of our modern existence inflicts severe environmental damage in one form or another," it warns, but the "battle fronts" where political action is most imperative include, at a minimum, highways, automobiles, airports, factories, waste treatment facilities, solid wastes, power generation, mining, oil pollution, noise, open space, and population."[2] As this list suggests, environmentalists have often stretched the meaning of "ecology" to embrace an enormous range of social problems; other environmentalists would prefer a less ambitious list. Yet this itinerary indicates how environmental considerations can be, and have been, superimposed upon an enormous number of public issues.

The federal government's growing involvement in environmental problems seems irreversible. In February, 1970, President Nixon delivered the first Message on the Environment ever presented to the Congress. Responding to growing national concern with environmental problems, Congress has since required that the President deliver such a message annually; it ranks with the State of the Union address and the National Economic Message as one of three addresses the Chief Executive is legally required to present the country.[3] As Washington has asserted more initiative in defining and resolving environmental issues, the environmental conflict has become national in its political scope and impact. In the year between the first environmental message and Birmingham, for example, federal officials made a number of unusual decisions indicating that ecology had major status on their policy agenda. Early in 1971, the Senate turned its back on a federal investment of $864 million, the pleas of the aircraft industry, and ten years of research by refusing to appropriate further funds for the mammoth Supersonic Transport (SST), thus grounding it permanently. Despite Presidential pressure, a threat of twenty-five thousand lay-offs among aircraft workers, and warnings of disaster for American technology if foreign interests were permitted to perfect the aircraft, opponents of the plan finally defeated it because, among other reasons, it might have dangerous environmental consequences. It was "Year One on the ecological calendar," exclaimed a jubilant senatorial foe of the plane.[4] A few weeks earlier, President Nixon, in an unprecedented move, halted construction of the Cross Florida Barge Canal in which the federal government had already invested $50 million. Citing the possibility of irreversible damage from the canal as his reason, the President made it the first federal public works project ever halted in peacetime specifically because of its environmental impact; in doing this, he also inflicted upon its builders, the politically powerful Army Corps of Engineers, a unique, totally unexpected defeat.[5] At the moment, the Alaskan North Slope reserves, one of the largest oil deposits ever discovered in the United States, lie untapped because oil companies have been restrained for more than four years by federal policy.[6] In 1970, the federal courts suspended construction of an eight-hundred-mile pipeline from oil fields on Alaska's North Slope at Prudhoe to the port of Valdez on the Gulf of Alaska while federal officials, oil interests, and conservationists attempted to determine the line's environmental impact; when the Secretary of the Interior finally approved the project in early 1972, environmentalists again obstructed it by initiating a series of court challenges based, ironically, upon federal legislation designed to protect the environment from ecologically damaging decisions by Washington officials. On a less elevated level, Washington has something for the children. The Forest Service's famous Smokey the Bear was joined in 1971 by Woodsey the Owl, who advises "Give a Hoot—Don't Pollute!"[7]

This environmental sensitivity is rather sudden; like their state and local counterparts, federal officials were slow to recognize most environmental problems and approached the few they did notice at a glacial pace. As early as 1912, for example, the International Joint Commission had warned Washington that pollution in the Great Lakes was "generally chaotic, everywhere perilous and in some cases disgraceful"; since then Lake Erie has become a "dead lake" ecologically, and a joint federal-state effort is only now underway to save endangered Lake Michigan from a similar fate.[8] The Donora air pollution disaster occurred in 1948 but it was 1955 before Congress passed the first, modest air pollution legislation; at the time there were no viable state programs at all. The first temporary water pollution control legislation was enacted by Congress in 1948; permanent measures came about in 1956. As late as 1964, the Democratic Party's platform gave slight attention to the environment and then spoke primarily of conserving natural resources and expanding recreational facilities; the Republican platform was silent about the environment.[9]

An interest in land and resource use came only slightly earlier and very unevenly to federal officials. Before 1900 the U.S. Government asserted little effective control over public lands and their resources; on the contrary, it handed over huge portions of the public domain with all its richly varied resources to a variety of private interests, usually through the principle of "preemption," which was written into a variety of federal statutes.[10] During the latter part of the nineteenth century, in addition, Congress bequeathed great swaths of public land to the railroads to encourage their expansion. During Lincoln's administration alone, more than 75 million acres of public land were disposed in this manner; before the giveaway ended, 180 million acres, an area larger than France, England, Scotland, and Wales, were devoured by railroad interests.[11] Despite a vigorous reform effort under Theodore Roosevelt (who coined and popularized the term "conservation"), the federal government continued to permit oil, timber, cattle, and mining interests to use federal reserves with little supervision, and, while outright resource giveaways were sharply abated, major private resource users still found that they could do business with Washington—legally and occasionally illicitly. (The Teapot Dome Scandal that fouled Warren Harding's reputation involved the selling of oil leases on federal reserves in return for bribes to major administration officials.) While the two Roosevelts were successful in getting more than 150 million acres of national land set aside for national parks and forests, Congress was a fitful and balky partner in the enterprise. "Uncle Joe" Cannon, the legendary Speaker of the House, had fought Theodore Roosevelt and William Howard Taft on every major Presidential effort to set aside public land for national parks with the battlecry "Not one cent for scenery"; this indifference to governmental stewardship of resources, coupled with an indulgence of their private use, was the dominant Congressional mood until recently.

A very useful measure of Washington's policy priorities is the federal budget. In 1955, environmental programs represented a minuscule portion of the federal budget—about 3 per cent including virtually nothing for pollution abatement. By the early 1970's, environmental programs had risen to only 5 per cent in appropriations; this still represented a very small portion of national spending and, by implication, a rather low national priority. Roughly, while the United States was spending 5 cents of every tax dollar in 1972 to finance pollution abatement, wilderness preservation, and water resource development, it was spending by comparison 32 cents for defense, 5 cents for veterans' benefits, and 8 cents for health, labor, and welfare matters. Thus, while environmental policy occupies a slightly greater portion of the national budget than previously, it is still far from a major national priority.

Although the federal interest in environmental protection developed tardily and conservatively, it seems somewhat enlightened when compared to the record of the states. Generally, the states have followed, rather than anticipated, federal environmental programs; environmental protection at the state level, consequently, was until recently very meager. Virtually no significant air or water pollution legislation existed in the states prior to 1960—in most, none at all. Between 1951 and 1962, only eleven states had any law relating to air pollution on their statute books; since then, thirty-six have added some form of air pollution control. Prior to 1966, only thirteen states had made any serious effort to regulate the emission of air pollutants within their boundaries, and, even more significantly, only a handful had begun to tackle the most essential problems, such as the regulation of sulfur oxide emissions and the establishment of ambient air standards. With the exception of some state regulation and support of municipal sewage treatment facilities, the situation in water pollution control until the late 1960's was equally void of incisive state action.

State stewardship of land and resources was somewhat better than pollution control, but land and resource management has only recently become a major preoccupation in most statehouses. More than 6 million acres of land had been set aside by the states for parks and recreational facilities by 1960, but millions of acres of public lands had been, or were being, surrendered to private interests. The states had been enthusiastic participants in the land giveaways throughout the nineteenth century. Maine and Pennsylvania sold enormous tracts for 12 cents an acre to the railroads and other commercial enterprises, while North Carolina auctioned hardwood stands to timbermen for 10 cents an acre. Such unbridled generosity gradually diminished, but the states, until very recently, did relatively little to prevent the transformation of open land, public and private, into commercial use. In recent years, rural land has been converted into urban developments, highways, airports, and other projects at a rate approaching 1 million acres a year. Wetlands—beaches, estuaries, tidal flats, lagoons, and the like—have been under equally intense pressure. Through dredging, filling, and other practices, the total wetlands once available in the United States, about 127 million acres, have been diminished to about 70 million acres—a 60 per cent decrease. Of the 3,700 miles of shoreline on the Atlantic and Gulf coasts, only 105 miles (or about 3 per cent) were available for public use in 1965. As will be noted later, a major effort among the states began only in the late 1960's to protect public lands and to regulate the use of natural resources in the interest of the environment.

The Public and Ecology. Public officials are both creators and instruments of public opinion; although at times they mold public sensibilities, at other times public officials must work within existing opinion climates that often shape their definition of policy priorities, set limits upon the actions they can take and the pace at which they must proceed in dealing with issues. All opinion studies indicate a recent, rising national consciousness of environmental problems; this can be attributed partially to the education of public thinking by ecologists and public officials proclaiming the need for environmental protection and partially to growing evidence of environmental degradation itself. In any case, environmental awareness has been a cue to public officials, goading them—sometimes reluctantly—into concern for ecology. So sudden has this surge of public interest appeared that some observers considered it a fad that would soon spend itself, and with its demise would go, as well, the sense of official urgency with environmental matters. Regardless of the long-range consequences, the dramatic rise of ecology in public awareness is extraordinary. Remarked one normally cautious observer, "Not since the Japanese attack on Pearl Harbor has any public issue received such massive support in all the news media, local as well as national."[12]

There were indications, large and small, that many public and private institutions had developed a new environmental consciousness. The Boy Scouts, anxious to be relevant as well as prepared, initiated Project SOAR (Save Our American Resources) in their national program. The Student Senate of the University of Texas at Austin passed a resolution changing the school mascot from the Long Horn to the armadillo, "a peaceful and ecologically minded animal," while puzzled school officials pondered if such could be done. There are ecology games. A soft drink manufacturer, having donated a new pollution control game to several grade schools, was avalanched by requests for additional copies; an innovative manufacturer of adult games offers two, "Smog" and "Dirty Water," for the older set. Several state universities established ecology majors, and one devoted its entire academic program to the topic. Older ecology journals prospered while new ones, like *Ecology* and *Environmental Quality Magazine,* made firm starts. Business, quick to propel the ship of its fortune on a strong breeze of opinion, rapidly acquired an environmental voice. Cleaning dirty rugs was now "fighting rug pollution." A major city bank bought a full page of the *New York Times* to assure readers that it was helping to clean up pollution; eight of the nation's largest corporations produced an expensive twenty-three-page insert in the country's largest circulation periodical to answer the title-page question: "What Are We Doing About Our Environment?"

Public apprehension about pollution was reflected, and stimulated, by dramatization and discussion in the media. A recent

TABLE 1
"Which three of these problems would you like to see government devote most of its attention to in the next two years?"

	Percentage of Public Mentioning Item		Five-Year Change
	1970	1965	
Reducing amount of crime	56	41	15%
Reducing pollution of air and water	53	17	36
Improving public education	31	45	—14
Helping people in poor areas	30	32	—2
Conquering "killer" diseases	29	37	—8
Improving housing, clearing slums	27	21	6
Reducing racial discrimination	25	29	—4
Reducing unemployment	25	35	—10
Improving highway safety	13	18	—5
Beautifying America	5	3	2

SOURCE: Gallup Poll *Index,* June, 1970, p. 8.

survey of editorials in five leading American newspapers over a twelve-month period revealed that environmental problems (principally pollution) were the major domestic issue of editorial concern. Articles on pollution in the *New York Times* doubled between 1965 and 1966 and continued to increase in every subsequent year.

How deep and durable is the public concern? Will it weather the test of time, withstanding the hard choices with which the public might be faced if genuine environmental protection is to be a reality? Let us consider the evidence of the public opinion polls. It is clear that the take-off period for major public interest in ecology was the era of 1965–70.[13] In Table 1 is a comparison of public responses to a question dealing with the domestic matters that ought to concern government as the public rated the issues from a list given to the respondents in 1970. A major leap in environmental concern is indicated during these years. Pollution control advanced from a modest position in 1965 (when 17 per cent of the sample mentioned it) to major interest in 1970 (when more than half the sample noted it); this was the largest advance in public attention among all issues listed. Public apprehension about pollution seems to have remained pervasive. In findings typical of later polls, two studies of respondents in Illinois and North Carolina revealed widespread concern: 90 per cent of the Illinois sample and 74 per cent of the North Carolina groups considered air and water pollution to be major national problems.[14]

This surge of pollution consciousness, however, projected a somewhat illusory image of massive public preoccupation and commitment to environmental restoration. It was difficult to estimate how much of this concern was genuine and durable. There is considerable evidence that ecology was far from dominating public interest, that the public was vacillating and uninformed on environmental matters. Polls indicated that the public's concern for the environment was generally confined to pollution and did not commonly embrace numerous other environmental issues that experts consider serious, such as solid waste management, noise control, better land management and control of open space and resources (note the low importance attached to beautifying the land in Table 1). Pollution was far from the most important social issue to most Americans. Each year for the past decade, the Gallup Poll has asked Americans to volunteer a list of the major problems facing the nation. With but minor variation, six issues were shown to dominate public consciousness: Vietnam, race relations, crime, the cost of living, violence, and poverty. The best showing made by an environmental issue on this spontaneous list was a ninth place in 1970, when pollution was mentioned by a scant 4 per cent of the sample.[15]

Americans appeared to shrink from the necessary financial sacrifices that might be required for environmental protection. Although polls in the early 1970's indicated that a majority of Americans believed the government was not spending enough on pollution abatement and other environmental programs, they did not seem very inclined to allot even small amounts for environmental protection themselves. In 1969, for example, almost two-thirds of a sample public told the Opinion Research Corporation that they would not spend one hundred dollars a year in taxes to control water and air pollution; the Gallup organization that year finally found a majority in favor of increased pollution taxes —if the increase did not exceed ten dollars annually. Even in 1971, with the environmental movement well underway, almost 40 per cent of one national poll indicated it was willing to spend "nothing" to banish air pollution.[16] This apparent public reluctance to make sacrifices for environmental protection is particularly notable because the questions asked generally concerned air and water pollution, which most people consider the most pressing environmental issue. This does not mean that the public's concern with ecology was necessarily unproductive. Citizen concern created favorable climates of opinion for state and local bond issues to finance pollution control facilities: In 1970, voters approved five such state issues for more than $1 billion total and accepted 90 per cent of local sewage treatment bonds compared with only 60 per cent of other bond issues nationally.

These vagaries in public attitudes mean that, despite the indisputable rise of public awareness, pollution control and other ecology programs are still second-order issues when compared to public interest in Vietnam, the economy, crime, and other matters commonly in the news. This implies that conservation can rather easily be displaced as a major public concern by many other matters and that environmental programs might suffer sagging public support if they had to compete with other policies for massive funding. The extent of long-range public pressure for effective governmental protection of the environment is an open-ended question. Public interest has now persisted too long to be dismissed as a fad, and major public and private programs now assure some continuing official concern for ecology. Yet the scope and pace of this attack on environmental degradation is still susceptible to opinion climates. It would be mistaken to reason that the public's new awareness will necessarily produce a continuing, incisive, and effective governmental attack upon environmental degradation, especially when the costs, direct and indirect, become more tangible.

Business and Ecology. Concurrently with governmental and public interest in environmental protection, business has become deeply anxious to demonstrate an ecological conscience. In many cases, unfortunately, this became a demonstration of bad faith when numerous corporations congratulated themselves through the media for accomplishments quite unsupported by deeds. Nevertheless, corporations have begun to invest substantial capital in environmental protection and to show the stirring of environmental sensibilities.

Opinion studies among business leaders indicate growing recognition of environmental problems and a professed willingness to revise production and profit priorities in the interest of ecology if necessary. *Fortune*'s 1970 survey of 500 top business executives found more than 80 per cent willing to restrain the introduction of new products, to forego increased production, or to reduce profits if doing so might contribute to environmental protection.[17] A later *Wall Street Journal* survey shows that almost half the nation's major corporations are now involved in environmental protection programs and that almost three-fourths of these companies' executives expected their company expenditures for environmental protection to increase substantially in the next few years. There was, additionally, considerable support for governmental pollution controls, for ecology groups, and for other things associated with good environmental usage.[18]

It is difficult to determine the sincerity or effectiveness of these expressions of concern, but American business, in any case, is progressing toward a major investment of capital, research, and technology in environmental control—whether spontaneously or with governmental prompting. The private sector of the economy must bear a major portion of the anticipated expense for pollution control in the future; the Council on Environmental Quality estimates that between 1970 and 1975 business must make a minimum capital investment of $35 billion in air and water pollution control equipment.[19] Beginning in 1970 and continuing through 1971, American business, with a few exceptions, began to divert increasing capital toward research on pollution control techniques; the manufacturing industry increased its pollution control research expenditures by 12 per cent between 1970 and 1972, the nonmanufacturing companies by a healthy 127 per cent. Although industries such as iron and steel, chemicals, and textiles seemed slow to respond to the need for pollution control research, most major sectors of the economy were increasing their investments in pollution control between 1970 and 1972 from 25 to 35 per cent. Arguments continue over the capital that industry should invest in environmental protection, with critics charging that most major industries are slow and niggardly in their expenditures on pollution, for example. Many industries, however, were reporting a sizable investment in actual pollution control equipment. According to estimates by the Council on Environmental Quality, some of the heaviest industrial polluters were spending a significant amount of their total capital expenditures on such equipment: the iron and steel industry, 10.3 per cent of capital expenditures; nonferrous metals, 8.1 per cent of capital expenditures; and paper manufacturers, 9.3 per cent of capital investment. Other measures of business response to environmental problems yield conclusions similar to these opinion polls and investment profiles.

The Political Anatomy of Environmental Issues

Looking upon this cumulative evidence of governmental, public, and corporate involvement in ecology, it seems apparent that between 1960 and the early 1970's the nation made an extraordinary rapid transition, in terms of social awareness, from environmental indifference to environmental concern; during this transformation, "ecology" rose from virtual political invisibility to political salience. As a nation, we are now involved in the complex and critical business of establishing a national public policy on environmental issues, having finally witnessed the success of environmentalists in forcing the issue itself onto the immediate policy agenda of government. In the remaining years of this decade, public officials will largely cast the shape of future environmental policy, and thus what remains in the 1970's may well be the most critical period in environmental policy formulation. To speak of how public officials make environmental policy is, from the viewpoint of this book, to speak of environmental politics, for we are concerned largely with the institutions, actors, and influences that now mold public environmental policy and with the policy's substance. This is not the whole story by any means, but it is the portion we shall emphasize. Let us briefly examine, in more specific terms, what shall concern us.

The bundle of issues bound together by the word "ecology" may have introduced new items on the governmental policy agenda, but the study of public policy-making itself is a venerable enterprise. Political analysts have created a multitude of schemes, many of great sensitivity and sophistication, in an effort to explain how and why public policies develop. Since our purpose is to create a relatively simple and serviceable model for identifying the important components in the policy process, we can borrow from the literature on public policy several widely recognized concepts that are useful in explaining the development of environmental policy.[20]

Issue Development. To explain how public officials respond to specific issues before them, it is profitable to examine several aspects of the issue's rise to governmental concern.

To begin, it makes a difference *whether one is dealing with a relatively new or old policy problem.* Generally, when public officials confront a major issue that has not previously absorbed much governmental attention, the breadth of the political battle may be quite wide, the possible solutions quite numerous, and the situation generally fluid. In a new policy area, for instance, there is likely to be keen competition among the various groups concerned with the policy to establish their influence and access to governmental decision-makers in order to set the course of future policy and strongly influence it subsequently. Legislators, bureaucrats, and executive leaders, often lacking a heavy investment in an established policy formula, may be more open to evaluating and enacting a broad range of policies than they will be after a policy line has developed. Various sections of the public may be strongly mobilized and intensely involved in the policy issue, adding another element that may be manipulated by the various participants in the policy struggle. Conversely, when policymakers deal with an issue upon which government has already acted, different conditions are likely to prevail. Lines of group access to officials are likely to be established, working relationships among the groups stabilized, and understandings reached. Moreover, an established policy often amounts to an agreement on, or settlement of, political conflict among competing interests concerned with that policy; these interests tend to resist a major revision of policy with the new blood-letting likely to follow. Public interest may be considerably diminished as well. Established policies, in addition, are enforced through bureaucratic agencies with often great commitments to the policy *status quo*, and legislators may, as well, have strong preferences for the established policy formula. Thus, policy changes in "old" policy areas are likely to be relatively modest and difficult to bring about, for there are strongly resistant, conservative pressures at work. In short, the political problems of *creating* a major policy are different from those in *changing* the direction of such a policy. This explains why it is useful to take time to examine the political history of various environmental policy problems.

This distinction between new and old policy areas might seem immaterial to environmental politics, for we have noted that ecology is a rather new issue. However, while the concept of ecology and the many issues it embraces are genuinely new, many other items now considered in the ambit of ecology have long concerned government. For instance, air and water pollution abatement in most respects is a new policy problem, but questions of land and water use, resource allocation, and related problems have long been grist for the governmental mills. Thus, the political context in which policy is made for different environmental issues currently in the news will differ to some extent among the issues. To understand the current policy struggle surrounding a specific environmental issue, therefore, it pays to examine its age.

Issue development also involves some concern with the nature of the policy problem itself. Obvious as this seems, it still deserves emphasis because the substance of a problem has at least two critical political implications: It defines the range of groups involved in a policy area and establishes some boundaries for policy alternatives. To the nonscientist and nonecologist, at least, even a modest examination of the complexities of an environmental problem may seem to lead into a thicket of technicalities unless the political implications of such details are emphasized. For example, during 1971 and 1972, Americans were treated to numerous television commercials, sponsored by petroleum companies, asserting that "the pulse of America" beat to the flow of refined petroleum. One showed a grandmother baking her pies (with natural gas), a jolly family outing in the station wagon (gas-propelled), and a community snugly warm on a frigid winter's evening (through heating energy from petroleum). This might have seemed, upon first inspection, a rather commonplace commercial, but it would seem considerably more to one moderately acquainted with the Alaskan pipeline controversy. During the period of these commercials, the nation's major petroleum refiners were locked in a struggle with conservationists over construction of the Alaskan pipeline to the largest oil reserves yet discovered in North America, reserves upon which the companies held leases. The focus of the struggle shifted to Washington, where public officials were then deciding whether, in light of the pipeline's environmental impact, the cross-Alaskan line should be permitted. The apparently innocuous appearance of grandmother baking her pies as a paean to petroleum appeared, in fact, to be a skillfully timed presentation to build public sympathy (and pressure) for the Alaskan development. As this example suggests, studying the nature of environmental policy problems can provide clues to which interests are likely to be involved, and in what manner, in the resolution of the issue.

The nature of environmental problems also sets some limits on solutions. Air and water pollution, for example, are so intimately associated with almost all industrial processes in the United States, and industry itself is so pervasive, that public officials must depend on considerable cooperation from American business if pollution abatement is to succeed; government cannot force, or enforce, pollution control unilaterally. In a different area, public policy-makers cannot reduce the growth of strip mining in the United States, despite widespread acknowledgment of its vicious environmental consequences, unless they are prepared to alter existing policy concerning the use of fuel by the electric power industry; these policy issues are interlocked because strip mining is an increasingly important fuel source for power generators and, hence, the problems cannot be realistically separated.

The Group Structure. To know how interest groups are involved in environmental policy-making is not to know all, or explain all; but an analysis of environmental policy devoid of attention to interest-group activities would be artless and quite unsatisfactory. The activity of groups in the policy process has been widely studied and its importance recognized. Groups are largely responsible for organizing and mobilizing demands for governmental policy, for exerting pressure on public officials to take action, and for organizing the various viewpoints on policy problems. In large part, therefore, the strength of group activity on various sides of policy questions determines how widely and effectively various policy issues will be represented to government. Indeed, it is largely through groups that issues are politicized in the first place—that is, brought within the ambit of public institutions. In order to understand which environmental issues are likely to be salient to public officials, or what conflicts are likely to develop over them within public institutions, or to predict the future importance of various environmental issues in government, some inspection of the strength, diversity, and viewpoint of interests organized in environmental policy battles is fundamental.

In addition, public policy-makers are very likely to weigh the costs and consequences of environmental policy decisions in group terms. This is not to suggest that various groups are the only components in the public officials' subjective map of the political world, but almost all studies of official decision-making emphasize that group viewpoints and the group consequences of policy choices do weigh heavily in official thinking much of the time. It is a matter of fundamental political intelligence for officials to discover, in any case, where important interests stand on policy questions, environmental or otherwise. All this underscores the fact that what groups do in the political arena—how they represent their interests, to which officials they speak—is likely to have substantial consequences in shaping public policy.

Finally, as we shall frequently emphasize, once policy decisions are formulated in general terms by legislators and executives, they are implemented, and in good part further developed, by the administrative arm of government in which organized interests play a major role. All administrative agencies have their "clientele groups"—those organized interests affected by the agency's responsibilities and working with the agency in making administrative policy. Once these clientele groups gain and stabilize their "access" to administrative officials (the variety of these groups may be great and their access patterns complex), they exert enormous influence in the creation and application of policy through the administrative branch. In short, there is no point in the policy-making process at which group activity ceases to be significant.

Such an abbreviated discussion of groups does little more than hint at their significance in the political process, but it should underscore, at least, why a separate chapter will be devoted to inspection of group involvement in the formulation of environmental policy.

The Governmental Setting. Anyone concerned with the making of environmental policy must, of course, turn to governmental institutions. As always, it is well not to be misled by the formal divisions of power in the Constitution. In theory, the federal government consists of three separate branches with differing responsibilities; in fact, however, the national government (and state governments, all of which follow the federal pattern) are actually composed of separate institutions that share many functions, and, more specifically, each has a major part in *making* policy. For example, the President assumes the initiative in much policy formulation, yet administrative agencies often promote legislation through the President or directly to Congress; thus, Congress is by no means the center of most policy formulation in government. The application of policy is primarily the business of the huge bureaucratic structure, but in the process of determining how policies—which are often written in very general terms—will apply in specific instances, the administrator often makes additional policy himself. Finally, although in theory the courts may only be declaring what the law is, in fact they often make policy in the process of interpreting the law. One must therefore look beyond the formal constitutional façade of the federal government into all branches in search of policy-making components.

It is also crucial to note that a governmental "policy" on any issue amounts to the way in which government deals with an issue through *all* branches. For instance, Congress may formulate a policy for dealing with air pollution by declaring that government's intent to limit the emission of certain pollutants from automobiles. This is merely a declaration; it will have no effect until it is administered through the executive branch and interpreted in the courts. In the administration and adjudication of the policy, in fact, will its actual impact be determined. This means, clearly, that there is often a difference—perhaps a great one—between what government declares it will do and what it is doing in a particular policy area. Any sophisticated analysis must approach governmental policy-making with an eye toward the cumulative impact of all branches in actually fashioning the operative policy.

Finally, it should be emphasized that, in order to understand the making of public policy, some attention must be given to the procedures that define *how* the decisions will be made. All decision-making rules are "loaded" in the sense that they will favor some policy outcomes over others. To an important degree, the rules make policy in that they preclude some decisions while encouraging others. For example, in the 1960's the federal government declared its intention to stop many serious cases of interstate water pollution. But virtually nothing was done by Washington to diminish many blatant instances of severe interstate water pollution. Part of the blame for this can be attributed to the cumbersome and time-consuming procedures that Congress ordained for acting against such pollution. In this case, Washington's passiveness was in good measure the result of rules for dealing with major interstate polluters.

The Substance of Policies. Finally, to understand how and why policies get enacted, one must turn to the substance of policies themselves. There are several aspects of policy that deserve particular emphasis.

It is clearly important to know *what policy alternatives are facing public officials.* In many cases, certain alternatives are impossible or so difficult as to be virtually impossible. Sometimes, courses of future action depend heavily on past policy decisions or on commitments made by policy-makers to politically influential parties in the policy process. All these considerations, among others, mean that policy-makers are never free to choose among all or most of the conceivable alternatives. To understand how policy is actually fashioned, therefore, one must often attend to past decisions and to the realistic constraints upon the decision-makers in the present. With these considerations in mind, it is easier to understand why some policy choices are more likely than others.

Also, all policy choices of consequence involve a *distribution of costs and benefits* among a multitude of important interests; how these costs and benefits are distributed by different policies often provides an important insight into how policy-makers will view their choices. Both costs and benefits can be tangible or intangible, hidden or obvious. One obvious tangible set of costs and benefits is economic. If there is to be a governmental ban on DDT, then chemical firms manufacturing that product are likely to absorb some high, short-run costs. If the government decides to discourage further increases in the amount of timber that commercial lumbering companies may remove from federal lands, the timber industry stands to lose future income while manufacturers of alternative building materials may profit. However, costs and benefits can also be reckoned in political terms. A policy may bestow political benefits by assigning the implementation of a new law to an administrative agency with which certain interests enjoy cordial relationships; in another case, representatives of an interest may be appointed to critical decision-making posts within the governmental structure as part of a policy concerning that interest. Conversely, political "costs" may be assessed against various interests by diminishing appropriations for programs of concern to them, or by reorganizing the agencies with which they have customarily dealt on various policy matters. Or, perhaps, a major piece of legislation will not include a set of interests within those granted some form of governmental favor. In any case, the variety of costs and benefits to flow from a particular policy can vary enormously. The important point is that the pattern in the distribution of such gains and losses will have a significant influence in shaping support and opposition to any policy formulated in government.

The many factors that shape public policy include numerous influences besides public officials and governmental institutions themselves. Even when one has a reasonably accurate idea of what factors enter into the making of policy, one may be uncertain of their relative influence. All this points to the complexity of environmental policy-making and underscores how rudimentary is the outline of these factors we have presented. Still, the factors we have discussed are clearly important in shaping the present and future course of environmental policy and will serve as organizing points for the subsequent discussion. We shall turn next to an examination of the environmental problem itself, the issue, as a beginning toward policy analysis.

Notes

1. The Birmingham story is adapted from reports carried between November 18 and November 25, 1971, by the *New York Times,* United Press International, the *Miami* (Fla.) *Herald,* and *St. Petersburg Times.* Additional data was supplied by the U.S. Environmental Protection Agency, *Progress in the Prevention and Control of Air Pollution* (Annual Report of the Administrator of the Environmental Protection Agency), March, 1972.
2. Sam Love, ed., *Earth Tool Kit: A Field Manual for Environmental Action* (New York: Pocket Books, 1971), pp. 102 ff. Environmental Action has organized the national Earth Day observances since 1970.
3. This message, technically the "Environmental Quality Report," is required by the National Environmental Policy Act of 1969, Public Law 91-190, signed by the President on January 1, 1970.
4. Ecology played a major part in defeating the SST but many legislators also objected to the aircraft's huge cost and uncertain economic returns. The ecologist's viewpoint is presented in William A. Shurcliff, *S/S/T and Sonic Boom Handbook* (New York: Ballentine Books, Inc., 1970), while a more complete summary of the principal issues is briefly but usefully contained in *Man's Control of the Environment* (Washington, D.C.: Congressional Quarterly Service, 1970), pp. 58–62.
5. Many of the issues involved in the barge canal case are examined in chapter 6. For a detailed analysis, see Walter A. Rosenbaum and Paul E. Roberts, "The Year of Spoiled Pork: Comments on the Role of the Courts as Environmental Defenders," *Law and Society Review,* August, 1972, pp. 33–60.
6. The environmental issues in this case are presented in the strongly partisan but informative study by the Sierra Club: Tom Brown, *Oil on Ice* (San Francisco: The Sierra Club, 1970).
7. *New York Times,* July 28, 1971.
8. Quoted in Charles R. Ross, "The Federal Government as an Inadvertent Advocate of Environmental Degradation," in Harold W. Helfrich, ed., *Agenda for Survival* (New Haven, Conn.: Yale University Press, 1970), pp. 178–79.
9. The history of federal pollution legislation is summarized in Council on Environmental Quality, *Environmental Quality, 1970: The First Annual Report of the Council on Environmental Quality* (Washington, D.C., 1970), pp. 43–44.
10. Such legislation includes the Pre-Emption Act of 1841, the Swamp Land Act of 1850, the Mining Act of 1866, and the Desert Lands Act of 1877. For a discussion of the political implications of these acts, see the

excellent summaries in Earl Finbar Murphy, *Governing Nature* (Chicago: Quadrangle Books, 1967), pp. 208 ff.; and Grant McConnell, *Private Power and American Democracy* (New York: Vintage Books, 1966), chapter 7.

11. A résumé of these "great giveaways" may be found in Stewart L. Udall, *The Quiet Crisis* (New York: Holt, Rinehart and Winston, 1963), chapter 5.
12. Harold Sprout, "The Environmental Crisis in the Context of American Politics," in Leslie L. Roos, Jr., ed., *The Politics of Ecosuicide* (New York: Holt, Rinehart and Winston, 1971), p. 49.
13. This trend is clearly evident in the compendium of polls found in Hazel Erskine, "The Polls: Pollution and Its Costs," *Public Opinion Quarterly,* Spring, 1972, pp. 120–35.
14. Rita James Simon, "Public Attitudes Toward Population and Pollution"; and Arvin W. Murch, "Public Concern for Environmental Pollution," *Public Opinion Quarterly,* Spring, 1972, pp. 94 and 106.
15. The Gallup Poll *Index,* February 1970, p. 5.
16. Hazel Erskine, *op. cit.,* pp. 132–35.
17. Robert S. Diamond, "What Business Thinks About the Environment," in Editors of *Fortune, The Environment* (New York: Harper & Row, 1970), pp. 55–65.
18. *A Nationwide Survey of Environmental Protection* (New York: The Wall Street Journal, 1972).
19. A detailed presentation of capital expenditures for environmental research and pollution control equipment may be found in Council on Environmental Quality, *Environmental Quality, 1971: The Second Annual Report of the Council on Environmental Quality* (Washington, D.C., 1971), pp. 82, 111, and 123.
20. While I make no pretense that this is more than a rudimentary scheme, I think it includes many concepts that policy analysts would consider important and does *start* the building of analytical policy studies on environmental issues. My own thinking has been influenced on this matter by Charles O. Jones, "From Gold to Garbage: A Bibliographical Essay on Politics and the Environment," *American Political Science Review,* June, 1972, pp. 588–95.

2 *The Environmental Toll*

Most Americans know now that we have an "environmental problem" although they might be vague about its details. The media in mounting volume have dramatized and disseminated information about environmental abuse, ecology is now commonly discussed from kindergarten through college, and public officials have preached protecting the environment almost to the point where not only the environment but the environmental issue surrounds us. The danger in this publicity is that Americans may become desensitized to the problem or begin to suspect that the constant emphasis exaggerates the issue. One purpose of this chapter is briefly to describe the nature of the nation's major environmental problems in order to lay at rest any doubts about their gravity. However, since the nature of the problems at hand creates many of the contours in the political struggle over policy, another purpose here is to provide some preliminary insight into environmental politics.

The current environmental movement, in its broadest view, represents a concern for the total environmental quality of the United States and the world. While various ecology activists may concentrate upon particular problems, they are also striving to move Americans toward an "environmental consciousness" in which environmental ills are viewed wholistically, as a totality of problems affecting both the quality and the feasibility of life. Most environmental experts, otherwise divided on many aspects of ecology, agree that the physical environment of the nation has seriously deteriorated and that grave, possibly calamitous consequences may follow unless effective countermeasures are immediately taken. Most Americans appear to equate environmental degradation principally with air and water pollution, but public and private leaders concerned with the environment see the problem more comprehensively. It involves not only pollution but, among other issues, poor land use, uncontrolled noise, rising waste, unrestrained use of chemical poisons, reckless population growth, and unthinking destruction of the wilderness. Most of these problems are related; in the end, they combine to make life increasingly unpleasant and may seriously threaten it.

Some critics, convinced that Americans have a perverted genius for environmental contamination, lay the blame on capitalism, the establishment, or some other American culture devil. To the contrary, environmental degradation is now worldwide. It is closely associated with Western culture (now global in its impact) and particularly with industrialization, a very "dirty" process ecologically. Both the Soviet Union and Communist China have admitted serious pollution problems. In a recent report to the United Nations Economic Commission for Europe, the Soviet Union noted that it would take more than two and a half times the present river flow in that water-rich nation to adequately dilute the existing water pollution there. Both desalinization of sea water and the use of melted polar glaciers were being considered by Russian officials as possible remedies to the pollution crisis. In Venice, the air and water are so fouled with sulfur oxides that the legendary canals have occasionally turned dark brown, silver exposed to the air tarnishes, and a third of the city's historic buildings and sculpture suffer from "marble cancer"—sulfuric acid corrosion from air contaminants. Experts have warned that the Sea of Galilee is "dying" of eutrophication (oxygen depletion), while eighteen nations along the Mediterranean have recently joined to save that body from irreversible pollution.

The global sweep of environmental damage is underscored by two unusual events. In 1972, the prestigious Club of Rome released a study prepared by experts at the Massachusetts Institute of Technology in which a mathematical model and computer simulation were used to forecast the future global impact of present environmental trends. After studying population growth, economic change, resource use, and numerous other worldwide phenomena, the MIT scientists made a chilling forecast:

> If the present growth trends in world population, industrialization, pollution, food production and resource depletion continue unchanged, the limits of growth on this planet will be reached sometime within the next hundred years. The most probable result will be a rather sudden and uncontrollable decline in both population and industrial capacity.[1]

Numerous economists and environmental experts challenged some of the assumptions that produced this forecast, while others defended it. Even though there were reservations about some of these conclusions, there was additional evidence of grave international environmental problems from the United Nations. In the summer of 1972, the first U.N. Conference on the Human Environment was held in Stockholm in response to mounting international apprehension about environmental damage. A 200-point program endorsed by 114 nations warned the world of possibly irreversible ecological damage that might be impending unless international measures were undertaken to abate it.[2]

The Major Problems

In the United States, it is increasingly difficult to find an environment unaffected by some sort of pollution; indeed, the federal government recently launched a program to save "samples of the full range of natural environments" in the country before they disappeared entirely. Federal and state efforts have concentrated on five related environmental problems that, while far from representing all, have seemed the most serious.

Air Pollution. Air pollution is the result of several contaminants appearing in differing concentrations and combinations in ambient air. Some, like the photochemical oxidents, react with sunlight, form smog, and become visible, while others remain invisible. These pollutants and the approximate proportion of each in emissions into the atmosphere during a recent representative year can be briefly listed:

1. *Carbon monoxide (CO)*—47 per cent: a colorless, odorless, poisonous gas produced by the incomplete burning of carbon in fuels. Most of this comes from internal combustion engines, usually gasoline-powered vehicles.

2. *Sulfur oxides* (*SO*)—15 per cent: a poisonous, acrid gas produced when sulfur-containing fuel is burned. Industry and electric generators produce most of this.
3. *Hydrocarbons* (*HC*)—15 per cent: represent unburned and wasted fuel that plays a major part in forming photochemical smog. Comes from both gasoline vehicles and industry.
4. *Particulate matter*—13 per cent: solid or liquid substances of variable size that remain in the air for long periods and travel enormous distances. Industry is the major source.
5. *Nitrogen oxides* (*NO*)—10 per cent: produced by fuel burned at very high temperatures. Electric power plants and transportation vehicles are the major sources.

A variety of studies suggests that short exposure to high concentrations of these pollutants singly and in combination, or prolonged exposure to lesser concentrations, can produce serious health hazards or physical impairment to many individuals; the annual property damage is also enormous. The federal Environmental Protection Agency has estimated that the total annual toll of air pollution to Americans now approaches $25 billion, including more than $9 billion in health costs, almost $8 billion in residential property damage, and an additional $7.6 billion in destruction to materials and vegetation.[3]

From a political viewpoint, an important aspect of air pollution is where it originates, which means, essentially, what interests are affected by air pollution controls. In Figure 1, the estimated contribution of various sources to the total United States air pollution load by weight is presented. It is noteworthy that three sources appear to account for more than three-fourths of the pollutants by weight: gasoline-burning vehicles (transportation), electric power plants (stationary sources), and industry. This means that any efforts at air pollution abatement must involve the automobile, petroleum, rubber, electric utility, and chemical industries among the major elements within the private economic sector, in addition to numerous other enterprises interlocked with these through product-sharing and investment structures. Equally important, to speak of such industries is to mention products that are basic to the American life style and that strongly determine

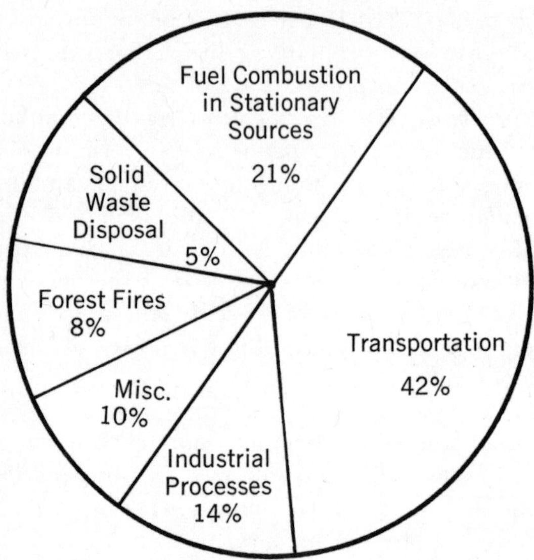

FIGURE 1. Major Sources of Air Pollutants, by Weight

SOURCE: Council on Environmental Quality, *Environmental Quality* (Washington, D.C., 1971), p. 64.

the nation's rate of economic growth and activity. For example, the electric power industry, producer of a commodity indispensable to private life and industry alike, has increased its output by 7 per cent yearly since 1947 to meet rising demand; this annual consumption of electric power is expected to quadruple by the year 2000.[4] Between 1964 and 1970—to cite a small yet instructive example of our electricity-dependent life style—the annual sales for window air conditioners doubled in the United States from 2.5 million to 5 million. Next to his shelter and daily bread, the average American spends more on his car than any other item. By 1980, Detroit will be producing about 44,000 cars daily to meet this transportation demand. So, in the end, air pollution abatement directly affects not only the largest corporate interests in the nation but almost all Americans whose convenience will be affected if regulation of major air pollution sources is to be a reality.

Water Pollution. Today, one eats Mississippi River catfish at his peril. Once a staple of local cuisine, it is increasingly suspect because of contamination to it and most other fish in the great river. The Mississippi, draining 41 per cent of the United States, has not proved too big to pollute; even swimming and fishing are now almost unthinkable along most of its meandering course. In one study of the river's southern end, sixty major industrial sources were found to be contaminating the water with eighty-nine organic compounds and significant quantities of cyanide, phenols, arsenic, lead, cadmium, copper, chromium, mercury, and zinc. In New Jersey's Raritan Bay, tests at several locations showed the water unsafe by state health standards; slightly south, one state official observed that vacationers along the Metedeconk River "are literally swimming and boating in their own sewage." In central Florida, when an industrial accident spilled 2 billion gallons of phosphate waste into the 75-mile-long Peace River (the third such spill in a decade), the investigating state officials had to steer their boats through miles of dead, bloated fish floating so densely that the water's chalky surface was often invisible. Such incidents, no longer rare, constitute only the more forceful examples of the nation's growing water pollution ills.

Totally unpolluted bodies of water are almost nonexistent in the United States. Federal estimates of pollution levels among waterways in major geographic areas of the country indicate that about a third of all stream miles and almost three-fourths of the total watershed area in the nation are polluted; in some regions, such as the Northeast, serious pollution has become almost rampant. The volume and combination of water pollutants vary enormously among the nation's waterbodies but it is possible to identify the major forms of pollution. Below is a brief description of these contaminants:

1. *Industrial wastes:* This includes almost every type of *organic compound* involved in industrial processes in addition to a wealth of *heavy metals* (mercury, cadmium, zinc, copper and the like) and, in recent years, *thermal pollution* produced by infusing streams, lakes, and rivers with heated water discharged by industries after its use to cool production equipment. The major source of thermal pollution is the electric power industry.

2. *Municipal wastes:* This consists primarily of human waste and detergents together with other organic compounds found in domestic effluent.

3. *Agricultural wastes:* The major components of agricultural waste are animal waste, fertilizers, and, particularly in the western United States, salt and other minerals leached from the soil during irrigation.

4. *Other sources:* Among these, *oil pollution* from oil spills in harbors and rivers is increasingly serious. The number of these spills rose sharply in recent years—in 1969 there were 1,007 such accidents in the United States in which more than 100 barrels of oil were involved. *Mine drainage,* mostly in Appalachia but wherever strip mining is practiced, produces sulfuric acid when sulfur compounds in the ground react with water; about 10,500 miles of streams in Appalachia have dropped below desirable quality levels in recent years solely because of this.

All authoritative studies predict a continuing rise in the volume of these pollutants. Within fifty years, there will probably be a fourfold increase in municipal sewage, while industrial wastes, barring a technological breakthrough, will more than double. Thermal pollution in particular seems destined to intensify. By 1980, the electric power industry, principal producer of heated water from industrial processes, is expected to require one-fifth of the total fresh water run-off in the United States to cool its generators.

The total cost of water pollution is impossible to estimate accurately because it includes both widespread tangible damages, which can be stated in terms of dollars, and aesthetic losses upon which a fair price is difficult or impossible to fix. Wherever accurate measures of water pollution damage have been determined, appreciable costs have resulted on a national scale. More than a fifth of the nation's shellfish beds have been destroyed by water pollution; the soft-shell crabfish industry has been almost totally eliminated in U.S. waters, while the annual harvest of shrimp from coastal waters has decreased from over 6.3 million pounds in 1936 to only 10,000 pounds in 1965. The losses suffered by western farmers due to increasing water salinity is expected to rise from $16 million annually in 1970 to $50 million by 2010. Taxpayers have borne and will continue to bear the major expense of purifying the nation's waters (over 80 per cent of the total, at least) through tax payments to local governments for waste treatment facilities. Between 1970 and 1974, total public expenditures for waste treatment facilities financed by taxes will increase from $800 million to $3.2 billion annually.

The water pollution issue clearly embraces most significant private and public institutions in American society. The 300,000 industrial concerns contributing to water pollution are distributed among all major sectors of the economy (although paper, organic chemicals, petroleum, and steel are the principal polluters). Municipal and state governments are deeply implicated in water pollution control as formulators of public policy and as the primary financers of water treatment facilities. The federal government, now assuming the initiative in water pollution policy, appears ready to use its own taxing powers to fund research, development, and construction of water treatment facilities on an unprecedented scale at state and local levels.

Resource Use. The first settlers in America encountered a virgin continent embracing, within the present United States, more than 3.6 million square miles containing some of the richest land, mineral, and water resources on earth. Until recently, Americans treated this inheritance as an inexhaustible cornucopia whose abundance should be used by the nation as private whim, economic advantage, or public expediency dictated. The culture, the law, and public officials treated nature as a "free good," an apparently limitless bounty costing nothing except the price of extracting its riches. Americans exercised little foresight in their onslaught upon this vast natural endowment. They were driven not only by hope of private reward or corporate wealth but also by a public policy inspired by the intense nationalism and the international insecurities of a new state. Not unlike the leaders of modern "developing nations"—albeit with far more promising opportunities and infinitely more resources—America's national administration pressed hard for domestic economic expansion, for the settlement and securing of the frontiers, for growth, wealth, and power of all kinds that would build the nation's international security and fortify its world economic position. In this respect, the nation's raid on resources was an environmental phase in nation-building and one which almost all the world's currently "developed" nations have experienced. The country was settled, timbered, mined, dammed, drained, dredged, filled, pitted, bored, bought, and sold with scant reflection on environmental consequences. For a century after the nation's founding, the westward frontier promised ever renewed resources over the horizon; one could abandon and thereby avoid environmental ravage by putting it to his back. "That is what the frontier has always meant to us—an escape from the consequences."[5]

For over a hundred years, prophetic voices were raised in unavailing warning against this reckless ethic. In this century, the two Roosevelts were the first leaders in American history to harness massive public concern and national energy to the task of redressing extensive damage to our natural resources. But it is becoming clear in the 1970's that the nation confronts land and resource problems requiring a far greater investment of public resources and more sweeping public policy than ever before. Environmental experts and ecology leaders have urged a rethinking of public policy concerning almost all major resources. We shall consider but a few issues currently important.

One major problem now facing the nation is the *growing scarcity of open land.* The nation is moving slowly but inexorably from an era of land abundance to an era of land scarcity, although the generous open space still visible may temporarily obscure this trend. With less undeveloped land available, however, conflicts over its use will grow more frequent and intense; there will no longer be sufficient land to satisfy all competing demands. As a result, more deliberate choices will have to be made about its use by public agencies. All this is plain enough in the statistics: About 1 million acres of rural land a year are now being converted to urban development, airports, highways, reservoirs, and flood control; suburban development alone accounts for half this annual land loss. This presents at least two significant problems. First, the disappearance of wetlands is acute. Wetlands are extremely vital areas not only for their aesthetic and recreational value, but for the continued existence of a multitude of plants and animals that could not breed or survive anywhere else. Moreover, the shellfish industry depends on the estuarine wetlands, especially as the breeding ground for its products.

Originally, the United States possessed 127 million acres of wetland, which has now shrunk by 40 per cent to only 70 million acres. In California, more than two-thirds of the wetlands once available for fish and wildlife has disappeared, while Florida and numerous other states have lost at least 15 per cent of their original estuarine environments. America's loss of wetlands has been concealed from full recognition because the disappearance is insidiously slow. Dredging and filling, conversion to industrial use, and residential development proceeds across wetlands at a measured, remorseless pace that absorbs relatively small land areas at a time. Over long periods, however, the toll mounts. In the decade 1954–64, for example, New York lost almost a third of its existing estuary land, Connecticut almost 13 per cent, and eight other northeastern states together about 8 per cent of all their wetlands.

Disappearing open land also means a decline in recreational opportunities and aesthetic enjoyment for many Americans. The recreation industry has, in some instances, attempted to manage open land for commercial purposes; more than three hundred American corporations are now in the business of creating recreation areas from open country. But much of this land has been lost, probably irrevocably, in its natural state, and much will never be open again. This means more than a diminished opportunity for relaxation and appreciation of natural environments; it denies many Americans, increasingly, the pleasure of living next to nothing "civilized."

Open land is only one of the nation's resource problems. Among others, strip mining, water resource development, and timbering have generated considerable ecological concern. *Strip mining,* or surface mining, is a technique for mining mineral seams (customarily coal) in hills and mountains by removing all soil, trees, and other "overburden," then blasting a bench into the hillside from which the mineral is easily extracted. Clearing and blasting continues down the slope until it is denuded of all original surface features. What remains is often a mound of bare, corrugated subsoil; sometimes the top of a hill is entirely removed and only the decapitated remnant is left for stripping. Harry M. Caudill, a native of Appalachia, writes about the viciousness of strip mining with the fire and eloquence of a man outraged. Though Caudill's anger is not impartial, few who have observed strip mining in action would disagree with his description of foothills after surface mining.

> The overburden is scraped off and the coal is scooped out. Inevitably such topsoil as the land affords is buried under towering heaps of subsoil. When the strippers move on, once level meadows and cornfields have been converted into jumbled heaps of hardpan, barren clay from deep in the earth. This hellish landscape is slow to support vegetation and years elapse before the yellow waste turns green.

When stripping is practiced on mountains, says Caudill, the damage is "fantastically magnified."

> Masses of shattered stone, shale, slate and dirt are cast pell-mell down the hillsides. The first to go are the thin remaining layer of fertile topsoil and such trees as still find sustenance in it. The uprooted trees are flung down the slopes by the first cut. Then follows the sterile subsoil, shattered stone and slate. As the cut extends deeper into the hillside the process is repeated again and again . . . After the coal has been carried away vast quantities of the shattered mineral are left uncovered. Many seams contain substantial quantities of sulfur, which when wet produces toxic sulphuric acid. This poison bleeds into the creeks, killing minute vegetation and destroying fish, frogs and other stream dwellers.[6]

Once a minor source of coal and confined to Appalachia, strip mining has advanced to a major industry because of increasing fuel demands for electric generating plants, the need for less polluting fuels, and an expected technological breakthrough that will make coal a major producer of natural gas. Stripping is, moreover, a comparatively inexpensive method of mining that enables the recovery of far more coal than would otherwise be possible. At present, strip-mined coal accounts for approximately half of all the U.S. annual coal tonnage; to produce this, 2 million acres—an area more than half the size of New Jersey—have been stripped of soil. A major push is now underway by the coal industry to purchase mineral rights in Arizona, Colorado, Montana, New Mexico, North Dakota, and Wyoming, where strip mining would begin when the expected mineral deposits are found. Since more than 77 per cent of the nation's strippable coal lies in the thirteen states west of the Mississippi, a major strip-mine industry is almost inevitable in the West. Without any restraint, this stripping will far surpass in area and coal tonnage produced anything found east of the Mississippi. Strip mining has aroused bitter opposition wherever it has appeared, even in eastern Kentucky, where coal has long been king; indeed, its proponents have frequently admitted many of its environmental ravages. As Harry Caudill's description suggests, environmentalists believe that strip mining almost totally destroys the natural ecology of entire regions, leaves ugly scars on the earth that are slow to heal, bleeds sulfuric acid from its remains to thwart soil regeneration, and contaminates nearby water until it impoverishes all about it environmentally and economically. Moreover, strip-mine operators are accused of callous negligence in failing to restore the stripped soil to better conditions. Defenders of strip mining, though acknowledging the truth in some of these accusations, argue that coal is a necessary American industry, and strip mining must eventually meet the mounting coal demand if it is to be satisfied. They also argue that environmental damage, though real, is often exaggerated and that their frequently successful efforts at environmental restoration are ignored or depreciated unfairly by their critics.

The controversy over *water resource development,* while older than strip mining conflicts, is no less intense. For almost two centuries, the federal government has been the principal developer of water resource projects. The current controversy swirls mostly about the work of the Army Corps of Engineers and, to a lesser degree, of the Interior Department's Bureau of Reclamation—the principal federal agencies in this area—although a larger issue is the whole system through which Congress funds water resource projects. Water resource developments—dams, navigable waterways, reservoirs, levees, flood walls, and recreation areas—have been generously and dependably funded. Such projects have regularly absorbed several billion dollars in appropriations and, until recently, were the most heavily supported of any federal program directly concerned with the environment. These developments, like other local public works projects collectively known as pork-barrel endeavors, are esteemed in Congress because of the real or alleged economic benefits they bring to constituencies and because they promote the political fortune of the legislator who bestows them upon his constituents. The Corps of Engineers, 170 years old and a formidable political force in Washington, dominates the planning and development of these projects and thus incurs the ire of environmentalists dissatisfied with the federal water resource program.

Those sensitive to environmental problems have long criticized Congress for authorizing, with the collaboration of the Corps, too many unnecessary, uneconomical, and ecologically damaging projects in an effort to keep federal money flowing to local constituencies. In essence, environmentalists have concluded that the continuation of water resource development along its present lines will result in progressively greater environmental degradation for the sake of projects of dubious worth. Some environmental spokesmen argue that if new projects were weighed carefully for economic and environmental value, it would be discovered that the most necessary ones have already been built.

Like water resource conflicts, arguments over the nation's present *timber policy* inevitably project the federal government into the middle of the dispute. This is not surprising, for national policy concerning most major natural resources is now largely, if not entirely, shaped by federal action. Conservationists have become increasingly critical of the federal government's administration of the national forests, a huge reserve of timber and other resources, which is the largest resource reserve directly controlled by Washington. The 187 million acres in the nation's 154 national forests constitutes about a tenth of the country's total land area and about 35 per cent of the nation's standing timber inventory; the federal government spends over a half billion dollars annually for the administration of this vast forest preserve.[7] Congress has declared that the national forests should be open for commercial and noncommercial uses: for recreation, conservation, and production of various resources needed for the nation's economy. The Forest Service, administrator of this vast federal preserve, cultivates large segments of the national forests for timber eventually sold to commercial lumbering companies; currently, timber from federal lands provides about a quarter of all lumber used annually in the United States. Environmentalists assert that the Forest Service has become so involved with commercial timbering that it runs the national forests essentially like a business and responds most readily to commercial lumbering interests in determining park policy, neglecting the development of the parks as recreational areas and wilderness preserves. This controversy involves, at one level, the question of proper priorities among a number of feasible forest uses, each of which is defensible in various ways. At another level, however, the argument also reveals the complicated web of political relationships that develops between government and private interests whenever government assumes responsibility for the administration of a major resource. We shall investigate in much greater depth both aspects of the problem shortly.

Wastes and Poisons. Solid waste is an unofficial measure of national prosperity: The more affluent the nation, the greater its volume and variety of solid wastes. It is hardly surprising, then, that Americans are the most prolific producers of solid waste on earth—4.34 billion tons in 1969 alone. Among the wastes produced in the United States, Americans annually throw away 30 million tons of paper and paper products, 4 million tons of plastics, 100 million tires, 30 billion bottles, 60 billion cans, and millions of major appliances including cars. Americans have regarded solid waste as an annoying but inevitable problem to be managed principally by government. The volume of solid waste is now rising at such a steep rate that the customary response—bury it—will no longer suffice.

Clearly, agricultural wastes (2.28 billion tons a year) are the greatest single source, producing almost twice the volume of all other waste sources combined; following (in order of volume) are mineral wastes (1.7 billion tons), residential, commercial, and institutional wastes (250 million tons), and industrial wastes (110 million tons). The variety of products represented in each of these sources is noted in the following summary:

1. *Agricultural wastes*—2.28 billion tons per year: manure and other animal products, slaughterhouse leavings, useless residues from crop harvesting, vineyard and orchard prunings, and greenhouse wastes.
2. *Mineral solid wastes*—1.7 billion tons per year: primarily from mineral and fossil fuel mining and including all the debris commonly found in slag heaps, culm piles, and mill tailings. Most comes from the production of copper, iron and steel, bituminous coal, phosphate rock, lead, zinc, aluminum, and anthracite coal.
3. *Residential, commercial, and institutional wastes*—250 million tons per year: paper and related products, plastics, tires, bottles, cans, grass and tree trimmings, food wastes, sewage sludge, and abandoned appliances.
4. *Industrial solid wastes*—110 million tons per year: scrap metal, paper and paper products, waste plastic, bales of rags, drums of assorted surplus products, and flyash.

While accurate data describing the total volume of national solid wastes over the years is scarce, considerable indirect evidence suggests that the volume is mounting. In general, there is an industrial and private trend away from recycling materials and toward higher materials consumption—both forecasting greater solid waste for the future. Indeed, when it comes to private consumption, the shape of the future seems to be a disposable container. By the mid-1970's, for instance, returnable bottles, the only container for soft drinks little more than a decade ago, will account for less of those sold as metal and glass throw-aways come to dominate the market. After the middle of this decade, according to predictions, seven of every ten beer containers sold in the United States will be nonreturnable as well.

As waste increases, more problems arise. The collection and disposal of the mounting waste from residential, commercial, institutional, and industrial sources—the most immediate health hazards—are becoming increasingly expensive, and the results are often unsatisfactory. The cost of manpower and machinery for waste disposal absorbs a progressively larger proportion of governmental appropriations (particularly at the local level, where most of this waste is handled), but, with the exception of the compactor truck, no significant technological innovations have appeared in waste management that might produce greater efficiency in operations. Moreover, dumps themselves are often poorly managed, unsanitary, and repulsive; open landfills—the most customary mode for disposing of solid waste—are getting scarcer and more expensive. Until now, Americans have expended little effort or imagination to develop more satisfactory methods of local waste disposal.

Recovering and reusing some portion of solid waste—customarily called recycling—is a desirable solution and may be essential. Recycling is partially a strategy for reducing the sheer volume of waste, but it may also slow the depletion of many natural resources, such as metals, timber, and minerals, through reconverting their end products to further use. Not least important, recycling may be a palliative for the junk and debris that clutters the American landscape in ugly profusion. Paper products, beverage containers, and automobiles, three major contributors to solid waste problems, illustrate the possibility for recycling. Americans deplete a large portion of their standing timber to consume more than 59 million tons of paper products yearly; eventually, much of this becomes the debris that amounts to half the roadside litter of the country. A large portion of this paper waste is technically reusable, yet the nation recycles less than a fifth of its paper production. In contrast, several other nations, including Japan, recycle almost half of theirs.

American industry manufactures about 45 billion disposable beverage containers annually and expects to avalanche the market with 100 billion a year by 1980. Between 1 and 2 billion of these are tossed away annually to decorate our highways. At the moment, only about 5 per cent of all nonreturnable containers are recycled, although it is technologically feasible to process almost all. Currently, somewhere between 2.5 million and 4 million abandoned automobiles embellish the American countryside while slowly rusting to powder; after motors and accessories have been stripped, the frames are often left to the elements because they are economically unprofitable for further recycling. Appalachia alone has the dubious distinction of being "Detroit's boneyard," where about three million junked cars (almost a fifth of all junked cars in the nation) now reside. As with other waste products, the technical capacity for recycling a used car exists, but not the economic incentives. Almost an entire automobile, including the oft-abandoned frame, can be and has been reused in some way when it proved profitable. What is now needed for massive waste recycling is an economic stimulus, together with additional research, to assure greater economy and efficiency. Government could provide such a stimulus, not only for recycling but for the elimination of many waste products, through tax incentives and research subsidization.

In 1962, Rachel Carson's informed, eloquent condemnation of indiscriminate pesticide use in *Silent Spring* opened the public debate over chemical poisons in the United States. The controversy involves a wide variety of chemical poisons—insecticides, herbicides, and biocides—widely used throughout the world and collectively called pesticides. Environmentalists and scientists have expressed acute apprehension about such lethal poisons as sodium arsenate and parathion, such "persistent" chemicals as DDT (chlorinated hydrocarbons), aldrin, dieldren, endrin, heptaclor, toxaphene, and the herbicide 2,4,5-T.[8] Like agriculturists around the world, American farmers depend heavily on chemical poisons to control plant and animal pests. In the United States, more than 900 active pesticidal chemicals have been formulated into about 60,000 preparations; more than 1 billion pounds of these pesticides are used annually here. There have been several reasons expressed for apprehension about chemical poisons. To begin, several persistent poisons such as DDT have proved extremely lethal to animal life. DDT has been responsible for large kills of shellfish, fish, birds, aquatic mammals, and land mammals; such toxicity may, the critics charge, ultimately destroy or seriously endanger entire ecosystems and eliminate several animal species entirely. The critics assert that persistent poisons are particularly deadly to the predators living at the top of "food chains." These "chains" begin with microscopic organisms forming the food base for more highly developed life which, in turn, supplies the food for still more developed organisms until, at the top of such a complex chain, there exist the large predators such as eagles, hawks, cats, and other carnivores with few enemies except man. The minute quantities of persistent poisons absorbed by organisms at the bottom of a "food chain" are concentrated in the bodies of their predators and this concentration continues until the animals at the top of this life pyramid may ingest massive doses of the poison into their system by eating their natural prey. Thus, persistent poisons may virtually extinguish predators at the top of a "food chain" if not controlled. DDT has been demonstrated to be a major cause in the death of hawks, eagles, pelicans, ducks, falcons, and ospreys among major predators. Equally important, critics of chemical poisons state that many pesticides may also be serious hazards to human life and that substantial enough evidence exists to suggest that a major study should be undertaken to determine the effect of pesticides on humans. Finally, those concerned with chemical poisons often assert that the federal government, though empowered to exercise some control over pesticides, has been lax in investigating the effect of chemical poisons and slow to assert tight control over their use.

The pesticide controversy involves not only a multitude of issues—of which we shall say much later—but numerous interests in both the public and the private sectors of society. Within the public sector, the U.S. Department of Agriculture, the Food and Drug Administration, and the Department of Health, Education, and Welfare, together with their counterpart agencies at the state government level, have been active participants from the beginning. Environmental groups, as well as scientific spokesmen, farming interests, commodity associations, manufacturers of chemical poisons, and many other private interests, are drawn into the debate. Moreover, it is a global issue. Recently, a variety of specialized United Nations agencies and representatives of most foreign governments entered the arena because any modification in the supply or use of chemical poisons, now almost universally the primary defense against agricultural damage, could have potentially profound effects on agricultural production in most nations.

The Governmental Imperative. It has been only a few years since public officials, citizens, and scientists, awakening to the gravity of environmental ills, began to consider their implications. Discussion has already reached the point where no informed analyst could suggest that the crisis can be resolved or even materially diminished without massive governmental participation. If a time ever existed when private—that is, nongovernmental—remedies were sufficient to check environmental deterioration, it is past. We have reached a point in history where only a nexus between government and ecology promises a chance for environmental restoration. Many of the reasons for this governmental imperative may be discerned by brief reflection on the problems we have analyzed.

The Exhaustion of Private Remedies. There are several reasons why a reliance on private means as the major cure for environmental ills is inadequate. One explanation lies in the technical nature of the problem: Almost all kinds of ecological ills are systemic and interdependent. Shrinking open space, mounting solid waste, resource depletion, and chemical poisons are not geographically bounded. Like other environmental problems, they are systemic in the sense of being spatially distributed throughout the whole national (and international) ecosystem and arise, in turn, from such cosmopolitan sources as population growth, technology, science, industry, and economic forces. Such problems exceed the capacity of private institutions to rectify, even the largest ones when acting in concert. Indeed, while corporate leaders may regard the federal government's intervention in environmental protection with ambivalence, they seem to recognize the necessity and inevitability of public institutions bearing the major initiative in this area. As one political analyst familiar with ecology has concluded, "Technologically related problems know no territorial bound, and they defy locally based efforts to deal with them."[9]

Reliance on private remedies is further negated by the interdependence of the problems. The first law of ecology, observes biologist Barry Commoner, "is that everything is connected to everything else." With a little reflection, one can trace out a multitude of cause-and-effect relationships among environmental ills. A brief illustration and a specific example can illuminate this in-

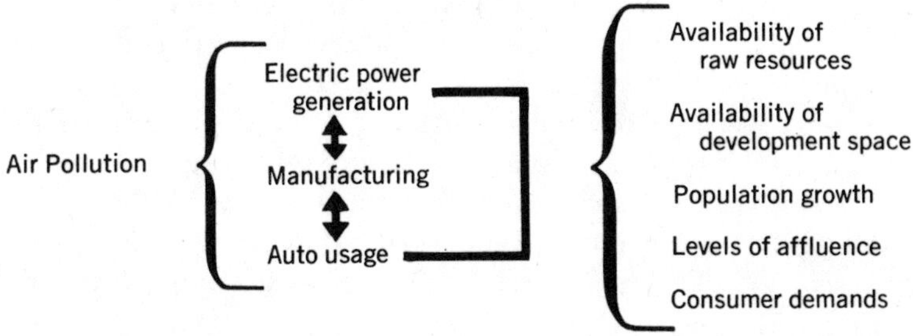

FIGURE 2. Some Major Factors Associated with Air Pollution

terdependency. Let us trace a few of the factors in the United States, using the diagram in Figure 2.

Clearly, one cannot reduce air pollution without treating its immediate sources: power generation, industrial production, and automobiles. All of these are interrelated: Industrial demand affects the growth of the power industry, but industrial growth is also affected by the market for automobiles in the United States. Further, the availability of electric power for domestic use is a determinant of suburban growth, and suburban sprawl increases the demand for transportation. Behind these primary causes of air pollution are a welter of secondary ones of which we have suggested but a few. A glance at these on the far right-hand column of Figure 2 indicates a number of other environmental problems ultimately related to air pollution: demands for natural resources, pressures on open space, population growth, and consumption patterns in the United States.

An Environmental Protection Agency (EPA) report on environmental problems in Helena, Montana, illustrates this interconnectedness more tangibly. The EPA discovered that two metal processing plants near the community had contaminated both air and water with sulfur oxides and heavy metals including arsenic, cadmium, and lead; these passed into the soil and vegetation, there to be absorbed into the bodies of farm animals. Eventually, these pollutants appeared in the bodies of Helena's adults and children. Metal refining, in brief, had triggered a complex chain of events leading from air and water pollution through agricultural contamination to potentially dangerous human poisoning. As these examples suggest, the interdependence of environmental problems means that the whole ecosystem is ultimately affected. As Barry Commoner concludes, "The environment is a complex, subtly balanced system, and it is this integrated whole which receives the impact of all the separate insults inflicted by pollutants."[10] Since one cannot attack a single environmental problem without simultaneously dealing with many others, it appears that environmental protection on a national scale requires a level of manpower, money, expertise, authority, and coordination vastly exceeding that of private institutions. In the words of the United Nations' first world environmental conference, "The very nature of environmental problems—that is to say, their intricate interdependence—is such as to require political choices."[11]

Even if the resources did exist for private remedies, the will to use them effectively while bearing the cost probably does not; it seems unlikely that private resources would ever be marshaled for environmental protection until ecological damage became so acute as to be irremediable. The environmental problem is, in the largest sense, a cultural problem. It arises from our economy, technology, science, attitude toward nature, and life style. So great is the force of culture on behavior that it is difficult to imagine a massive, spontaneous surge of feeling for environmental protection permeating American society to such a degree that it could effectively throw off its own traditions without being forced by the weight of governmental authority. For these reasons among others, governmental leadership seems to be the only likely path.

The Primacy of Government. If governmental activity is now so crucial to environmental protection, several major consequences follow.

To begin with, a failure to find the governmental means for environmental restoration is likely to produce an ecological disaster. This is not a foregone conclusion, but it seems obvious when one considers the magnitude of our environmental ills and the limitation on private means for their solution. In effect, the nation is entering a critical period when it can solve its ecological crisis only by developing two concurrent technologies—scientific and governmental. Only when the scientific skills and resources are combined with the proper authority, organization, and action by government does a long-range restoration of environmental quality seem possible. There is no assurance that governmental efforts at environmental protection will prove ultimately effective, but without government the effort is likely to fail.

As it asserts increasing responsibility for environmental management, government must declare what environmental degradation is and what environmental quality will be. As Clarence Davies notes in his study of pollution control, governmental bodies are defining, in effect, what the nation will consider "pollution":

> Not only is control of pollution a political problem: the very definition of pollution hinges on politics. . . . While we may be able to scientifically define what level of environmental quality is necessary for particular uses, the definition of what constitutes pollution is dependent on the public's decision as to what use it wants to make of its environment. It becomes a political decision, a voicing of the community of its concept of the public interest.[12]

In the name of the public, governmental bodies will also decide how much poison in air, water, and soil constitutes an environmental danger, what rate of resource use is compatible with good ecology, how much solid waste we can continue to produce, and other determinations that define what the nation will consider environmental degradation and restoration. Essentially, this amounts to government's defining, in most important respects, what kind of ecological quality the nation will accept.

Government must also determine the priority of ecological issues in the agenda for public action. However urgent the nation's environmental problems may seem to ecologists, environmental issues must compete among themselves and with other social problems for a position on the governmental agenda. Public officials must make numerous hard choices in determining the priority for environmental issues. In what order should environmental problems be tackled? How important is environmental protection in comparison to foreign aid, defense, or welfare? What level of funding, manpower, and organization should be achieved if various environmental programs are to be successful? While environmental issues may seem of great urgency when considered by themselves, public officials are constantly confronted with spokesmen for various interests who feel other matters are equally urgent. Government must therefore determine how much of the national resources and effort will be allocated to ecology when it must compete for support on the political marketplace against other major issues.

Critical and frequently contentious governmental decisions must also be made about the distribution of costs for environmental restoration. As we shall observe often, there are at least two aspects to this problem. First, the federal government must decide how costs will be apportioned between the public and private sectors of society for environmental protection. In pollution abatement, for example, how much of the cost for research, development, and operation of facilities should be borne by industry and how much by government? Second, an equitable method must be formulated for assigning the cost of environmental restoration to a specific polluter. This is by no means a simple problem, especially in cases where it is difficult to determine how much of a pollution problem is attributable to a particular source (as in air pollution) or where it is difficult to assess environmental damage in financial terms (as in open land loss).

Finally, government may ultimately have to decide what "trade-offs" we must make as a nation for environmental protection. Ecologists generally assert that Americans cannot have a healthy environment and continue to live as they have in the past; there must be some trade-off for environmental protection. Demand for electric power and automobiles, for example, cannot continue indefinitely, nor can the consumer's appetite for absolutely unblemished fruit be satisfied much longer if air pollution or chemical poisons are to be abated. If we continue to demand natural wood in increasing supply, we cannot hope to protect the nation's forest lands from depletion.

Thus, there is no socially costless ecology. As these examples show, to achieve real advancement in environmental protection or restoration almost assumes that the nation can in some manner successfully reduce its demands for various goods and services or abandon some cherished values. To the extent it is possible to engineer such trade-offs on a national scale, one looks toward government as the most logical agent. It can encourage, if not force, environmentally advantageous trade-offs through many methods: by taxing goods and services to enhance or diminish their desirability, by regulating resource use, by subsidies to various industries, and by its enormous capacity to stimulate research on new, environmentally advantageous technologies. Environmentalists are currently pressing federal officials to force a trade-off between the public's demand for private transportation and the need for air purification by channeling much of the money now subsidizing highway development (a major incentive for car usage) into the development of mass rapid transportation. State and local governments are taking the first tentative steps toward another trade-off: between consumer convenience and solid waste management. Several state and numerous local governments are considering, or have already enacted, laws that outlaw the use of nonreturnable beverage containers. In any event, the important point is the great potential government has, and will hopefully exercise, to force national trade-offs for environmental protection.

No Ecology Without Government. A few years ago, "ecology" and "environmental protection" did not exist in American public discourse; they were non-issues to most citizens and public officials. Now we are in the midst of a new "environmental decade" whose meaning and broad implications we have briefly sketched. More importantly, the nation has moved in a relatively few years from a general governmental indifference about environmental protection toward a new governmental involvement. The remainder of this book is concerned with the politics of ecology, with the actors, issues, and processes involved in governmental efforts at environmental protection. Clearly, the politics of ecology is a crucial component in any successful solution to the nation's environmental dilemmas; indeed, governmental action looms so large in determining the outcome of the struggle that to speak of ecology makes little sense unless one deals with its politics. Thus, we now turn to the events and processes through which we will either win or lose the environmental battle.

NOTES

1. *New York Times,* March 12, 1972. The study has now been published: Donella H. Meadows *et al., The Limits of Growth* (New York: Universe Books, 1972).
2. See the "Declaration on the Human Environment," summarized in the *New York Times,* June 17, 1972.
3. U.S. Environmental Protection Agency, *The Economics of Clean Air: Annual Report of the Administrator of the Environmental Protection Agency* (Washington, D.C., 1972), pp; 1–11. This is an extremely conservative estimate because it states the annual costs in terms of 1977 figures, when the EPA assumes a significant air pollution abatement program will exist.
4. John Noble Wilford, "Nation's Energy Crisis: It Won't Go Away," *New York Times,* July 6, 1971. This may be a rather conservative estimate. See comments by the chairman of the board of New York's Consolidated Edison Co. in Charles F. Luce, "Energy: Economics of Environment," in Harold W. Helfrich, Jr., *Agenda For Survival* (New Haven, Conn.: Yale University Press, 1970), pp. 107–18.
5. Robert Rienow and Leona Train Rienow, *Moment in the Sun* (New York: Ballentine Books, 1967), p. 245.
6. Harry M. Caudill, *Night Comes to the Cumberlands* (Boston: Little, Brown and Co., 1963), pp. 311 and 312.
7. The timber controversy is succinctly and informatively summarized in two articles by Gladwin Hill: "National Forests: Physical Abuse and Policy Conflicts," *New York Times,* November 14, 1971; and "National Forests: Timbermen vs. Conservationists," *New York Times,* November 15, 1971. The ecologist's viewpoint is aptly argued in Nancy Wood, *Clearcut: The Deforestation of America* (San Francisco: The Sierra Club, 1971).
8. For ecologists, the bible in the pesticide battle remains Rachel Carson, *Silent Spring* (Boston: Houghton Mifflin Co., 1962). A useful update, in the same vein, is Frank Graham, Jr., *Since Silent Spring* (Boston: Houghton Mifflin Co., 1970), especially chapters 7–12.
9. Harvey Wheeler, "The Politics of Ecology," *Saturday Review,* March 7, 1970, p. 63.
10. Barry Commoner, *Science and Survival* (New York: The Viking Press, 1966), p. 122.
11. *New York Times,* March 17, 1972.
12. J. Clarence Davies, *The Politics of Pollution* (New York: Pegasus Press, 1970), p. 18.

3 *Beyond Birdwatching: A Political Profile of the Environmental Movement*

The environmental movement caught most social prophets looking the other way. A decade ago, no social analyst could have predicted ecology's rise to major national attention. As late as 1968, the gathering of experts associated with the prestigious Brookings Institution did not list ecology among the most pressing issues that ought to be tackled immediately by the Nixon administration. In part, this lack of foresight appears to be a failure to perceive major changes that might occur in the American social climate that would make ecology more attractive to the public than previously. But there has also been a fundamental transformation in the character of group support for environmental protection, a transformation that could not have been easily discerned until recently. In this chapter, we are concerned with understanding both the social climate and group structure that buoy up the environmental movement, as well as their future implications.

Why Here? Why Now?

The United States might now seem like a logical place for an environmental movement. Americans consume more than half the world's important resources and might be expected, if only from self-interest, to be acutely sensitive to any depletion of the materials upon which the nation's prosperity depends. Moreover, since severe pollution is closely associated with industrialization and technology, the United States—the world's leader in both respects—might seem ripe for a grave pollution crisis that would awaken public sensibility to environmental abuse. Also, the nation's large scientific community might appear to be a special public capable of articulating an ecological concern of particular persuasiveness to others.

Yet, environmental protection is a bitter potion. Many of the movement's objectives are incompatible with current cultural norms; indeed, the movement's success might seem to ask for some form of cultural suicide. Effective environmental protection, as former Secretary of the Interior Stewart Udall has remarked, requires a value revolution in American society. A moderate by the standards of the current environmental movement, Udall still speaks with numerous other environmentalists of the need for a radical recasting of American values: "The times demand nothing less than a sustained, life-centered effort to reshape the attitudes, laws and institutions that have produced the mess that is man-made America."[1] Numerous Americans probably greet such pronouncements with skepticism, but almost all environmental experts agree that the roots of the environmental crisis lie deep in our culture. The President's Council on Environmental Quality cites among the principal causes the nation's dedication to unlimited industrial production and economic growth, an affluence that stimulates an apparently insatiable appetite for consumer goods, a burgeoning population, and technology. Other analysts add to the list our belief that nature is property to be used at its owner's discretion, our faith that science can solve any social problem before it becomes catastrophic, and our fierce dedication to private rights over public ones. A major alteration in the American life style seems to be the price of environmental clean-up, and Americans have a powerful incentive to resist paying it.

Environmental protection would also demand changes in the nation's economic structure. Major corporations would probably be required to submit to governmental controls on their use of resources, would have to invest billions of dollars in pollution controls, and might have to restrict the volume and variety of their production. No longer could unlimited production and constant growth be economic gospel; transformation in the profit structures of major industry, of course, would necessarily follow any change in this growth ethic. Most business leaders do not welcome such changes and may, in various ways, seek to delay or blunt their impact. Not least important, the basic political institutions and norms of society would be affected by any major effort at environmental protection. Governmental planning and controls over the economy would have to be extended, the ascendancy of corporate interests in governmental chambers would be challenged, and public officials would have to make hard, controversial choices between ecological values and such previously sacrosanct goals as full employment and production, continual growth of the gross national product, expanding highways, new housing starts, and a multitude of other policies no longer consistent with good ecology. Still, we are now witnessing a major environmental movement. Why has it arisen here and now? Let us examine several suggested explanations.

Environmental Degradation. The increasingly tangible evidence of environmental ills and, more particularly, the crises that finally erupt from this degradation have played a part in the mounting environmental concern. In American politics, it often takes a crisis to prompt public officials to act on social problems. Thus, a bill to control oil pollution languished in the 90th Congress until the disastrous Santa Barbara oil platform blowout of January 28, 1969, released 235,000 gallons of crude oil into Santa Barbara harbor, blackened thirty miles of white beach, and enraged normally apathetic local residents. Pressure on public officials quickly convinced Congress to pass the measure that now controls oil spills, provides new safety standards for platform drilling, and levies heavy fines on corporate violaters of its provisions.[2]

In the Pacific Northwest, environmentalists had vainly fought for decades against many of the forty dams erected across the Columbia River and its tributaries. Despite their warnings that great stretches of scenic wild river and irreplaceable animal habitat would be sacrificed to the dam builders and that major ecological damage would be inflicted upon the affected states, most public officials in the states involved remained unresponsive to such pleas. But when the Federal Power Commission in 1971 licensed two dams in Hell's Canyon that would have flooded the last remaining wild stretch of the Snake River, destroying most of its sixty-six rapids, the governors of Oregon, Washington, and Idaho were finally convinced that dam building had progressed too far at the expense of their states' natural resources. Joining with conservationists, they protested to Washington and promised to fight the projects until their abandonment. Such instances of environmental degradation triggering governmental action are not uncommon over the last decade.

Nonetheless, the gravity of environmental problems alone cannot explain the current environmental movement. Many environmental problems now on the agenda of public agencies—such as disappearing open space, the depletion of resources, pesticide use, and waste management—have not become so pervasive or visibly ominous to reach the stage that customarily arouses immediate public alarm. Moreover, Americans have lived with many serious environmental ills in the past without demonstrating much apprehension. Air pollution may have been more lethal in many communities a few decades ago, but little public concern was evident; the people of Appalachia watched the daily rape of their once lovely land for generations without much significant protest. And, as we have noted, the public's current concern over environmental matters should not be overrated. We have observed that many Americans do not seem greatly alarmed by environmental deterioration, if one judges them by their willingness to make a personal sacrifice for ecology. Perhaps many regard environmental protection, like the state of their souls, as an important issue that nonetheless fails to concern them very often.

The End of Industrialization. Some commentators believe that ecology is important because the United States, now past its great industrializing push, has room for it on the social agenda. In the view of these interpreters, ecology is most likely to be a major national issue in postindustrial societies. Not only is environmental blight likely to be serious, but such nations have attained many desired national goals: economic productivity, a measure of international political and military influence, rising education, scientific competence, and reasonable affluence. In this case, political and economic leaders need no longer concentrate on industrialization, with all the political and economic sacrifices it entails, at the expense of conflicting national policies. For, having arrived at a high plateau of economic development, the leaders are free to ponder the environmental effects of industrialization and the economic controls necessitated by environmental protection without surrendering the benefits of industrialization itself.

International affairs lends some support to this thinking. The industrialized ("developed") nations are currently far more preoccupied with global environmental ravage and its control than less industrialized ("developing") nations, which also suffer environmental blight. The developing areas apparently fear that international environmental controls might restrict or entirely arrest their own economic growth. Some of these nations assert that the industrialized nations' concern with ecology is a selfish luxury that would permit affluent countries to maintain a superior domestic and international economic status while assuring that other nations remain economically inferior; in the end, as Anthony Lewis has remarked, ecology would then become a "fortress of the privileged" against new nations wanting wealth.[3] In effect, the industrialized nations are sometimes viewed as ecologists with a tainted conscience: Having cut the wood to timber their own mansions, they now propose to protect the forests at the expense of neighbors whose dwellings are hardly more than blueprints.

Changing Power Structure. Another explanation for environmental politics suggests that there has been a derangement—perhaps only temporary—in the traditional power structure of the nation that had previously inhibited the emergence of ecology as a salient issue. This argument asserts that power at most governmental levels has customarily resided in different constellations of private interests, primarily major corporations and trade associations, which could force "nondecisions" upon government. They usually kept objectionable issues from engaging major governmental attention, which, in turn, prevented the issues from acquiring public importance. This "off stage power to enforce political inaction" usually prevented the passage of governmental policies that would adversely effect their reputation, economic structures, or political status.[4] These interests allegedly preferred that governmental agendas favor "private" policies that conferred benefits on a specific, limited set of economic interests, rather than "collective" policies with benefits for a diffuse, collective group such as an entire community or most of a nation. Under such conditions, this argument contends, ecological issues were seldom given much governmental attention because they were "collective" in the sense that they bestowed diffuse benefits on a large, amorphous public (in the form of a healthier environment) while imposing heavy costs on a number of specific economic interests (the expense of pollution control devices, for example). After recently studying two communities where air pollution regulations were gradually, and grudgingly, enacted, Matthew Crenson concluded that private "veto" groups were the major obstacle to pollution control in both communities long after air contamination became serious. Crenson suggests that his findings, though limited to two communities, may depict a relatively common situation at most American governmental levels.

Some commentators believe that these veto groups have suffered a gradual power deflation over the last decade severe enough to impair their previous ability to inhibit the development of collective issues they found objectionable. This power deflation, suggest the analysts, has resulted from the Vietnam War, race crises, economic problems, and other recent issues that mobilized many Americans against the real or suspected influence of private interests on public policy. Once these interests were thrown on the defensive, room was made for the emergence of such collective issues as the needs of the poor and minorities, consumer affairs, educational problems, and ecology. Commentators also note that when a few collective issues gain widespread attention, others soon follow. Once public awareness of collective problems is stimulated, a public mood is apparently created; public consciousness of yet other collective problems occurs while groups expand the scope of governmental agendas.

The environmental movement clearly draws part of its inspiration from a larger movement that might be called public interest politics, which represents a militant concern for a multitude of public needs. This movement is personified today by Ralph Nader, whom many would consider the foremost national spokesman and organizer of public interest movements in the political arena. It is revealing that Nader speaks about ecology in the larger context of public needs versus private interests, as if to underscore the fact that ecological concerns stem from a broad concern with public needs in general. "Our institutions, public and private, are not really performing their regulatory functions," he noted in a recent full-page *New York Times* advertisement. "They tend not to control power democratically, but to concentrate it, and to serve special interest groups at the expense of the voiceless citizen."[5] What the public must do, he advises, is to demonstrate an awakened concern not only about pollution but about urban decay, deceptive advertising, shoddy consumer goods, unequal employment opportunity, and a host of other collective American grievances. As this advertisement suggests, one ought to project the environmental movement against the larger background of public rights politics in the late 1960's and early 1970's to fully appreciate the source of the issue's impetus. Perhaps, also, the ecology movement reflects or intensifies a renewed public interest in domestic affairs that has been largely subordinated to international considerations since World War II. The bitterly controversial, prolonged Vietnam War together with other international fiascoes may have soured the public on global politics and rekindled an interest in domestic problems. Americans are turning inward, so some suggest, and reversing their domestic and foreign priorities. In such an era, environmental affairs will assume a saliency previously lacking. The environmental problem, growing more ominous for years, can now be "discovered" because public officials are no longer distracted by global preoccupations.

Finally, education and, particularly, educated youth may contribute to the mobilization of ecological concern. Some commentators link environmentalism to increasing public education. Public opinion studies reveal that a sensitivity to environmental problems is closely associated with education. This relationship was demonstrated, for example, in one of the first careful studies of public opinion and pollution, done in St. Louis in 1963.[6] The investigators found that the respondents with a post–high school education showed a greater frequency of concern with air pollution than any other social group in the study, including even those who were exposed to high concentrations of the pollution; many recent studies further verify the link between education and environmental sensibilities.[7] Reasoning from such familiar findings, some analysts conclude that the rising levels of public education in America must contribute to the vigor of the environmental movement. Others, noting the decidedly youthful cast to the movement, point to youth's distinctive contribution in mobilizing ecological concern. They note that there are currently more young Americans between eighteen and thirty-five years than ever before in the United States and that these young people are a large, available, and politically sensitized manpower pool for the environmental forces. America's young people, the argument runs, are well-educated and therefore environmentally alert. Many are veterans of political protest and election struggles; moreover, with the winding-down of the Southeast Asian conflict and major draft reforms, they are ready to engage their energy in other political issues. All these circumstances result in an unprecedentedly large base of youthful eco-activists with political skills.

Regardless of how one accounts for the new environmental movement, it is not only a reality but a very different phenomenon from earlier efforts at environmental protection. This is more apparent if we briefly examine its philosophy and political tactics.

Beyond "Conservation"

The present environmental movement is more than a newer, reinvigorated edition of the earlier "conservation" crusade. Current environmental activists often make a point of emphasizing the distinction by calling themselves ecologists, environmentalists, or eco-activists rather than conservationists. Many of the goals and much of the material strength in the older conservation movement have been absorbed into the new environmental crusade, to be sure, but the differences between the two are real and continuing.

The Environmental Ethic

The current environmental movement is unified more by a mood and shared attitudes than by a carefully wrought creed. Within the movement, one can discern a great diversity of groups espousing different, sometimes conflicting ecological priorities and philosophies of political action. Yet, amid this pluralism exists a common outlook that might be called the ethos of the movement.

A Concern for Life's Quality. When environmental spokesmen speak of ecology today, they are apt to be concerned with the total quality of the human environment and its effect on man's survival. This truly encompassing definition of ecology, with the breadth of problems and activities it embraces, comes from expanding the original meaning of the term "ecology," which once referred to a rather exotic, obscure branch of biology concerned with the mutual relations between organisms and their environment. In this respect, the focus of the environmental movement is a major qualitative leap beyond earlier conservation interests.[8] Conservationists gave paramount attention to land use. They committed much of their energy to wilderness preservation, to the wise use of natural resources such as forest and rivers, and tended to see the problems they confronted in rather fragmented terms. "Pollution" was not in the movement's vocabulary, nor was "ecology" in the sense of a comprehensive vision of man's environment and its interrelated problems. From the viewpoint of current eco-activists, the conservationists, notwithstanding their many admirable achievements, were too narrow in their vision of environmental degradation and too unsophisticated in their understanding of its causes and consequences.

Environmental spokesmen have attempted to express the scope of their current concern in various ways. "Today, we recognize that man has been engaging in activities that affect the whole life system of the planet," says one leader; "instead of focusing upon a single resource . . . we must paint on a canvas that might be a river valley, a region, a continent—or the planet itself."[9] To another spokesman, environmentalists must concentrate on "how to preserve the general ecological balances" of the planet; a third analyst speaks of ecology as "conserving resources for human use."[10] Such definitions of ecology seem to leave nothing in man's world outside the ambit of attention; some environmentalists, indeed, don't want much excluded.

> The human environment is an immense complex of natural elements, man-made structures, institutions, societies and other people. . . . Environmental quality and human welfare are not two independent values. . . . It is not possible for one to remain good while the other is bad. . . .
>
> Under this broad definition of environment all of the ills of man emerge as environmental problems—poverty, prejudice, public education, health services, militarism, inner circles and pollution all qualify as environmental crises.[11]

As a practical matter, few environmental leaders actually propose to tackle the whole catalogue of human miseries in the name of "ecology" but prefer to concentrate instead on such specific maladies as pollution, waste disposal, pesticides, and land use. Still, modern eco-activists approach individual issues with a characteristic logic. They tend to see each problem in a wholistic perspective, in relation to other environmental problems and forces. They speak of air pollution in the context of industrialization and technology, frequently link these to our culture and economy, and may, finally, view all these issues in a worldwide framework. The environmental activists may also bring to their discussion a rather sophisticated synthesis of political, economic, and scientific perspectives that allows them to move from one context to the other freely in interpreting the issues before them. With these perspectives, environmentalists increasingly talk of problem-solving in terms of broad social planning, long-term trends, and interrelated social forces. In short, their view of environmental ills tends to be total, systematic, or integrative in its definition of problems and prescriptions for their resolution.

The Time Is Now. A sense of urgency pervades the ecology movement. This apprehension ranges from cautious warnings of environmental degradation to tense predictions that the United States has reached the edge of an ecological catastrophe and will soon plummet over the precipice unless radical action is immediately initiated. The President's Council on Environmental Quality, steering a mid-course between complacency and exaggeration, represents the moderate view:

> The public has begun to realize the interrelationship of all living things—including man—with the environment. The Santa Barbara oil spill in early 1969 showed an entire nation how one accident could temporarily blight a large area. Since then each environmental issue —the jetport project near the Everglades National Park, the proposed pipeline across the Alaskan wilderness, the worsening blight of Lake Erie, the polluted beaches off New York and other cities, smog in mile-high Denver, lead in gasoline, phosphates in detergents, and DDT—flashed the sign to Americans that the problems are everywhere and affect everyone.[12]

Still, the Council did not entirely eschew dark judgments; at one point it spoke of the "deadly, downward spiral of environmental quality." Many environmentalists, particularly scientists and other professionals associated with the movement, favor such a balanced, cautious assessment of ecological damage. While admitting the seriousness of environmental abuse, they point to the complexity of ecological relationships, the primitive state of man's ecological knowledge, and the limited environmental data available as reasons for restraint in making dire judgments about ecological ills.

Numerous other laymen and professionals in the movement, however, predict an imminent ecological crisis with few misgivings that they might be "hysterical." They forcefully assert that man is an endangered species whose existence is threatened by population pressure, technology, materialistic culture, and all the environmental ravages that follow. They would agree, at a minimum, with the judgment of the famed microbiologist and Pulitzer Prize winner René Dubos:

> It would be easy, far too easy, to conclude from the present trend of events that mankind is on a course of self-destruction. I shall not discuss this real possibility but shall instead focus on the certainty that . . . all over the world, technological civilization is threatening the elements of nature that are essential to human life, and the values that make it worth living.[13]

Such pronouncements do serve the movement nicely. They capture the media's attention and stimulate popular imagination while imparting a doomsday tone to the movement's rhetoric; they also enlist manpower, particularly when the warning comes from spokesmen with considerable stature such as Dubos. And there have been many who speak similarly. One is former Secretary of the Interior Walter J. Hickel, a minor hero among ecologists for his vigorous attack on numerous environmental problems. "We are rapidly approaching a civil war of priorities in our nation: neighbor against neighbor, man against need, over the preservation or use of our resources," he has written. "Bitter voices are being raised—on the one side pleading 'Give us work, give us energy for our homes'; and, on the other side shouting 'Stop the rape of our environment.' "[14] David Brower, among the movement's most militant and effective organizers, has repeatedly predicted "destruction in a decade" unless radical steps are taken to alleviate environmental ills. Among the newer militants, Stanford University biologist Paul Ehrlich, whose book *The Population Bomb* became the best-selling bible for population control advocates, has predicted a grim future:

> I *am* an alarmist, because I'm very goddamned alarmed. I believe we're facing the *brink* because of population pressures. I'm certainly not exaggerating the staggering rate of population growth; it's right there in plain, round numbers. Whatever problems I'm diverting attention from will be academic if we don't face the population-environment crisis now.[15]

Ehrlich, like other environmental militants, has often been called an alarmist, yet it is only his extreme pessimism that distinguishes him from more moderate voices in the movement. While ecology leaders and experts may disagree over the extremity and implications of environmental damage, they are seldom divided over the existence of currently serious problems.

Social Reconstruction. Within the ecology movement, one can detect a deep disillusionment with existing American values and institutions that seem responsible for the nation's ecological problems. Radically new forms of social organization are often proposed and older ways rejected. Whether this criticism is explicit and articulate or merely implied, it betrays a social radicalism in the movement's *mystique*—even on the part of many who would not consider themselves "radical" in political terms. The movement is too heterogeneous to agree on a detailed, comprehensive formula for social reconstruction, but it does agree on the cultural causes of environmental ills. In its most extreme form, this critique of American culture represents an alienation from Western culture in virtually all respects and a yearning for an alternative culture more congenial to ecology.

Most ecologists realize that they are on a collision course with contemporary American life. They generally regard the dream of unlimited economic growth as a malignant illusion; this "growth psychology," with its emphasis on continually expanding production, demand, and resource use, is seen as the accelerator of environmental degradation. Environmentalist Robert Rienow suggests that the growth myth produces a "superficial dazzle and glamor" and caters to American influence without accounting for ecological costs:

> A major evil in this national worship of the GNP is the lack of discrimination that marks its acceptance. The economist prodding the nation to growth is not disturbed by the beer-can-littered landscape or the unsightliness of the strip mining location. His concern is to stimulate the appetite, not to cultivate the taste. His is a kind of science of collective gluttony. It has been aptly remarked that "one of the weaknesses of our age is our apparent inability to distinguish between our needs and our greeds."[16]

Technology and science are viewed as serious problems because they produce environmental damage even when most other sources of environmental degradation can be controlled. "If the population declined and technology continued to breed, without any improvement in our arrangement for its prudent use," states one ecology writer, "a small fraction of the present U.S. population could complete the destruction of the physical environment."[17] The American market economy is also condemned. It does not take adequate account of environmental damage in producing and pricing goods for the market; this encourages too much demand for products that eventually create great environmental damage by failing to take account of these damages in the cost of the items. A recent national conference of environmental experts concluded:

> In the terms of familiar economic analysis, the injuries done to the environment and to the society by pollution are "external costs" or "social costs," not taken into account in the ordinary business calculations of income and expense. They have been "external costs" not for reasons inherent in the nature of things or derived from the fundamentals of economics but because the legal system has so provided.[18]

All these contributors to environmental degradation are also abetted powerfully by a government that, in the view of many environmentalists, has lacked the will, organization, and authority to deal with environmental degradation effectively. One major reason is that governmental officials, consciously or not, have usually shared the values of American business and therefore have collaborated in the economy's destruction of the environment. Complained a former member of the Federal Power Commission to an environmental conference:

> The relationships of industry . . . with government, in effect, have actually determined the inadvertency of the environmental degradation. In order to put together the complicated, long-range plans for tomorrow, an almost incestuous relationship between these unholy partners has developed and such "minor" problems as the environment have been lost in the shuffle.[19]

Many environmental leaders believe that major governmental restructuring must be accomplished if public officials are now to combat environmental deterioration. We need, suggests one ecologist, "a political economy for Spaceship Earth" in which the government undertakes this restructuring for environmental protection as a first priority. Rarely does a spokesman conclude an analysis of ecological problems without calling for a transformation in government policy, organization, or ethics in the name of environmental preservation.

Almost all environmentalists recognize the cultural components of ecological problems and admit the need for some cultural change. However, the movement's reaction to American culture, especially to prevailing economic and political institutions, has been intensified and in some instances radicalized by a partial overlap between the environmental movement and what has been called the American New Left. The New Left emerged as a significant political force in the United States during the mid-1960's, enlisting its manpower primarily from college faculties and student bodies, the intellectual community, and other groups. The movement marched under many organizational banners, followed a great diversity of leaders, and often espoused inconsistent political philosophies; it was united by shared attitudes rather than by a pervasive, coherent philosophy. The New Left bitterly condemned the nation's prevailing political and economic institutions. It asserted that the country was scourged by materialism and capitalism, that its political and economic leaders were a selfish, often corrupt elite governing in their own interests, that it was an inhuman society for the disadvantaged, the nonwhite, and the young; the cure most often proposed was a radical reconstruction of all the nation's major institutions, usually along lines derived from socialist or communist principles.

Many among the New Left discovered a strong affinity between their view of the nation's social malaise and the environmental movement's diagnosis of the country's ecological problems; the ranks of environmental groups were swelled by New Left activists joining the ecology crusade, especially on college campuses. For many of these recruits, the environmental struggle is simply an old battle on a new front. "Capitalism" had created Vietnam, militarism throughout the country, the repression of minorities, and other evils; it was responsible for environmental degradation, too. The same political leaders and institutions that had irresponsibly led the nation into foreign war, racial discrimination, and other immoral situations had permitted environmental degradation. Materialism and affluence had blinded the nation to its abuse of the poor at home and to the needy nations abroad; so, too, had it caused an ecological crisis. Many New Left activists quickly imposed upon ecological issues the same philosophical framework they had used to interpret other social problems, while some of the most militant environmental spokesmen borrowed liberally from New Left ideology to fashion a radical environmental rhetoric, as in the following remarks by one eco-activist:

> . . . the politics of ecology must start from the premise that present day reality is increasingly a product of a structure of economic and political power that consolidates and sustains itself through the systematic destruction of man and his physical world. The exploitation of man by man and nature by nature are merely two sides of the same coin. . . . The task of ecological radicals is to continually raise those issues which sort those who seek to patch up the status quo from those who struggle for basic transformation.[20]

Other political radicals in the environmental movement are equally militant. Says California poet Gary Snyder, "You can't be serious about the environment without being a revolutionary. You have to be willing to restructure society."[21] Another exhorts, "Liberate the ecosystem."

The New Left does not dominate the environmental movement numerically or philosophically but the earth movement has been sufficiently attractive to young radicals to arouse apprehension among some New Left intellectuals. Richard Neuhaus, a radical Lutheran clergyman, asserts that environmentalism is "a seductive diversion from the political task of our time," distracting radicals from the task of liberating the poor from economic bondage and leading unthinking radicals into espousing policies in the name of environmentalism that are, in fact, hostile to the underprivileged. Population control, for example, is close to war on the poor. Pollution control, which requires an economic slowdown, is a selfish, middle-class wish that would deny the less advantaged an opportunity for material advancement. Indeed, argues Neuhaus, the ecology movement is largely inspired by the nation's political and economic establishment, which wants to blunt the force of radical protest by diverting its attention from economic inequalities to quests for a cleaner environment.

While environmentalists offer a variety of prescriptions for cultural change in the United States, one salient feature of the movement as a whole remains its probing, questioning, and critical stance toward the nation's basic values and institutions. Even as they disagree about remedies for our environmental ills, most environmental spokesmen sense that they are raising a profound issue: "All our problems seem to have a common root. Something is wrong with the way this nation uses its human and natural resources. And I believe that it is always healthy to reexamine, to test, the basic mechanisms we have created to run our affairs. . . . How should our society be organized to resolve the crisis of survival?"[22]

Environmental Politics

Environmental groups have experimented with many political tactics ranging from such traditional strategies as lobbying to newer techniques borrowed from protest movements of the 1960's. This cosmopolitan approach to political action has created a profusion of political techniques unknown in earlier efforts at environmental protection.

New Tactics. The variety of new political techniques found among environmentalists is suggested by some incidents in the early 1970's:

• The seventeenth President of Rutgers University interrupted his inauguration speech to condemn fifty student demonstrators whose hooting, clapping, and whistling was, the President complained, "hooliganism reminiscent of the Nazi hordes of the nineteen-thirties." The students had not come to protest the Indochina war, racial inequality, or repression of youth. They were indignant because a proposed state highway would cross the campus, bringing noise and air pollution. After their brief demonstration, they left peacefully.

• In California, two hundred major industries spent more than $1 million fighting an initiative petition on the state ballot called "The Clean Air Environment Act." The petition proposed a five-year moratorium on the building of new nuclear power plants, a ban on offshore drilling within three miles of the state coast, and removal of all lead in gas sold within the state by 1975, among other items. It had been placed on the ballot by environmentalists who obtained the necessary 500,000 signatures at a cost of only $8,000.

• In Washington, D.C., environmental groups succeeded in obtaining a temporary injunction halting the Army Corps of Engineers from constructing a 170-mile waterway between Tennessee and Alabama at a projected cost of $386 million. A federal district court, in granting the delay, agreed with environmentalists that the Corps had failed to investigate the environmental impact of the project, as it was now required to do by Congress.

Current environmental tactics depart noticeably from earlier ones in several respects: (1) activists are much more willing to get involved in elections and partisan politics; (2) mass demonstrations, protest rallies, and civil disobedience are ocasionally utilized to gain attention and to dramatize ecology issues; and (3) legal strategies, particularly the "environmental lawsuit," have gained support. In these respects, environmentalists display a greater sophistication in using the mass media than was common to earlier conservationists. While ecologists remain active lobbyists at all governmental levels, they have recently shown an interest in more direct political action through electoral involvement on behalf of candidates sympathetic to environmentalism and against those with unsatisfactory conservation records. To do this, some groups have had to sacrifice the tax-exempt status they previously enjoyed as "nonpartisan" organizations. The influential Sierra Club, one of ecology's most effective organizations, several years ago abandoned its tax shelter to enter the electoral arena. Recently, the former executive secretary of the Sierra Club, David Brower, created the new League of Conservation Voters for the principal purpose of soliciting funds and organizing manpower to elect ecology-minded candidates; a coalition of ecology groups in New York and several other states has formed for statewide electoral action. Such explicitly partisan groups are still experimental, their impact on candidates and policy still unproved; however, they represent a movement toward partisan politics rather new to ecology-minded interests.

Few techniques have done more to dramatize ecology than

mass demonstrations and other attention-getting activities borrowed from the style of protest politics in the mid-1960's. The rise of ecology to national prominence might well have begun with the "Earth Day" celebrated on April 20, 1970; the first Earth Day was a coordinated program of environmental teach-ins at major academic and urban centers across the nation. Large audiences were treated to addresses by distinguished, nationally renowned scientists, public officials, educators, and environmentalists who reaped plenty of media attention. College campuses have spawned major environmental demonstrations, often promoted with a fine eye for theatrics. "Strive for far-out symbolic actions on meaningful, relevant issues that will seize the imagination and commitment of the press and the public," advises one organizer of campus ecology demonstrations. "Don't just demonstrate against water pollution: pick a nearby polluted stream and wage a cleanup campaign. . . . Shine a giant searchlight on belching smokestacks." At the University of Minnesota, one student ecologist dressed in a page's costume and accompanied truckloads of empty cans to St. Paul, where he presented an American Can Company executive with a golden can on a velvet cushion. In New York, a "mock trial" was held in which "The People vs. Technology" was the topic. Business, scientific, and academic leaders were invited as jurors for the "trial" at which the distinguished lawyer Louis Nizer presided and several scientists associated with the atomic bomb's development were among the "witnesses." In the frigid waters off Amchitka Island near the Alaskan coast, sixteen protesting environmentalists anchored a small boat near the spot where a large underground nuclear blast was to be detonated, forcing attention on their concern for the environmental damage they expected to follow. Environmental leaders have recognized the limitation of demonstrations, even though they did generate media interest and public attention and undoubtedly aided in enlisting ecology activists. By 1973, Earth Day ceased to be a nationally organized event, an indication that the public had tired of ecology demonstrations and that its sponsors had wisely turned to other forms of political action. Demonstrations, in fact, were largely an ephemera associated with the movement's early, mobilizing days, when they served a useful purpose. Undoubtedly, demonstrations will be tried again if public support for ecology seems to be sagging badly.

"Environmental lawsuits" met with early success, encouraging environmentalists to use the courts with increasing frequency for environmental protection—a distinct reversal of the past. Environmental lawsuits are court actions initiated by private citizens or ecology organizations seeking to protect the public from various types of environmental degradation. These suits are customarily aimed at government agencies to prod them into action against private interests allegedly destroying the environment or against the agencies themselves if they seem responsible for environmental damages.[23]

Until recently, frustration and disappointment was the customary result. Judges had been reluctant to hear such suits. They often ruled that environmentalists did not have the "standing" to sue (that is, the right to a court hearing) because the alleged environmental damage was suffered by the "public" and was, therefore, the responsibility of legislators and administrators, or because no laws explicitly give citizens the right to sue for environmental protection in the public interest. Judges were not anxious to substitute their judgment for the determination of administrative agencies whose decisions were often the point at issue. Then, too, many jurists felt unqualified to render decisions on the many technicalities involved in such actions and felt uncomfortable in the role of social planners. When it came to "judging between the birds and people," as one lawyer put it, judges preferred to let other governmental bodies make the choice.[24]

There are several reasons for the court's new receptivity to such suits and its willingness to judge in favor of environmental interests. The growing national awareness of environmental problems has undoubtedly sensitized many jurists to what the Council on Environmental Quality has called "a history of administrative decisions that ignores environmental impacts and . . . a tide of legislative delays in developing pollution control law."[25] Federal and state governments have also passed laws in the last few years explicitly granting citizens the right to sue governmental agencies to protect the environment, thus removing the "standing" issue as an impediment to such litigation; among these laws are the National Environmental Policy Act of 1969 and the Clean Air Amendment of 1970, to be discussed shortly. Many states have recently enacted statutes or constitutional amendments conferring upon their citizens the right to sue state agencies to protect the public against serious environmental damage; New York, Illinois, and Michigan were among the first. Lastly, the feasibility of environmental lawsuits has also been enhanced by the creation of several groups specializing in environmental litigation, such as the Environmental Defense Fund (EDF). The EDF, like several other organizations with a similar purpose, seeks out environmental cases for presentation to the court and organizes many professionals—lawyers, ecologists, and scientists—into a team for the court battle.

Who Wants Ecology? The ecology movement speaks in middle- and upper-class accents. Those most often counted in the ranks of ecology groups are usually white, middle- to upper-class, well-educated, relatively young Americans. Public opinion polls and surveys indicate that the ecology movement depends heavily on these groups for manpower, financial support, and political effectiveness. Conversely, ecology draws relatively meager interest among most blacks, the poor, and the least educated. Efforts to bridge this gap have been largely unproductive, so that the ecology movement still has no significant base in this stratum of society.

Ecology's failure to engage less advantaged groups seems ironic when projected against the environmental realities confronting the poor, blacks, and the underprivileged generally. The highest sustained rates of air pollution are often found in the core of cities where large numbers of such individuals live; the inner cities, more often than not, are grim models of "visual pollution" in the form of urban decay and suffer the most from "noise pollution." Pesticides are used there in especially heavy dosages to combat flies, roaches, and rodents. In general, whether they live in cities or not, the least advantaged Americans suffer as much or more from environmental degradation than the relatively affluent, educated citizen.[26] Nonetheless, ecology remains a peripheral concern to most disadvantaged Americans because their more urgent needs are adequate employment, decent diets, better housing and education, health care, and other essentials. It is not surprising, given these elemental needs, that improving the quality of the air might seem less compelling than getting food for one's family or protecting one's children from disease. Many spokesmen for the disadvantaged believe that the ecology crusade may divert the nation's interest and resources from the greater task of improving the lot of the disadvantaged. As black leader Whitney Young asserts:

> The war on pollution is one that should be waged after the war on poverty is won. Common sense calls for reasonable national priorities and not for inventing new causes whose main appeal seems to be in their potential for copping out and ignoring the most dangerous and most pressing of our problems.[27]

Those responsive to the needs of the disadvantaged often argue that a massive attack on environmental degradation would mean diminishing the nation's rate of economic growth, cutting back on affluence, and in general drastically reducing new forms of wealth, capital, and opportunity that the poor desperately need to improve their condition.

This division of social support has produced mixed political consequence for the ecology movement. On the positive side, the middle- to upper-class base of the movement includes the largest number of Americans, brings to it those citizens with the greatest political experience, resources, and interest, in addition to giving the movement support from those social sectors to which American government has traditionally been the most responsive. At the same time, its feeble appeal to the disadvantaged not only deprives the movement of additional manpower, political weight, and social appeal but creates a potentially dangerous cleavage that, under the right circumstances, could become a socially polarized struggle pitting the more affluent's demands for environmental protection against the less advantaged's desire for social advancement.

Even with its fairly homogeneous social base, however, there is a pluralism of viewpoints among groups representing environmentalism in politics. A brief examination of this organizational diversity reveals the pluralism often concealed within the ecology movement.

The Organizational Base. During ecology's rise to prominence, environmentalists could draw on ready public emotion when they wanted political strength for environmental programs; public sentiment, however, is unlikely to remain so pervasive and intense, for it can seldom be kept deeply involved in a public issue. The long-range fortune of ecology depends more on the skill, strength, and determination of the organized interests that promote environmental protection and represent its continuing base of stable political support. More than 3,000 organizations in the United States are concerned with some aspect of the environment. The majority of these—about 2,500—exist on the local level and seldom assume national visibility or importance. National environmental policy is most often affected by the 250 national and regional organizations and the 400 state environmental groups with the membership, resources, and status to fight major political battles. With the sudden awakening of national environmental concern in the early 1970's, many of these groups—particularly the large national organizations—experienced rapid, sometimes spectacular membership growth. Between 1970 and 1971, membership in the five largest environmental groups jumped by 400,000, a 33 per cent increase in one year. The politically active Sierra Club, among the best known of ecology organizations, grew by annual increments of more than 25 per cent during the early 1970's.[28] The influx of members has somewhat abated now, but the rapid increase has given the movement its largest manpower base in history and has also produced several new, politically active organizations.

Almost all major environmental organizations have entered the political arena occasionally, but the most involved today constitute a relatively small but growing segment of the ecology movement. These politically active groups will become familiar to anyone following current environmental policy.

The Sierra Club. Politically militant and aggressive, the Sierra Club has gained a reputation as a tough, sophisticated political opponent. Founded in 1892 by the great American naturalist John Muir, the club remained relatively small and active primarily in the West until recently, when it climbed to 135,000 members in forty-one chapters throughout the nation. The club's reputation was fashioned, in good part, during the years when it was led by David Brower, its executive secretary for seventeen years before leaving the organization in 1969. Under Brower's direction, the club defeated an effort to place dams across the Colorado River that would flood segments of the Grand Canyon, and thwarted numerous other efforts to develop wilderness areas commercially. The club asserts a hard-line "preservationist" viewpoint that resolutely opposes destruction of any wilderness area for almost any purpose; this fundamentalist position has often separated the club from more moderate environmentalists who favor multiple use of wilderness areas and caused most of its opponents to call it extremist. In recent years, the club has fought the proposed Alaskan oil pipeline, the development of California's Mineral King Mountain by commercial recreation interests, and further hydroelectric dam construction. In the late 1960's, the club sacrificed its tax-exempt status to enter election contests. Although it has had to cut back activities somewhat because of a recent decline in membership growth, it remains the most well-known environmental group in politics.

The Audubon Society. Founded in 1905 and with a current membership of approximately 210,000, the society is a federation of state and local chapters, many of which (like the Massachusetts state chapter) exert considerable political influence within their own regions. The society is primarily concerned with the enjoyment, preservation, and enhancement of wildlife in all varieties. It has been especially active in fighting pesticides and other poisons that affect the food chain, in gathering funds from public and private sources to buy wilderness preserves, and in encouraging public agencies to use existing public resources to protect animal life, particularly endangered species. The society maintains a lobbying office in Washington and many state capitals; in many communities, its local chapter is often the only environmentally active organization. While usually moderate on most environmental questions, the society has often sided with more militant groups such as the Sierra Club in political combat.

Izaak Walton League. The league represents a mixture of straight conservationists and sportsmen. Founded in 1922, the league has 56,000 members distributed among state chapters in a loose federation that gives the local units great autonomy; in many respects, the league has been far more effective at the state level than in national politics. Since it is a confederation of sportsmen and conservationists, the state units tend to take positions according to which of the elements dominates the membership. Generally, it favors the development and enhancement of recreational facilities on public lands but not without some attention to wilderness preservation. Thus, it helps to bridge the gap that sometimes develops between sportsmen and conservationists on resource use. Operating principally through lobbying, publications, and other familiar forms of political action, the league leans toward a more traditional, "conservationist" view of environmental problems.

National Wildlife Federation. Generally considered the only militant and effective sportsmen's group, the organization is a federation of state councils representing rod-and-gun clubs. Although the affiliated clubs represent about 2.5 million members, few are active in the organization and most of its money comes from conservationists who buy the club's attractive magazines, wildlife stamps, and other publications. The federation has very close ties with state fish and game departments, commercial recreational interests, and other groups concerned with the enhancement of recreational fishing and hunting activities. The federation maintains a Washington lobby but is more effective at state levels. Since it usually sides with those wanting to expand hunting and fishing opportunities, it often opposes strict "preservationist" organizations like the Sierra Club and sometimes incurs the criticism of conservationists for its relatively mild position on wilderness development.

Friends of the Earth. Created by David Brower after a split in the Sierra Club resulted in his dismissal as its executive secretary in 1969, the FOE is hard-line preservationist and vigorously political in its approach to ecological issues. The organization, according to Brower, wants "conservation to go on the attack, to . . . reclaim shopping centers, not swamps, cities, not mountains, polluted rivers, not free-flowing streams. More space and less development, more wild animals and fewer people are the political aims of Friends of the Earth." The organization tries to provide information to environmental groups for ammunition in their battles in legislative halls and other political arenas. Current membership is less than 15,000, but it's growing. Following Brower's philosophy, the FOE fights its political battles wherever major political decisions affecting the environment are made. Already active in Washington, the FOE is becoming a presence in many state capitals.

League of Conservation Voters. Originally an electoral arm of Friends of the Earth, the league became fully autonomous in 1972. A nonpartisan organization, the league published appraisals of the environmental record for most members of the House of Representatives, raised and distributed $50,000 in campaign contributions for selected Congressional contenders in 1970, and published evaluations of environmental views for the major Presidential contenders in 1972 (although it endorsed none). The league is still small, its electoral impact uncertain; it has promised to be increasingly active in state and national elections as the 1970's progress. At the moment, the league represents the first national environmental organization committed to a wholly political program.

The Environmental Defense Fund. When he founded it in 1967, flamboyant lawyer Victor Yannacone assured its fame among ecologists by his unofficial motto: "Sue the bastards." Though Yannacone left the group, it has grown in activity and impact until it is today the most effective legal weapon in the environmental movement. The fund is a coalition of sixty lawyers, 700 scientists, and other experts who collaborate in preparing and presenting cases before the nation's courts in which they seek to protect public rights to a safe environment. Although the fund operates on a modest budget, mostly dues from its 25,000 members, it has been extremely successful in achieving its objectives. Relying on a mixture of well-presented, carefully prepared scientific testimony and imaginative, vigorous legal argument, the fund has succeeded in getting DDT banned in several states, in halting the Alaskan pipeline until careful environmental studies could be made, and in halting construction of three major federal canal-and-dam projects in an unprecedented defeat for the Army Corps of Engineers. Most significantly, the fund has apparently succeeded in establishing the right of citizens to defend a claim to a clean environment as a "public right" in the courts. In 1972, the fund had more than forty suits in the courts or under consideration.

Zero Population Growth. Created by biologist Paul Ehrlich in 1970 to proselytize for population control as the only alternative to a major world catastrophe, ZPG has been particularly active on college campuses. New and relatively small, the group is zealous, forceful, and colorful in proclaiming its message. Concentrating almost exclusively on population problems, ZPG follows a philosophy of active political involvement but is too new to have yet demonstrated what political muscle, if any, it possesses.

In addition to organizational diversity, there are several important philosophical divisions among environmentalists. There is a fundamental, persisting division between preservationists who want wilderness and other resources saved from almost all man-made alterations and moderates who accept "multiple use" (for preservation, recreation, and commerical interests); this not only results in a difference in organizational philosophies—the Sierra Club's hard-line preservationism against the Audubon's less militant position, for instance—but often divides groups internally. There are also differences among priorities for environmental action: The Izaak Walton League and National Wildlife Federation tend to be responsive to the concern of sportsmen, Zero Population Growth places population problems above all other considerations, and the Audubon Society pays particular heed to wildlife issues. Also, as we shall shortly note, the interest of governmental bureaucrats involved in ecology may diverge in significant respects from those not committed to particular governmental agencies or politics.

Besides ecology groups, a great variety of other interests are continually involved in the politics of environmental protection. American business and governmental agencies, in particular, are among the most important of these interests that also shape the political pattern of environmental struggles.

Business, Bureaucrats, and Ecology

Except for government, no other institutions in American society are more deeply implicated in the struggle to make environmental policy than are the nation's corporations. Whether considered as single firms, trade associations, or entire industrial groups, businessmen have become increasingly aware of environmental issues and alert to their political interest in ecology.

Corporate Politics. American business has reason to be deeply involved in environmental politics. First, since industry is the principal source of many pollutants, it will be heavily regulated by any governmental policy to abate pollution; industry produces about three-fourths of the most damaging air pollutants and more than half the volume of oxygen-demanding wastes discharged into municipal sewage systems. Much of the cost and initial responsibility for installing pollution control devices must also be borne by business. The Environmental Protection Agency estimates that corporations must invest $42 billion by 1975 to meet present air quality standards (almost 90 per cent of the total national investment needed) and an additional $13.5 billion for water pollution abatement (more than a third of the national requirement);[29] in the primary metals industry, pollution control costs in 1970 reportedly had already reached 10 per cent of total capital expenditures.[30] The consumer will eventually pay much of this cost in higher prices, but corporations are nonetheless affected; business must absorb some of this cost, may be adversely affected in some cases by the increased cost of their products, may have to close economically marginal plants when pollution control equipment is required, and may have to "write off" some future projects as losses.

Business is also a major resource consumer, vitally concerned with any restrictions on resource availability that government might impose for ecological reasons. A number of industries, for instance, will be affected by any changes Washington may dictate in corporate access to federal lands. The lumber industry obtains more than 35 per cent of all its commercial softwood from federal forests, cattle and sheep raisers graze their herds on 273 million acres of federal reserve, while an additional 64 million acres of public domain is leased for private mineral exploitation. If tough environmental safeguards are imposed on oil companies developing new fields such as the Alaskan reserve at Prudhoe Bay, the cost and volume of petroleum production would be significantly affected. Not least important, American industry has been thrown on the defensive by the environmental movement. Numerous environmental experts have harshly assailed industry for its pollution and alleged callousness regarding environmental protection; the public commonly views business as the source of environmental ills and often as the villain in environmental politics.[31] Corporations, extremely anxious to demonstrate that they are maligned by environmentalists, want to prove they are also working for a cleaner environment.

Since 11 million corporations speaking through 3,000 trade associations constitute the American business community, it is far too pluralistic to possess a single voice on environmental issues. The largest corporations and trade associations that frequently set the policy stance for most business have, however, demonstrated some fairly consistent political strategies on environmental issues. Although many environmentalists regard any statement of corporate environmental concern as a case of the devil quoting scripture, business leaders profess a will to cooperate with governmental efforts at environmental protection and appear to accept, if not always welcome, ecology as an enduring political issue. This is apparent not only at the top stratum of business leadership, but also at middle and lower levels as well. A fairly typical attitude was expressed by one large southern land developer: "I'm not even sure what ecology means. But whatever it means, it's here to stay and it will enter into all future development projects." Business seldom welcomes federal intervention in the economy, but in the case of pollution control, major corporations generally prefer the federal presence because it prevents the confusion of fifty different state regulatory systems while assuring that no major corporation will escape regulation and thereby enjoy a market advantage. For these reasons, the auto industry did not oppose federal emission standards for new cars, and industrial users of fossil fuels prefer that Washington take the initiative in establishing air quality standards.

American business may profess its commitment in principal to environmental protection, but it has been considerably less enthusiastic about the practical details. The public record reveals considerable corporate resistance and dissatisfaction with initial governmental efforts to protect the environment; conflict, not concord, has most often marked the relationship between business and its regulators, just as it has the corporate community's attitude toward ecology activists. Business has adopted several common attitudes toward the environmental issue. To begin, businessmen frequently argue that environmental experts exaggerate our ecological problems and demand excessively harsh regulatory policies that will dangerously retard the nation's economic growth and impose unjustifiably heavy costs on individual firms. A variation on this theme is a statement by the Western Environmental Trade Association, an Oregon coalition of business and labor pledged to fighting "environmental hysteria" and "environmental McCarthyism." After Oregon's legislature required a deposit on most beer and soft drink containers and established strict new air and water pollution controls, the group complained:

> There have been a great many ill-conceived and unsound [environmental] programs which seriously endanger the public welfare. . . . As a result of over-zealous, erroneous governmental regulations and actions, that segment which produces jobs and profits has been rendered a serious economic blow.[32]

A conviction that ecologists have exaggerated environmental problems and may jeopardize healthy economic growth is apparently widespread within management. *Fortune*'s survey of 270 major corporate leaders in 1970—a time when environmental concern was extremely high—revealed that most of these leaders placed the environmental issue in fifth place among national problems, feared government would overreact to ecological issues, and agreed that environmental groups did not represent the opinion of most Americans. As soon as other interests perceive that ecology will bring new economic difficulties, they are usually quick to take a similar position. When state and local governments sought to prevent billboards from defiling the natural beauty along American highways, the opposition included not only such predictable elements as the Outdoor Advertising Council and the American Hotel and Motel Association but also the Brotherhood of Painters, Decorators, and Paper Hangers (AFL-CIO). The environmental movement's opposition, in general, is usually determined by the distribution of costs for environmental protection.

Despite the considerable initiative that some American corporations have taken in pollution control, American industry's general response to ecology has been a grudging, passive resistance to most governmental policy. The auto industry balked and delayed so long in developing auto emission control equipment that the government finally had to file suit against Detroit's four major auto makers in 1969 to force a more cooperative attitude; in subsequent efforts to achieve further controls by 1975, the industry was only slightly more cooperative.[33] The oil industry emasculated much of the 1966 Clean Waters Act by getting it written in a manner that made it almost impossible for the federal government to sue successfully an oil company responsible for a major oil spill; massive efforts by environmental interests in 1970 finally changed the bill.[34] The nation's steel firms have generally opposed existing federal air and water pollution standards; earlier efforts by local government to achieve air pollution abatement was frequently thwarted when major steel corporations expressed willingness to accept "reasonable" controls but refused to make any effort to promote them, thus denying their considerable support to pollution control and delaying it through the power of inertia. Business leaders frequently complain that they have been unfairly accused of environmental negligence, but their public record often seems to justify the indictment. It is hardly surprising, then, that one study of community leaders in fifty-one important American cities in the early 1970's revealed that almost 95 per cent of them listed industrial corporations and their executives as the opponents of air pollution control.[35]

Whatever the truth may be, business is also spending millions of dollars in advertising to convince Americans that it is a conscientious environmental guardian with impressive accomplishments. This is an important strategy. If successful, it can create public good-will that may be tapped and directed to industry's advantage in policy struggles; it can delay or diminish efforts to achieve greater governmental control of industrial pollution by undercutting popular support. All major American industries subject to environmental legislation have paid handsomely for media space to assure the public they are on the side of the angels in environmental affairs. Here is a sampler of such advertising:

STANDARD OIL: "Great strides are being made in the control and reduction of automotive pollution by the automobile manufacturers and the petroleum industry, assisted by Federal, State and local governments. . . . The development of F-310 is . . . an important advance. To our knowledge, F-310 is the most significant step taken to date by any oil company to provide a gasoline which helps reduce air pollution."

REPUBLIC STEEL: "We were concerned about ecology long before it became a household word. Our program began more than thirty years ago."

PRIVATE ELECTRIC INDUSTRY: "Building with *the electric climate* put nothing into the air around them . . . because electricity is the cleanest source of energy."

GLASS INDUSTRY: "Working toward the ULTIMATE recycling system. Which means a system that will channel the components of trash into a new useful life."

CAN INDUSTRY: "Cans are good guys. We've already set up recycling centers for used cans. . . . More are coming. This costs us money but doesn't cost you anything."

So useful has a virtuous ecological image become that even corporations with seemingly minor environmental responsibilities —watch companies, manufacturers of duplicating equipment, and brokerage firms among them—have recently strained to prove they are fighting the good fight. Industry has further utilized massive advertising to influence public opinion on specific environmental issues. The Rural Electric Cooperative Association placed full-page ads in major newspapers and magazines to convince the public that the power industry's growth should not be halted during a period when Congress was contemplating air pollution controls that might inhibit the industry's expansion; the consortium of companies anxious to exploit the extensive oil reserves in Alaska's Prudhoe Bay placed material on television and in news magazines to demonstrate that a continuing supply of oil was a vital national priority. In an effort to counteract public criticism of corporate pollution, many of the nation's major businesses formed Keep America Beautiful, Inc. (KAB), "to urge more individual anti-pollution action and less criticism of business and government." Predicting it would obtain more than $450 million in free media time and space for its programs, the KAB's chairman announced the group's theme would be "People start pollution. People can stop it."

Many corporations have made themselves vulnerable to charges of misleading or blatantly false advertising. In an unusual move, the Federal Trade Commission investigated vigorous complaints that a major steel corporation's advertisements in *Time, Newsweek, Business Week,* and *Saturday Review* falsely claimed that its strip mining in Appalachia had produced recreational and aesthetic improvements. Critics charged that a dam and lake for which the company took credit had been built by the state of Kentucky; that the state's Fish and Wildlife Department was unable to stock the lake, while the ad claimed there was good fishing; and that the water was badly contaminated from mine runoff, although the company said one could safely swim in it. Other instances in which corporations "improved" on the truth were cited by a nonprofit, independent research firm:

- A large western public utility depicted a lobster, apparently content in power-plant water wastes, that in fact came from "nowhere near the plant."
- A major petroleum refiner represented the Palm Springs courthouse as the company's research center.
- A large timber company offered as an example of its pollution control a clean stretch of Idaho's Clearwater River quite unconnected with the company's activities.

Corporate leaders often assert in rebuttal that such deception is a regrettable, but very small, portion of all corporate environmental advertising. They point out that the public often blames industry for environmental problems that the public itself helps to create, and too often believes the worst allegations of environmentalists rather than considering the commendable environmental achievements of industry. Advertising, industrial spokesmen maintain, is the major means by which they can present their side to the nation and thereby create a balanced picture of environmental affairs. Despite these protestations, there is little doubt that many major corporations have taken considerable liberty with the truth in their environmental presentations. Unless Congress or such agencies as the Federal Trade Commission enforce higher standards, there seems little prospect that environmental advertising will decrease in volume or improve in quality.

Beyond such general approaches, the philosophy and tactics of American business vary considerably according to the specific policies at issue. This matter we can leave to the chapters on policy that follow. An examination of the group structure of environmental politics would be incomplete, however, without briefly mentioning the activities of governmental bureaucrats. These interests are intrinsically important and have often been ignored in public interpretations of ecology issues.

The Bureaucratic Structure. It is difficult to estimate accurately the number of federal, state, and local governmental agencies with a strong interest in environmental politics. For instance, a recent federal study indicates that air pollution policy directly involves the Department of Health, Education, and Welfare, the Department of Agriculture, the Environmental Protection Agency, the Department of the Interior, the Department of Transportation, the Coast Guard, and the Federal Aviation Agency; pesticide regulation vitally concerns four federal departments and the Environmental Protection Agency; the handling and transportation of hazardous materials affects four major federal departments and five independent commissions or agencies. To this list should also be added the multitude of state agencies with responsibilities within their own jurisdictions that would overlap that of the federal government. In short, any significant environmental issue is bound to engage the interest and activity of a great many governmental officials.

Administrators have many reasons for being concerned with

environmental policy. They may be charged with the responsibility of implementing and enforcing environmental legislation enacted at federal or state levels. Thus, the Department of Agriculture's Forest Service and Interior's National Park Service are likely to have a vested interest and strong views about any contemplated change in land management of federal reserves; similarly, the "fish people"—the National Marine Fisheries Service (Department of Commerce) and the Bureau of Sports Fisheries and Wildlife (Department of Interior)—will be greatly concerned with water pollution control and water resource development. Moreover, bureaucrats are often creators and advocates of environmental policies, often working in conjunction with sympathetic private interests. In federal and state government, it is common to find that many legislative acts begin with, or are substantially shaped by, the work of administrative specialists in government whose expertise alerts them to the need for various environmental measures. Finally, most administrative agencies have developed strong political alliances with private interests involved in environmental politics and may be drawn into policy conflicts through such coalitions. Often, for example, foresters, fishery managers, fish-and-game officials, and water resource planners actively support the governmental policies advocated by the commercial interests with which such officials must deal constantly; sometimes, environmental groups have collaborated with insurgents within governmental departments wanting a major policy reform or change in traditional agency procedures. In any case, policy struggles among various private interests almost always draw various governmental agencies and their representatives into the fray. This is too common to be surprising, but it explains why an examination of governmental policy struggles must take account of these bureaucratic interests.

Environmental groups look with mixed emotion on the governmental agencies responsible for environmental programs. Environmentalists recognize that the expertise, experience, and cooperation of these bureaucracies are essential for environmental protection; ecologists frequently acknowledge that most bureaucrats attempt to discharge their responsibilities with reasonable good faith. Yet, environmental interests often assert that these administrators too often side with the *status quo* against new policies, identify too often with the private interests that cause serious environmental degradation, and use their influence to stifle innovation within their own departments. Thus, it seems to many environmental leaders that the established governmental agencies involved in environmental management and protection are, at best, fitful allies and frequent adversaries. However, it is a fact of environmental politics that ecologists need the collaboration of these agencies if environmental protection is to become a reality, and they must find a means of satisfying this large, important set of interests if new ecological policies are to be created.

The Group Basis of Environmental Politics: A Summary

We have witnessed in the last few years a transformation in the character of groups espousing environmental protection, a change that marks the end of the "conservation" movement and the onset of the "ecology" crusade. One manifestation of this has been a notable alteration in the political philosophy and tactics of groups concerned with environmental quality. In general, there has been a proliferation of new groups committed to explicit, wide-ranging political activity and a growing receptivity among older groups to more aggressive political action. Newer, militant political tactics have won growing acceptance within environmental groups; electoral action, environmental lawsuits, protest marches, and mass demonstrations, in particular, have proved popular and effective as new means of action. Moreover, environmental groups have considerably broadened their base of support and improved their political resources by enlisting the assistance of a large number of young people, a fact that has had much to do with the transformation to greater political militancy within the movement. All this has also been accompanied by a very ambitious definition of issues for which ecologists should work politically; the list of problems now embraces almost any matter that may affect the quality of man's environment. In short, the *mystique* of the movement is more political, more militant, more comprehensive in its social concerns.

At the same time, the group structure of the movement is not monolithic in its environmental priorities, its preferences for political strategies, or its militancy. It is divided internally on all these issues, so that one is likely to find a significant consensus on the existence of grave environmental problems, but not on the proper remedies, tactics, or order in which the problems are to be solved. The group pluralism is hardly surprising—one does not find any major socioeconomic or ideological interests with a monolithic group structure—but it does point to serious internal political cleavages within the movement that are often neglected by observers.

Whatever its character, the long-range outlook for environmental protection will depend, in good measure, on the group structure of the ecology movement. Organized groups have been largely responsible for mobilizing discontent with environmental degradation, for proselytizing to increase the political strength of the movement, and for bringing sustained pressure to bear on governmental bodies to remedy environmental ills. The vigor, imagination, and dedication of these groups in political struggles of the future represent the most important political resource the environmental movement has at its disposal. All these resources will be severely tested in the battle to achieve and enforce environmental protection through government.

Notes

1. Stewart L. Udall, "Total Environment: A New Political Reality," in Harold W. Helfrich, Jr., ed., *Agenda for Survival* (New Haven, Conn.: Yale University Press, 1970), pp. 10 and 11.
2. The political pressure generated by the Santa Barbara incident is described from an insider's viewpoint in Walter J. Hickel, *Who Owns America?* (Englewood Cliffs, N.J.: Prentice-Hall, 1971), chapter 4.
3. *New York Times,* March 8, 1972. For an interpretation of this "third-world paranoia" from an observer of the recent U.N. Conference on the Human Environment, see Robert Bendiner, "Third-World Ecology," *New York Times,* June 23, 1972.
4. This theory is most explicitly applied to the pollution issue in Matthew A. Crenson, *The Un-Politics of Air Pollution* (Baltimore: The Johns Hopkins Press, 1971), pp. 23 ff. The intellectual heritage, however, reaches into more general theories of elite structure in American society. See, for example, Peter Bachrach and Morton S. Baratz, "Two Faces of Power," *American Political Science Review,* December, 1962, pp. 947–52; and Theodore Lowi, "The Public Philosophy: Interest-Group Liberalism," *American Political Science Review,* March, 1967, pp. 5–24.

5. *New York Times,* September 12, 1971.
6. Thomas B. McMullen *et al.,* "Air Quality and Characteristic Community Parameters" (Paper delivered at the annual meeting of the Air Pollution Control Association, Cleveland, Ohio, 1967), Appendix. Cited in Matthew A. Crenson, *op. cit.,* p. 12.
7. See, for example, Rita James Simon, "Public Attitudes Toward Population and Pollution," *Public Opinion Quarterly,* Spring, 1971, pp. 93–99.
8. The difference between the current "ecology" and the earlier "conservation" viewpoint is best appreciated by reading a sampler of each ethic side-by-side. A good contrast would be a comparison between Alde Leopold, *A Sand County Almanac* (New York: Oxford University Press, 1940) and Gene Marine, *America the Raped* (New York: Simon and Schuster, 1969). In literary terms, Leopold's graceful prose is far superior to Marine's outraged, if eloquent, polemics, but the substance of the two books fairly represents the differences in the two movements.
9. Stewart L. Udall, *op. cit.,* p. 1.
10. Harvey Wheeler, "The Politics of Ecology," *Saturday Review,* March 7, 1970, p. 52; Daniel R. Grant, "Carrots, Sticks and Consensus," in Leslie L. Roos, *The Politics of Ecosuicide* (New York: Holt, Rinehart and Winston, 1971), p. 104.
11. Frederick E. Smith, a Harvard ecologist. Cited in Fred Carvell and Max Tadlock, *It's Not Too Late* (Beverly Hills, Calif.: The Glencoe Press, 1971), p. 5.
12. Council on Environmental Quality, *Environmental Quality, 1970* (Washington, D.C., 1970), p. 6.
13. René Dubos, "The Human Landscape," *Bulletin of the Atomic Scientists,* March, 1970, p. 31.
14. Walter J. Hickel, *op. cit.,* p. 298.
15. Paul Ehrlich, "A Playboy Interview," in *Project Survival* (Chicago: The Playboy Press, 1971), p. 77.
16. Robert Rienow and Leona Train Rienow, *Moment in the Sun* (New York: Ballantine Books, 1967), p. 233.
17. Max Ways, "How to Think About the Environment," in Editors of *Fortune, The Environment* (New York: Harper & Row, 1970), p. 202.
18. *Man's Impact on the Global Environment: Report of the Study of Critical Environmental Problems* (Cambridge, Mass.: MIT Press, 1970), p. 232.
19. Charles R. Ross, "The Federal Government as an Inadvertent Advocate of Environmental Degradation," in Harold W. Helfrich, Jr., ed., *The Environmental Crisis* (New Haven, Conn.: Yale University Press, 1970), p. 173.
20. Barry Weisberg, "The Politics of Ecology," in Robert Disch, ed., *The Ecological Conscience* (Englewood Cliffs, N.J.: Prentice-Hall, 1970), p. 154.
21. Quoted by Peter R. Janssen, "The Age of Ecology," in John G. Mitchell and Constance L. Stallings, *Ecotactics* (New York: Pocket Books, 1970), p. 55.
22. Barry Commoner, "Beyond the Teach-In," *Saturday Review,* April 4, 1970, p. 63.
23. The purpose and philosophy of environmental lawsuits are fully discussed in Joseph L. Sax, *Defending the Environment* (New York: Alfred A. Knopf, 1971).

24. The problem of standing is examined at considerable length in Norman J. Landau and Paul D. Rheingold, *The Environmental Law Handbook* (New York: Ballantine Books, 1971), chapters 2, 3, and 4.
25. Council on Environmental Quality, *Environmental Quality, 1971* (Washington, D.C., 1971), p. 155.
26. A typical socioeconomic profile of ecology enthusiasts may be found in Roos, *op. cit.* Evidence on the environmental degeneration of the inner city may be found in Council on Environmental Quality, *Environmental Quality,* 1971, pp. 189 ff.
27. Harold Sprout, "The Environmental Crisis in the Context of American Politics," in Roos, *op. cit.,* p. 46.
28. The group structure of the ecology movement is explored in Jeremy Main, "Conservationists at the Barricade," in Editors of *Fortune, op. cit.,* pp. 167–80. Estimates of the Sierra Club's growth provided by Congressional Quarterly Service, *Man's Control of the Environment* (Washington, D.C.: Congressional Quarterly Service, 1970), p. 4.
29. The air pollution cost estimate is found in U.S. Environmental Protection Agency, *The Economics of Clean Air* (Washington, D.C., March, 1972), p. 101; water pollution costs are summarized in Council on Environmental Quality, *Environmental Quality, 1971, op. cit.,* p. 111.
30. Council on Environmental Quality, *Environmental Quality, 1971,* p. 126.
31. Indeed, the public appears to see little else but industry as the environmental villain. See Hazel Erskine, "The Polls: Pollution and Industry," *Public Opinion Quarterly,* Summer, 1972, pp. 263–80.
32. Quoted in *New York Times,* December 25, 1971.
33. A detailed discussion of the emission control controversy is found in John C. Esposito, *Vanishing Air* (New York: Grossman Publishers, 1970), chapter 2.
34. This is fully described in J. Clarence Davies, *Politics of Pollution* (New York: Pegasus Press, 1970), pp. 46–48.
35. Matthew A. Crenson, *op. cit.,* p. 89.

4 *The Pikes of Politicians: Setting Environmental Policy*

The politics of ecology is ultimately a struggle to control the exercise of public power in the United States; in Washington, contending environmental interests converge in their efforts to exploit the authority of public agencies to their own advantage. Washington may not be the seat of the nation's environmental wisdom, but it is the only place where officials can create and enforce a national environmental policy; here, where the ambit of public power is greatest, the most critical policy decisions and conflicts occur. Ecologists know that their movement's energy will dissipate into a futile spasm of arrested reform unless the firm, continuing weight of federal authority is brought to bear on environmental protection. The nation's corporate managers, too, recognize that Washington sets the policy trend for all governmental levels in environmental affairs; if they are to shape that policy to their satisfaction, they must be effective in Washington.

Environmentalists commonly face the prospect of working with Washington's officialdom with varying degrees of wariness, frustration, and bitterness. "Perhaps I am a cynic," writes a veteran conservationist, "but in my lifetime I have seen too many potentially good leaders in the field of conservation come with high hopes to Washington only to be impaled on the pikes of politicians." To many in the movement, this is gospel: The pikes of politicians will impale not only good men but good policies, good agencies, and good intentions. Among conservationists, there is an unspoken conviction that something in the American political process is inherently inhospitable to environmental protection, that "politics" undermines sound environmental policies established in the public interest while nature's private exploiters profit. Many who do not share such pessimism still recognize they are operating in a milieu where the opposition has historically enjoyed the greater advantage and success. Under the most favorable conditions, environmentalists expect a hard, uncertain battle in an unfriendly arena before winning, if such is their luck, major environmental victories.

Ecologists, as we shall often note, have reason for disenchantment with past federal programs and grounds for reservations about the rewards of future effort. Why should this be so? And what, then, are the prospects for effective environmental protection through government? To answer these questions, one needs some acquaintance with the governmental process, together with an understanding of the particular problems this process poses for the environmental movement. Such an approach helps to explain not only what occurs in making environmental policy but *why* it happens.

Ecology and the Governmental Process

A customary style in the making of public policy in the United States, a recurring logic, marks the way in which our public institutions handle most policy issues. Although exceptions enough suggest that they are not locked into an immutable policy-making mold, powerful conservative forces inhibit most policy questions from departing very far from traditional procedures for their resolution. Most importantly, this decisional style is likely to have a significant impact on the making of environmental decisions.

The Bias of the Rules

In governmental policy-making, as economist Charles Lindblom suggests, it is important to know not only who makes policy but *what* makes policy.[1] Lindblom, like many analysts, suggests that the policy outputs of government are powerfully shaped by the principles and rules that govern decision-making—the "what" of the system. These principles include both the formal rules that dictate how decisions must be made and the informal understandings, or "rules of the game," that are shared by decision-makers and shape their relationships with one another. In any governmental system, these rules are biased in the sense that they will favor some policy decisions over others, will promote the consideration of some issues and encourage the neglect of others, and will generally "load" the governmental process in favor of some interests. The bias of decisional rules can be observed abundantly in Washington. The Congressional seniority system, which confers on southern interests an unusually large voice in legislative committee deliberations, or the electoral college's apportionment, which bestows such great influence on the populous states in Presidential elections, are garden-variety examples of "loaded" rules. Because decisional rules shape policy outcomes so strongly, it is understandable that those wanting to alter governmental policy often attempt to revise the rules by which decisions of concern to them are made.[2] It should also be apparent that a conflict over what rules shall prevail for making decisions in governmental bodies is actually a contest to determine which array of interests will be favored by governmental decisions.

Despite the great profusion and complexity of decision-making procedures in American government, in the United States—as in other governmental systems—the rules tend to correspond with certain principles or values that are considered essential to the governmental process. Thus, the apparent diversity of rule-making procedures is undergirded by what has been called an "inarticulate ideology," an informal set of beliefs that provides a common logic to the many different decisional arrangements. This logic, of course, engineers a bias into the making of environmental policy as it does in other matters. Among the major components of this "inarticulate ideology," we shall briefly mention those that exert particular influence on governmental responses to the environmental movement.

Incrementalism. Both formal rules and informal understandings among public officials promote public policy by "increments." Incrementalism favors the making of new policy on the basis of past experience, careful and prolonged consultation among all the major parties affected by decisions, bargaining and compromise among interested parties, and modest policy change rather than comprehensive or radical alterations in policy. Incrementalism also means that few policy problems are ever solved; indeed, final solutions are seldom expected. "In the United States," writes Lindblom, "policy-makers nibble endlessly at taxation, social security, national defense, conservation, foreign aid. . . . Political analysts assume that their problems are never solved, and hold themselves in readiness to return to them again and again."[3] A number of governmental arrangements encourage incrementalism or reflect a belief in its importance. Important policies in both the executive and the legislative branches cannot be formulated and ratified without consultation and eventual concurrence by numerous officials and agencies at many governmental levels. The division of powers among the three major branches of government forces bargaining, compromise, and time consumption in fashioning policy; the collaboration of numerous informal power holders (private interests) is usually essential if policy affects them. Moreover, the federal system puts brakes on rapid or radical policy innovation in favor of incremental changes engineered through consultation and the creation of consensus among differing governmental levels. This system does not wholly preclude major change, particularly in foreign and military affairs, where Presidential innovation often prevails. Still, radical or rapid policy change customarily occurs only under such extraordinary circumstances as depression, war, or other emergencies when decisive innovation may be necessary to meet urgent national needs.

An incremental system has several appeals for officials. In terms of policy planning, it concentrates their attention on a limited set of policy alternatives, reduces the complexity of factors they must consider, and permits them to draw on past experience as a guide for future decisions.[4] There are also political virtues. Once policy is fashioned, the coalition of supporting interests is likely to prefer an incremental change rather than a drastic revision that upsets established understandings, triggers more political bloodletting, and opens the possibility for undesirable new interests to gain some advantage. Incrementalism, additionally, seldom pushes change to the point where the public or major private groups balk at the new situation. Then, too, there is always the risk that constituents may react to drastic change by deposing the policymaker or by altering the rules of decision-making to his disadvantage.

Thus, incrementalism is generally conservative in that it favors the perpetuation of the existing political framework, its dominant policies and interests. Since incrementalism places a drag on rapid or radical policy change, those who want major departures from the *status quo* will chafe under the restraints imposed by this system. Those excluded from the company of the elect who benefit from an incremental approach will view the system with equal prejudice. Especially for the reformer, incrementalism is frequently a cross to bear because the demand for reform is almost always a demand to alter the *status quo* in ways costly to vested interests. Not surprisingly, many ecologists believe that one of the most formidable pikes in the politician's arsenal is labeled "incrementalism."

Organized Interests and Public Policy. One explanation for Washington's incremental style is that public officials customarily engage in extensive consultation and negotiation with the major organized interests affected by a policy before any significant decisions are formalized. If many organized interests are affected, decision-making is likely to be protracted and contentious, with only those policies enlisting substantial support among most of the significant interests likely to prevail.

Although it has never been stated as an explicit doctrine, most political analysts recognize that governmental officials operate on the premise that major organized groups affected by public policy should have an important voice in both shaping and administering it. To many analysts, such as Theodore Lowi, this deference to interests has reached the stage where their control of public policy is considered legitimate and desirable. Today, he suggests, "The role of government is one of insuring access particularly to the most effectively organized, and of ratifying the agreements and adjustments worked out among the competing leaders and their claims."[5] Analysts who reject such a sweeping judgment would nonetheless find little quarrel with Grant McConnell's assertion that we have witnessed "the conquest of segments of formal state power by private groups and associations. . . . Although it would be impossible to state with any precision what portion of the power of American government has been taken possession in this way," he observes, "it is certain that the portion is substantial and that the control involved is considerable."[6]

Many arrangements illustrate how organized interests penetrate the governmental process at strategic points in ways sanctioned by law and custom. In the legislative arena, lobbying constitutes the most familiar exercise of group influence on public policy; the dominion of organized groups is further extended by the tendency of legislators to assume that important policy issues can be most satisfactorily clarified and resolved through the interaction of organized group spokesmen. Group influence is designed into the administrative branch in many ways. More than 1,400 "advisory committees"—usually dominated by representatives of major interests affected by agency programs—exist to give agency officials information on group reactions and preferences on policy;[7] thus, when the Environmental Protection Agency was created in 1971, President Nixon created a National Industrial Pollution Control Council, an advisory panel of big business executives, to give industry a voice in agency decisions. Some of these committees are merely ineffectual administrative decorations, but others exercise considerable influence on the actual decisions of public officials. Private groups also profit through the recruitment of their own members as administrators in many federal departments and agencies. Yet another enhancement of group influence is the creation of semi-public organizations that intermingle private group leaders and public officials with common policy concerns. One of the best examples of this is the Rivers and Harbors Congress, a private agency whose membership consists of public officials and group leaders concerned with water resource development; this organization's recommendations on water resource development have customarily been the agenda followed by Congress and administrative agencies in the water resource field.

This pervasive group presence has not always produced a group monopoly on policy to the exclusion of other sources of influence, but group activity at all governmental levels is so widely practiced and accepted that it has become, in effect, part of our constitutional order. This situation poses several problems for the environmental movement.

The Diffusion of Power. Authority and influence in the making and enforcing of public policy are parceled out among numerous agencies, governmental levels, and unofficial power wielders. This dispersion of power has been created by deliberate constitutional and legislative means and through the informal arrangements used by public officials and important group leaders to facilitate their negotiations in formulating policy. The division and subdivision of governmental power amounts to a fragmentation that is a basic structural trait of the American governmental process.

The Constitution ordains a fragmentation of governmental powers in two important directions. Federalism distributes power "vertically" among national, state, and local government levels, while the separation of powers within the federal government apportions authority "horizontally" among the three branches. In this era of vast federal power, federalism is often supposed to be an antique fiction disguising the actual poverty of power among state and local governments; however, in formulating and applying policy, all levels continue to exert considerable influence and to share major responsibilities. "It is difficult," writes a veteran observer of the governmental process, "to find any governmental activity which does not involve all three of the so-called 'levels' of the federal system."[8] As a result, no governmental level enjoys a monopoly of control over policy. "There has never been a time when it was possible to put neat labels on discreet 'federal,' 'state' and 'local' functions."[9] The separation of powers, as Richard Neustadt has aptly remarked, has not actually fashioned three institutions with separate powers but three separate institutions *sharing* powers. This shared power is readily apparent in such routine procedures as the enactment of legislation in which the President ordinarily proposes, Congress disposes, and—if legislation becomes law—the courts often interpret. The important point is that the vertical and horizontal divisions of power in government create numerous centers of authority that, whether in cooperation or in competition, disperse power in policy-making.

There is also a diffusion of power in other important directions—"inward" and "outward." A careful examination of Congress or the administrative branch of the federal government will reveal that power is internally divided so that there is an inward fragmentation of power and influence. This is most clearly revealed, in the case of Congress, by the committee system in both houses; committees are nuclear units of power within the Congressional system whose members can, and frequently do, wield influence independently of one other. Within the executive branch, the bureaucracy is an organizational constellation of units with different magnitudes of power and influence; departments, agencies, and bureaus acting alone and in differing combination are capable of exercising considerable influence in making and implementing public policy. Finally, the outward distribution of influence relates to the influence that private interests customarily exercise in the governmental process—a matter discussed in Chapter 3. Public officials make a few important policy decisions without extending consultation outwardly to incorporate the major private interests in the process; few of these interests enjoy an absolute veto over policy proposals, but many enjoy the right to be consulted and to have their preferences honored in some degree before policy is formalized.

Fortunately, the fragmentation of power vertically, horizontally, inwardly, and outwardly seldom ends in paralysis, deadlock, or impotence in governmental responses to important policy issues. Major power holders in and outside government have stabilized their relationships, routinized decision-making, and reached numerous understandings that facilitate reasonable cooperation. Presidential leadership often serves as a catalyst to draw these disparate power centers into collaboration. In emergencies—wars, depressions, or international crises—the routine policy process can often be short-circuited and major decisions reached with great dispatch. However, the fragmentation of power has imparted several significant traits to the governmental process that affect the making of most policy. To begin, fragmentation encourages time consumption and incrementalism in policy-making. Moreover, extensive negotiation among many participants—the price of securing support for major policy in a fragmented power system—means that the policy that emerges is often the common denominator of many different preferences. Fragmentation of power gives a great tactical advantage to those who wish to defeat major policy initiatives; while the proponents of a policy must ordinarily struggle to coordinate and satisfy many interests throughout the government if they are to succeed, the opponents can often inflict a crucial defeat simply by withholding the support of only one power center. Thus, proponents of major policy change must often invest far greater resources, time, and political ingenuity in their efforts than need their opposition. Not least important, fragmented power frustrates comprehensive policy planning and implementation because it prevents the concentration of authority in the hands of a few individuals or agencies essential for continuity and deliberation in the unfolding of governmental policy. Without the goad of crisis, policy is customarily short-range, uncoordinated, and seldom possessed of the coherence that results from central direction and planning.

The Administrative State. The flow of the policy process does not necessarily follow the constitutional channels intended to guide it. The Constitution appears to vest the principal power to formulate public policy in Congress, while leaving the responsibility to see that it is "faithfully executed" to the President and his agents in the executive branch. Political realities are different. Public policy is *made* in both branches. "In many ways policymaking within executive agencies is indistinguishable from the process that takes place within legislative assemblies," writes one observer. "Agencies respond to group pressures by modifying existing policies or by developing new ones. Bargaining or the adjustment of conflicting interests is as constant a feature of administrative politics as it is of relations among legislators."[10] Policy is *implemented* and *enforced,* however, primarily within the executive branch (with judicial participation). In the last four decades, the administrative branch has burgeoned in responsibilities, manpower, and impact on the nation under the stimulus of increasing federal responsibilities for social needs. Once a modest enterprise of 600,000 civil servants in 1930, it is now a mammoth institution of more than 3 million employees distributed among 11 major departments, 27 independent regulatory agencies and boards and over 100 other specialized organizations. Today, any interest that wishes to influence the shape of public policy must be prepared to understand and cope with the administrative complexities of the policy process.

Why does the administrative establishment loom so large in the making of public policy? One reason is that Congress frequently enacts legislation only in broad outline, stating general purposes and guidelines while leaving administrators with the responsibility of filling in the details and eliminating the vagaries as their more technical training dictates. The delegation of authority to administrators is unavoidable and often wise, for legislation customarily deals with technicalities and complexities in which all likely contingencies cannot be anticipated or understood. The result of this delegated authority is to bestow on administrators many options in interpreting and applying general policies in particular cases—which amounts to making policy. Moreover, legislators often prefer to let administrators work out policy details and to negotiate among interests to arrive at an acceptable interpretation of policy; it may take some political heat off the legislators, satisfy important interests, or affect the nature of the policy in a manner legislators cannot achieve through legislative means.

Since policy is implemented in the executive branch, the actual scope and impact of any policy formulated by Congress will depend on how administrators handle it. In short, policy is not effective until it is administered; how it is administered will determine how effective it will be. This political maxim is lost least of all on the interests affected by public policy. The administrative apparatus in Washington is the focus of an intense interplay of group pressures on agency officials leading to a complex pattern of political understandings and relations among administrators and pressure groups. Those who want policy, those who hope to stifle it, and those who want its modification all invest considerable energy and resources in continuing efforts to affect administrators' interpretation and implementation of programs concerning them. The interplay of interest groups with administrative agencies is almost as old as the Republic and as fundamental to politics as the law of gravity to physics.

Since we shall extensively discuss the administrative process in environmental policy later, our purpose here is only to establish the importance of this process in policy-making. There are, however, certain implications that merit emphasis. First, because administration is crucial in policy-making, much of the actual policy-making process is remote, if not totally unknown and inaccessible, to many groups and individuals. As Francis Rourke observes, the bureaucratic policy process is often the least visible part of government.

> The environment of bureaucracy is a cloistered sanctuary as compared with the limelight of publicity in which a legislative assembly normally operates. . . . The meetings, conferences, negotiations, and agreements through which bureaucratic policy decisions are reached can only be dimly seen through the opaque exterior which an administrative agency presents to the outside world.[11]

This "opaque exterior," though seldom the result of a bureaucratic conspiracy, nonetheless often conceals or obfuscates the locus of important policy decisions from those vitally concerned with them. Groups lacking established bureaucratic influence or political expertise often experience extreme difficulty in knowing when and where decisions concerning them are made.

Second, given the importance of administration, it follows that policy battles apparently won in Congress may yet be lost in the administrative labyrinth; those vanquished in the legislative arena can, and often do, resort to the administrative forum where they successfully undercut the effectiveness of policy at the point where it is interpreted and applied. Thus, political logic dictates that both friends and foes of public policy must fight a two-front war if they are to be effective. Those favoring a public policy must take care that not only is it made in Congress but also "faithfully executed" administratively. The moral is that those who rejoice in the passage of legislation, confident that they have accomplished a major task in their quest for a public policy, are often deceived. In the end, a bill may become a law, but the law is still only a proclamation of possibilities, a declaration of intent that may or may not be realized. To be successful in Congress but ineffective in the administrative sphere is to be ineffective indeed.

Finally, this discussion suggests that vigilance over administration is the price of victory in the policy process, and that successful interests in the struggle are those that can create stable access and influence within the administrative branch. There are many ways to accomplish this. Groups may develop sufficient political weight to be able to offer agency officials desirable support and encouragement in the political in-fighting common to the bureaucracy—administrators always welcome allies. Groups may find formal or informal methods for placing sympathizers within the administrative process, perhaps through appointment or recruitment to administrative positions. Sometimes interests find that influence flows to them in administrative affairs if they can acquire and exploit Congressional or White House alliances. Whatever the technique, a strategy aimed at developing a measure of political power for the group within the administrative process is virtually a prerequisite for interests seeking long-range influence over the administration of policies vital to them.

Whatever else may be said of these procedures in making our public policy, they have often proved in the past to be the major stumbling blocks of sound environmental programs. At the same time, the character of the policy process is a "given" to the contemporary proponents of environmental protection, an unyielding reality that must be confronted and, if possible, surmounted in the present effort for a new environmental policy. In essence, the environmental movement places a set of demands on Washington policy-makers that the policy process has so far not been well adapted to meet. Environmental protection through the federal government largely depends on whether the policy-making apparatus is now capable of responding to these demands appropriately. Let us examine the most important of these and the particular stress they place on our policy process.

The Challenge of Environmentalism

If Washington's efforts at environmental protection are to be something more than a charade, public officials need to find a method to respond affirmatively and effectively to some basic challenges posed to them by the environmental movement.

Protecting the Public Interest. Proposals to abate air and water pollution, to protect national resources, to reduce waste—indeed, most measures needed for environmental protection—are commonly considered public interest legislation. Those concerned with public policy have never reached a satisfactory agreement regarding what "public interest" means in general or in relation to some specific policy domain. However, as a practical matter, public interest policies are understood to be those intended to benefit a great many people or the entire public—this in distinction to policies whose benefits are rather narrowly distributed among a relatively small set of groups or economic interests.[12] Theoretically, most measures enacted and implemented in public agencies are supposed to be in the public interest but actually benefit a rather limited public. Nonetheless, environmental protection measures clearly fall into the category of policies whose benefits are presumed to flow to the public at large in the form of a safer, more enjoyable environment; these are collective benefits in the sense that "they must be available to everyone if they are available to anyone."[13]

Those who, like environmentalists, promote public interest policies confront formidable obstacles in their efforts to have such policies legislated and enforced. First, public interest legislation poses many political difficulties because, as a rule, the benefits are often intangible, long-range, and distributed among a very large public, while the costs are often very tangible, immediate, and imposed on a specific set of organized interests. Pollution abatement measures are an excellent example. Benefits from cleaner air and water will presumably accrue to each member of the public in some important but intangible manner, but the immediate expense, a very tangible one exceeding several hundred billion dollars, will be borne almost entirely by industry. The numerous private interests absorbing the immediate cost of these measures are likely to belong to existing political organizations with great influence, skillful leadership, and long experience in the political process. They also benefit, as we have observed, from some basic traits of the process itself. They enjoy many opportunities to modify or defeat such legislation, as they usually attempt to do, because the policy process "deals in" organized private interests at most strategic points and assumes that their voice should be important in policy decisions. Moreover, the diffusion of power within government allows wide latitude for such interests to delay or defeat public interest proposals by playing centers of power against one another or by occupying a crucial "veto point" among the many power centers that must be brought into the policy-making process. Thus, when public interest proposals create diffuse public benefits and specific group costs, they are likely to stimulate an intensive and extensive group mobilization that usually works against the broad objectives of a policy's supporters.

The task of securing effective public interest legislation is further compounded by the fact that groups promoting "public" measures are at a tactical disadvantage in organizing their support. Such groups are often *ad hoc organizations* that lack a continuing structure and an established access and reputation among policy-makers; it is, moreover, an arduous task to keep large segments of the public mobilized, vigilant, and active in support of such measures even if they are enacted into law. Interest wanes, the details and complexities of politics demoralize or bore many; often the "benefits" that the public expects to derive from policy are not sufficiently tangible or immediate to keep enthusiasm and political pressure strong. Then, too, the diffuse publics that often support public interest legislation can often be satisfied too easily with policies that give them largely symbolic reward but actually deliver few tangible, desired benefits; in effect, this can amount to buying off the public through "symbolic legislation." This might happen, for example, when the legislature declares that there will be a balanced use of publicly owned resources to assure that environmental protection is not sacrificed to commercial demands, but fails to provide operational standards for enforcing the rule. Supporters of environmental protection might be mollified by such a symbolic gesture, while the private interests seeking to exploit the resource largely for commercial advantage may still determine its actual use by their political influence in administrative agencies.[14]

According to an old political maxim, "money can wait." Organized special interests unsympathetic to public interest policies can often defeat them legislatively by outlasting the patience and interest of the mobilized public. Or the policies, once legislated, may be quietly frustrated within administrative agencies where the public is often uninformed or unconcerned about policy decisions. Often, notes one analyst, administrators charged with protecting the public interest discover that "the public interest must usually be identified without the constructive assistance of an organization representing the public. The organized public which eventually secured the passage of regulatory legislation quickly evaporates leaving only an inchoate, unorganized mass."[15] Thus, while environmental leaders have tried to make those concerned with environmental protection into a "constituency of conscience," such a constituency is quite vulnerable to impotence or slow dissolution.

Not least important, these policies often suffer a vagueness that leaves administrators without clear guidelines to follow in protecting the public interest. As in Gifford Pinchot's famous instructions to the Forest Service—"The public good comes first"—administrators are often given a mission to protect the public interest but not much assistance in determining what decisions are to be made, and in what manner, to this end. Not all administrators are set adrift in such a sea of ambiguity as Pinchot's directive suggests, but administrator's often find it difficult or impossible to create a satisfactory operational definition of the public's interest in a particular policy matter. In such cases, it often happens that administrators, for many reasons, must rely on the competing claims of private interests to arrive at a formulation of acceptable policy. This is especially true when administrators representing agencies with relatively weak political support must negotiate with politically potent private interests. What often happens under such circumstances is that an agency may be "captured" by the interests it is supposed to regulate for some public purpose. This has been the typical situation in the independent regulatory commissions: "Left largely to its own resources . . . a commission will probably be guided by dominant interests in the regulated industry in its formulation of the public interest. Thus the public interest may become more private than public."[16]

The capture of agencies charged with environmental programs has been frequent in the past. Over a considerable period, the Forest Service's stewardship of the federal government's public lands has come to be dominated in many respects by the commercial lumbering interests with which the service must deal; the Army Corps of Engineers has, in large measure, yielded any independent control of water resource development in favor of active collaboration with numerous private interests and Congressional leaders in the development of projects desired by these groups. The fate of the Forest Service and the Corps is perhaps an extreme illustration of public agencies whose public responsibilities have been subverted to largely private ends, but they symbolize a persistent trend in governmental affairs that environmentalists consider pernicious.

Concentrating Environmental Authority. If a "clean environment" is to be more than an official piety, it requires public officials to achieve substantial changes in the content and organization of policy-making. Such innovation, while not impossible, is difficult in our typically incremental decision-making system. It is, in general, a demand that moves in two directions. In the case of air and water pollution, it is a quest for new administrative agencies with broad, potent policies to deal decisively with problems that government has largely ignored in the past. In the case of other environmental issues such as resource use, land use, waste management, and pesticide control, the objective is to reinvigorate the agencies responsible for these matters with a sense of mission—to resurrect, especially, a concern for the public interest—while providing new resources and powers to agency officials. Both goals are difficult because they represent an effort to advance policy content and procedure well beyond the *status quo* and thus generate the inherent resistance to change that is part of the incremental system.

Probably the greatest single impediment to administrative innovation, regardless of where or when it is attempted, is the strong bureaucratic resistance to major change resulting from the "sunk costs" built into existing policy and procedure. These sunk costs have mounted over a long time in an agency's bureaucratic history and have produced some very crucial rewards that are not easily or willingly jeopardized. As Anthony Downs explains:

> . . . bureaus have a powerful tendency to continue doing today whatever they did yesterday. The main reason for this inertia is that established processes represent an enormous investment in time, effort and money. . . . Years of effort, thousands of decisions (including mistakes), and a wide variety of experiences underlie the behavior pat-

> terns a bureau now uses. Moreover, it took a significant investment to get the bureau's many members and clients to accept and become habituated to its behavior patterns.[17]

Nonetheless, sound environmental protection appears to require a sacrifice of some sunk costs as the price of administrative innovation.

Several innovations appear particularly imperative. The need for *comprehensive planning* and *comprehensive authority* for environmental use and protection is very great; broad environmental planning is largely a futile enterprise unless planners have enough power to implement their programs. The need for comprehensive environmental planning arises from the interdependence of environmental problems themselves; the environment, as ecologists emphasize, is a unity in which problems and solutions are all related. In governmental terms, this means that policy arrangements ideally should assure that various environmental programs are coordinated through some agency or agencies with a broad view of environmental problems and an awareness of how individual programs interrelate. Comprehensive authority would then be the necessary complement that assures planning will be implemented.

Achieving a comprehensive governmental approach to environmental management is a formidable task, for environmental policies have been neither comprehensively planned nor controlled. Rather, planning and authority have been fragmented into a bewildering mosaic of different agencies and levels of government, producing frequent confusion, contradiction, and frustration in environmental management. Planning has often proceeded by fits and starts owing to the diffusion of power within the system; incremental change was the easiest to engineer and, hence, the common element in most environmental programs. Both federalism and fragmentary authority within the national administration impede comprehensive environmental planning. The distribution of authority over most major environmental programs among national, state, and local agencies has commonly produced inconsistency or failure in the planning effort. As the President's Council on Environmental Quality noted, independent local governments, each exercising its own tiny ration of authority, cannot attack water degradation adequately:

> . . . their focus is often too narrow to cope with the broad environmental problems that cut across many jurisdictions. Agencies dealing with water pollution, for example, typically do not have jurisdiction over the geographical problem—the watersheds. Control is split, instead, among sewage districts, municipalities, and a multitude of other local institutions.[18]

Not only the authority but the will to enforce effective water pollution controls is often absent at local levels. Upstream polluters, whether private or municipal, seldom feel the need to abate water degradation as urgently as do the recipients of the pollution downstream; communities competing for industry are often reluctant to initiate stringent water pollution controls that might discourage business from settling in their area.[19]

Congress's penchant for delegating authority over water pollution abatement to state and local governments has aggravated the planning problem. The U.S. Comptroller General's 1969 study of all federal grants to upgrade state water treatment facilities between 1957 and 1969—a $1.2 billion program involving 9,400 grants—illustrates how the planning that Congress had encouraged failed to materialize. According to the report, the states, rather than planning for the best funding of facilities, commonly listed all municipalities needing funds in alphabetical order, left the initiative for seeking such funds to the local governments, and failed to encourage local planning for sewage treatment. Congress again showed its preference for decentralized authority over comprehensive planning in the important Water Quality Act of 1965, which left to each state such important decisions as the most desirable use for its waters and acceptable pollution levels within its jurisdiction.

A more promising approach to air and water pollution abatement would be the creation of regional authorities with comprehensive control over whole watersheds or "airsheds." This, however, would require that state and local governments relinquish some authority to regional agencies—a proposal they stoutly resist. Currently, only five river-basin authorities exist in the

United States—none with very impressive credentials. The Ohio River Valley Water Development Authority, often considered the best of these regional entities, has seldom initiated proceedings against major water polluters mainly because action requires virtual unanimity among the many representatives of the eight states constituting the authority; similar requirements for near consensus on action have hampered other regional agencies.

While decentralization of authority obstructs comprehensive environmental planning, it is usually favored by major industries and other interests that bear a major cost for environmental clean-up. Industrial influence is especially strong at local and state levels; hence, business can exert considerable influence in shaping environmental policy when state and local governments are empowered to do this task. Also, state and local governments have less sophistication and fewer resources to deal with industry than has the federal government; often, in fact, major industries are better equipped with technologists and resources in the pollution control area than are governmental units. Thus, the decentralization of environmental planning authority through federalism generally works, intentionally or not, to the advantage of major polluters, while frustrating extensive planning.

At the federal level, efforts at comprehensive planning have usually been grounded in the past by the dispersion of environmental authority within Washington's bureaucracy. Many environmental problems fail to respect organizational charts and cut instead across the jurisdiction of several agencies that seldom approach solutions through coordinated efforts. Agencies with one primary environmental mission—commercial fishing, water resource development, or forest management, for instance—often work zealously within a narrow view of their task that desensitizes them to the wide-ranging ecological consequences of their endeavors. Additionally, some agencies have acquired an operational independence that insulates them from the influence of attempted comprehensive planning. The need for centralized federal environmental planning has long been recognized by administrative analysts, but their exhortations were largely ignored until recently. In 1971, President Nixon responded to the mounting gravity of environmental problems by proposing in his Environmental Message that a cabinet-level Department of Natural Resources be established to plan and coordinate federal resource programs and, thus, to end the welter of existing agencies and departments sharing environmental authority. The lack of this authority has resulted in some of the following situations:

- The 1969 Santa Barbara oil spill was the responsibility of three different agencies within the Interior Department: the Bureau of Land Management (which issues federal land oil leases), the U.S. Geological Survey (which oversees the technical aspects of federal oil leases), and the Federal Water Pollution Control Administration. The Federal Water Pollution Control Administration stayed out of the crisis to avoid further confusion, and Secretary of the Interior Hickle, irritated by the lack of action in the other agencies, finally intervened directly in the crisis.
- A gypsum company requested a permit to dig into four miles of Los Padres National Forest in California, basing its request on a claim bought in 1963. The nesting grounds of the rare California condor were threatened. While the Department of the Interior's Land Management Bureau could issue mining exploration permits, the forests were under the jurisdiction of the Department of Agriculture's Forest Service. The Forest Service could only advise the other bureau on issuing the permit but would have to supervise any regulations issued by Land Management. Further, the U.S. Geological Survey had at least a technical oversight of the mining efforts. The agencies could not agree upon issuing the permit and consultation continues.
- The departments of Agriculture and the Interior share extensive authority over timber cutting on federal land, control of pesticides, dam building, and soil conservation; the competition and division over policy has been continual and frequently acrimonious.

Disagreements over environmental policy would undoubtedly persist in federal agencies regardless of the degree of centralized environmental planning and authority achieved in Washington; better planning arrangements would, however, reduce the instances of deadlock, confusion, and contradiction now common with agency policies.

Even should greater centralized planning and authority be accomplished within government, such innovations—like other purely administrative alterations—would hardly be more than cosmetic touches in the name of ecology unless there also takes place some transformation in the nature and priority of administrative values among those concerned with environmental protection. Obviously, to wait until administrators acquire a set of values certified as ecologically acceptable would be to wait forever. However, a significant advance in environmental protection does seem to require that some *relative* rearrangement of values occur. Most analysts suggest that environmental protection requires at least the following changed priorities among those responsible for decisions affecting the environment:

1. *Greater emphasis on long-range environmental consequences of decisions, less on the short-range economic consequences.* For many reasons, administrators have customarily been guided in environmental decisions by short-range economic considerations. Local officials confront almost irresistible pressure to "develop" land and other resources to increase jobs, expand employment, broaden the tax base, and satisfy local interests benefiting from economic growth. State and federal officials have often sanctioned resource development and exploitation because of short-term economic advantages—especially in creating dams and canals and in leasing rights to public land by private interests. Pollution controls were often minimal and minimally enforced out of concern for consequences. A new environmental ethic would require a greater "balancing" of interests if not an absolute priority to long-run environmental values.

2. *A devaluation of the growth ethic.* "The most primordial fact of American culture," notes one observer, "remains its emphasis upon production." Production, or "growth" in all its economic dimensions, has been an orthodoxy of American business and public officials; it is imbedded in the logic of American public policy at all levels and, with few exceptions, in the cultural outlook of most Americans. The environmental movement, however, demands that growth no longer be viewed as an unqualified good or a goal to be approached as speedily as possible—though

never fully attained. Instead, wise resource use and environmental protection appear to require some restraint on growth and very thoughtful reflection on its proper course and dimensions; unless these constraints are created by public officials, resource use is likely to proceed at a pace so rapid and unguided that irreversible environmental damage and dangerous resource depletion will occur.

3. *Less emphasis on the politics of compromise.* Public officials cannot long function effectively unless they are able to routinize and stabilize their relationships with the important private interests and other governmental agencies with which they must deal. We have seen that our governmental process encourages bargaining and compromise among these competing interests, with the result that administrative policies usually represent a moderate mid-position among the contending sides of a policy issue. However, this process of seeking the middle ground in policy conflicts often works against sound environmental policy. Effective environmental protection may require that administrators advocate and enforce politics that do not belong in the mid-range of options—that they find, in brief, means to push ahead without resorting to the politics of compromise as the primary tool of administrative decision-making.

Many administrative experts would regard these prescriptions as a counsel of perfection unsuited to the harsh realities of administrative politics in Washington. It is an intriguing question whether such changes can be achieved and to what extent. What is important, however, is that most of these alternatives are implied by any significant proposal for environmental protection—that is, genuine environmental protection seems to demand both changes in substantive policy and alterations in the way decisions are made. This is one reason the environmental movement constitutes a major challenge to Washington's decision-making apparatus.

Enforcing Administrative Responsibility. Environmental administrators are rarely deliberate assassins of the public interest in a wholesome environment. They are usually conscientious, reasonably diligent, and well-intentioned individuals trying to fulfill their mission under circumstances that have often contrived to produce undesirable environmental policy. Without impugning the integrity of most administrators, however, it seems imperative that new policies aimed at environmental restoration be attended with greater emphasis on assuring accountability and reasonable faithfulness within the administrative branch in the implementation of these policies.

The need for increasing accountability arises from the field of political forces in which administrators operate in making environmental decisions. Our earlier discussion amply illustrated the considerable advantage that private interests enjoy in pressing their claims in environmental matters upon administrators. Additionally, legislators are also major participants in the administrative process, often exerting pressure to sway administrative decisions in directions incompatible with the intent of environmental legislation. A former commissioner of the Federal Power Commission describes how legislators often collaborate with important constituents to submit administrators to the "hard sell":

> . . . if it becomes necessary, industry can turn to its true friends, those representatives or senators who understand the role of government and business. For the hard sell, discreet phone calls from distinguished senators from the "oil patch" or the current impoverished area as to the status of a particular case usually are informative enough for a good political regulator or administrator to get the message. Or possibly someone in government needs more money which can be obtained from bonuses for offshore oil and gas concessions. There is even the possibility that upon leaving government you can secure a good consulting contract for your new firm with either industry or the local, state or federal agencies—if you are a good boy. It is tempting.[20]

To these persuasive influences must be added the administrator's frequent vulnerability to outside pressure. This situation is most often created by the ambiguity of the goals he is supposed to achieve and the absence of effective group support for decisions more consonant with environmental protection.

Faced with these conditions, administrators often cope by resorting to strategies that environmental lawyer Joseph Sax calls "nibbling" and "suboptimizing"—strategies used quite often, without conscious intent, to defeat sound environmental management. "Nibbling," suggests Sax, is a process whereby administrators continually make little compromises with their environmental responsibilities by allowing the intrusion of wrong values into their decisions. "It is so easy for an administrator to adopt the position that this is the last intrusion to be permitted, that no bad precedent is being set, and that the line will be drawn at the next case."[21] But the line is often never drawn decisively, with the result that serious environmental responsibilities are compromised severely. "Suboptimizing" is a strategy for making a decision when "all the many constraints, pressures and influences at work are taken into account."[22] This is often decision by common denominator; the policy that best satisfies the most demands is made, and, in the process, the administrator often responds most readily to whatever combination of interests can generate the most compelling pressures upon him. Such approaches to decision-making, of course, can represent a willful effort to subvert policy intended to protect the environment, but, probably in most cases, they represent simply the best approaches administrators feel they can use and still function in their own milieu.

The point is not to judge the motivation of administrators but to suggest why concern for accountability in environmental affairs arises so often in discussions of sound environmental management. There are many procedures through which greater accountability might be obtained. One is vigorous legislative oversight of administrative decisions, an exercise of authority well within Congress's power to investigate and monitor administrative activity. How much this would accomplish would depend on many factors: the will and ability of Congress to conduct such oversight and the dedication of legislators to sound environmental use. Based on past experience, most environmentalists do not consider such a procedure the most promising means to achieve administrative accountability. Yet another procedure might be the creation within the administrative branch of an administrative unit with the specific responsibility for reviewing the conduct of environmental policy; alternatively, a new super-agency for environmental affairs might be established and staffed with administrators at the top level who would assume comprehensive authority over most environmental programs, together with sweeping planning powers. This last suggestion, in effect, is an effort to make a new start toward environmental management with a new administrative institution and personnel lacking the vested interests and established political alliances of older agencies.

Many environmentalists, however, believe a more promising approach lies in enabling environmental groups to use the courts as an instrument to enforce accountability—a procedure that might at first seem doomed to failure since it has worked poorly in the past. In general, the federal courts have so far been reluctant to review thoroughly or overturn administrative decisions relating to the environment, partly because judges did not consider themselves sufficiently knowledgeable in the frequently technical problems involved in environmental policy and partly because, following well-established legal precedent, judges viewed such determinations as policy issues that should not be resolved in the courts.[23] The practical effect of this judicial stance was to make it difficult, and usually impossible, for ecologists to challenge administrative decisions on environmental matters through the initiation of suits. Many ecologists now believe judicial methods to enforce administrative accountability may be more promising. They cite the government's growing ecological concern, which may incline judges to greater interest in environmental affairs, the enactment of new legislation—much of which we shall discuss in Chapter 8—that encourages citizen suits against administrative agencies to enforce environmental protection, and the enactment of bills that charge administrators with detailed, specific environmental responsibilities.[24]

Regardless of which strategies, if any, prove effective in securing a significant measure of administrative accountability in the handling of environmental policy, the issue will remain of utmost importance in the long-range effectiveness of current governmental efforts at environmental restoration.

No response yet made to the environmental crisis by the federal government has greater potential significance than the enactment of the National Environmental Policy Act of 1969 and the creation of the Environmental Protection Agency. They represent the most sweeping attempts yet to deal with environmental degradation at the level of the federal government and to solve the policy-making problems that, as we have seen, could obstruct or defeat sound environmental policy. While it is far too early to assess the impact of these measures, their unusual promise and influence on the course of all major environmental policy issues sets them apart for special emphasis.

The National Environmental Policy Act of 1969

The National Environmental Policy Act of 1969 (NEPA), an unprecedented bill, declared the federal government's commitment to a broad range of environmental protection goals and measures; it is the most thorough and comprehensive statement of environmental protection policy enacted by Congress.[25] Borne through Congress on a peaking tide of public environmental concern, NEPA encountered relatively little opposition, receiving the massive legislative support usually given only to measures of the utmost gravity or triviality. Far from trivial, NEPA set in motion a series of events that would have caused many Congressmen apprehension had they anticipated the consequences soon to be evident.

NEPA begins with a very general and generous federal pledge to environmental protection. The opening section declares:

> . . . it is the continuing policy of the Federal Government, in cooperation with State and local governments, and other concerned public and private organizations, to use all practicable means and measures . . . to create and maintain conditions under which man and nature can exist in productive harmony, and fulfill the social, economic, and other requirements of present and future generations of Americans.

Congress then pledged itself to assure healthy and pleasing surroundings to citizens, to avoid degradation of the environment, to preserve historic cultural and natural aspects of our national heritage, to achieve a balance between population and resources, and to enhance the quality of renewable resources, among other specific goals. Toward these ends, the act required the President to deliver an annual Environmental Quality Report to Congress. The cutting edge of NEPA, however, is its provisions requiring "impact statements" for all federal actions affecting the environment and its creation of the Council on Environmental Quality.

The Environmental Impact Statement. The provision in NEPA that has had the greatest immediate impact on governmental policy is its requirement of an "environmental impact statement," set forth in Section 102(2)(C). This section declares that all federal agencies must accompany "every recommendation or report on proposals for legislation and other major Federal actions significantly affecting the quality of the human environment" with a detailed report that describes:

1. The environmental impact of the proposed project
2. Any adverse environmental effects that cannot be avoided should the proposal be implemented
3. Alternatives to the proposed action
4. The relationship between local short-term uses of man's environment and the maintenance and enhancement of long-term productivity
5. Any irreversible or irretrievable commitments of resources that would be involved in the proposed action should it be implemented

These "102 statements" must ultimately be made available to the public and filed with the President's Council on Environmental Quality; according to guidelines established by the Council on Environmental Quality, initial drafts of these statements must be available to the public and other agencies at least ninety days prior to the contemplated action, and final statements—taking account of comments from public and private agencies—must be available to the public at least thirty days in advance of the action. After "102 statements" are properly filed with the council, it may advise the President or the concerned agency about the desirability of proposed action in light of its environmental impact.

The requirement for impact statements had a number of clearly important purposes. It was an effort to force agency administrators to make a careful, searching appraisal of the environmental effects of their activities, to give the President and his advisers a comprehensive view of the environmental impact of federal activities, and to open federal actions to challenge on grounds of environmental impact—all of which was to apply categorically to *all* federal agencies and *all* activities that might effect the environment. Moreover, the rather exacting language of the requirement left administrators with fairly clear guidelines to follow in their appraisal. If these purposes are achieved to any important degree, the act would clearly represent a major attack on many of the policy-making problems that would seem to interfere with effective environmental protection.

The impact statement in its early operation has been a unique challenge to federal administrators. Administrators long accustomed to the role of advocate for their particular agency projects were now expected to engage in self-criticism and searching examination of the ecological value of their efforts. The specific requirements that agencies had to meet to produce a satisfactory impact statement were far from clear and are still being clarified through administrative channels and court action. Many agencies lacked the technical resources and experts that seemed necessary to conform to the requirements of Section 102. There was, moreover, the usual uncertainty at the beginning of the program concerning how consistently and rigidly the demands for impact statements would be enforced. Despite such inevitable confusion, some early trends were apparent. To begin, although 1,300 impact statements were filed during the first full year of NEPA's operation, many agencies were slow to initiate impact statements, either through ignorance concerning their exact responsibilities or through reluctance to subject themselves to environmental impact studies. One large question, therefore, concerns how thoroughly the impact statements will affect all agency actions. Moreover, many of the impact statements were far from satisfactory. "Too often," noted the Council on Environmental Quality, "the environmental impact statement is written to justify decisions already made, rather than to provide a mechanism for critical review."[26] In particular, agencies filing impact statements were often reluctant to consider seriously the alternative of abandoning their proposed actions or projects when environmental damage seemed likely. Sometimes, even agencies with the capacity to produce respectable impact statements produced slapdash affairs that indicated an unwillingness to make a serious impact study unless external sanctions were applied.

Notwithstanding all this, environmentalists found several reasons for encouragement in the early application of the impact statement to federal activities. The most important positive result was that it provided citizens and conservation groups with the means to challenge administrative decisions concerning the environment in the courts. Early rulings on impact statements generally upheld the right of citizens to challenge these statements in the courts and to require that impact studies on projects be properly made; moreover—in a very significant reversal of history—the courts also asserted that as a rule administrators had to take account of conservationists' objections to projects in making impact statements.[27] As a result of this judicial attitude, a number of major federal projects, including water resource developments, were temporarily or permanently halted by the federal courts because agency sponsors failed to produce satisfactory impact studies. Environmentalists were further heartened by the courts' frequent willingness to go beyond a simple determination that impact statements had superficially followed the steps required by law and into a more thorough inspection to assure that statements actually investigated environmental impact carefully. Also encouraging was the courts' opinion that impact statements would be required for projects under way but not finished. One immediate effect of the impact statement, in short, was to expose administrative decisions concerning the environment to court inspection and citizen challenge—an important step in breaching the protective wall that has long insulated administrators from effective influence by environmentalists.

It is too early to assess the long-run significance of the impact statement, for early trends could easily be reversed or substantially altered by subsequent events. It is very likely, for instance, that if the impact statements continue to affect major federal projects significantly, there will be an effort in Congress to rewrite Section 102 in order to diminish its influence on policy. There is already evidence that Congress may have written into the NEPA a more effective law than it intended, for many congressmen have been surprised and irritated by the effect of the impact statements so far. A number of dams, canals, and other pork-barrel projects much esteemed by legislators have been casualties; most of these projects—as we shall see in later chapters—were halted temporarily or permanently by the courts because agency impact statements were absent or inadequate. In the wake of these decisions, a backlash of Congressional sentiment, still of uncertain strength, has developed to relax the impact statement requirements in the NEPA or to exclude entirely many local public works from the law's jurisdiction.

The Council on Environmental Quality. A second major provision of the NEPA created the President's Council on Environmental Quality (CEQ), the highest level advisory body to the President on environmental affairs. The CEQ is part of the Executive Office of the President and thus shares a formal status equal to that of the President's Council of Economic Advisers and other bodies that are top-level staff arms of the Presidency. The council, appointed by the President with the advice and consent of the Senate, consists of three members (one of whom is designated the chairman) serving at the pleasure of the Chief Executive.

The National Environmental Policy Act assigns many potentially important functions to the CEQ. It is expected to advise the President in the preparation of the annual Environmental Quality Report, gather "timely and important information" regarding environmental problems and transmit it to the President, review federal programs for their environmental implications, recommend legislation to the President, create independent environmental studies, and review environmental impact statements from the other federal agencies. In later legislation, Congress added to the CEQ a small professional staff, the Office of Environmental Quality, to assist it in discharging these responsibilities. The CEQ's actual influence will largely depend on how the President chooses to use the council. Like other White House advisory groups, the CEQ has the prerogative to inform, advise, and warn the President, but it has no right to be heeded and no operating authority over other agencies; it has no constituency of its own, nor funding for more than a modest level of independent activity. To its inherent weakness caused by a lack of political or administrative strength is added its dependence on the President to define what role it should play in the decision-making process. Since President Nixon had opposed the council's creation and Congress appropriated very limited funds for it, its initial prospects did not seem bright. Nonetheless, the council has taken the initiative in creating detailed specifications for impact statements, for reviewing them and advising the President on federal programs in the light of these statements. Moreover, the council appears to have largely shaped the President's 1971 and 1972 legislation proposals on the environment, and its advice was cited by President Nixon as a major reason for his unprecedented decision to halt the Cross Florida Barge Canal because of its detrimental environmental impact. From the viewpoint of environmental specialists, the council's annual reports constitute a very important source of data and policy information on environmental affairs.

The Environmental Protection Agency

In December, 1970, President Nixon officially created the Environmental Protection Agency (EPA) with the concurrence of Congress, and thereby initiated the most imaginative, sweeping federal effort to restructure and revitalize the making of pollution control policy. The EPA, now the most important "action" agency in Washington's attack on pollution, has rapidly acquired great attention and exposure nationally because it is usually the organizational arena for major pollution policy conflicts.

The EPA represents an effort to combat the decentralization and fragmentation of power in the field of federal pollution control; it is intended to provide a framework in which long-range policy planning and policy coordination can be achieved. To centralize the administration of pollution control in Washington, the EPA absorbed five major pollution programs that had previously been parceled out among various agencies. Specifically, it acquired authority over (1) water pollution policy formerly administered by the Federal Water Quality Administration in the Interior Department; (2) air pollution policy supervised by the National Air Pollution Control Administration in the Department of Health, Education, and Welfare; (3) solid waste management programs that had been part of Health, Education, and Welfare; (4) the setting of standards and guidelines for radiation control previously done by the Federal Radiation Council; and (5) the registration of pesticides and standard-setting for other toxic substances previously under the jurisdictions of the departments of Agriculture and Health, Education, and Welfare. Unlike the Council on Environmental Quality, the EPA is a "line" agency with great operating authority and resources. Not only has it acquired the authority and responsibility for pollution problems that were previously bestowed on the agencies it supplanted, but it is likely to have operational authority over most new federal pollution policies. With a budget of $2.5 billion in fiscal 1972 and more than 7,000 employees, the EPA had more appropriations and manpower than several cabinet departments. Like the Atomic Energy Commission and the National Aeronautics and Space Administration, the EPA is an independent agency outside the jurisdiction of any existing federal department.

Since the effectiveness of federal pollution control will largely depend on the aggressiveness and initiative of the EPA, the long-run political status of the agency is crucial. The EPA began its organizational existence with many political problems that may eventually diminish the vigor of its pollution controls. As a new agency lacking an organized constituency of its own, it was vulnerable to the slow attrition of support for its programs that has occurred with other regulatory agencies charged with public interest policies. It inherited the policies of other pollution control agencies, and in many cases those agencies had reached understandings with their regulated interests that undermined the force of pollution regulation. The EPA, moreover, was bound to experience intense pressure as major private interests subject to pollution controls worked to assure themselves of a voice in policy-making; indeed, within a few months of the EPA's creation, the Iron and Steel Institute suggested that a "policy review board" with industry representatives should pass judgment on water pollution standards set by the agency. Although the review board was stillborn, most regulated interests were actively seeking various ways to gain some leverage with agency administrators. In many respects, the EPA was beginning in a position similar to that of other regulatory agencies whose "life cycle" ended with their capture by the regulated.

The EPA's leadership believed that the agency could be effective if a sense of mission developed among its personnel and if it took a tough stance toward pollution control during early encounters with industry, thereby establishing its credibility as a pollution fighter. To the surprise of many observers, the EPA under its first administrator, William D. Ruckelshaus, did take a firm stance against pollution. During his early months in office, Ruckelshaus ordered action against 185 air and water polluters, including U.S. Steel, ITT-Rayonier, and the cities of Detroit and Cleveland; the administrator had purposely chosen large polluters in keeping with his philosophy to "single out violators with the greatest visibility in order to get the message across." The EPA also exerted its influence to convince the Secretary of the Interior to engage in a more searching examination of the ecological effects from the Alaskan oil pipeline before approving its construction. While the EPA did make some accommodation with industry in a few regulatory matters, the agency seemed determined to establish a reputation as a hard-liner on pollution regulation through dramatic, early encounters with major polluters. Whether the credibility of the agency has been established and will be justified cannot yet be determined. To date, the agency has been considerably more dedicated to its mission than many veteran observers could have predicted.

Summary: Ecology and the Politics of Procedure

It should now be apparent why the creation of a truly operative policy of environmental protection is an arduous task, though not an unattainable goal. The struggle must proceed at two levels. At the policy level, it is a drive to assure that the stated ends of policy and its actual substance are compatible with environmental protection. At the procedural level, it is a struggle to assure that the way in which policy decisions are implemented will be conducive to the principles of environmental protection to which policy is ostensibly committed. The procedural issue, as we have seen, has been a formidable impediment to environmental protection in the past, for the design of the policy process has been one of those pikes upon which sound environmental policy has been impaled, a structural feature of our basic policy process that environmentalists cannot easily design out of the governmental system. In effect, there is a "politics of procedure" in American government, a distribution of advantage and influence ordained by the architecture of our traditional decision-making system that has worked, and may well continue to work, to the disadvantage of ecology.

The creation of the National Environmental Protection Act and the Environmental Protection Agency indicates the stirring of efforts to break out of traditional decision-making forms. Yet, there is no assurance that these acts may not in the end become "symbolic legislation" that fails to deliver the real rewards of environmental protection desired by the environmental movement. What seems apparent, in any case, is that both substantive and procedural changes must take place in Washington policy-making if the federal government's very uneven record of past ecological achievements is to be improved. Whether this can be accomplished, and to what extent, will largely be written in the record of Washington's attack on particular environmental problems. Let us turn, then, in the remaining chapters to a number of specific environmental issues in an effort to ascertain what has been accomplished, substantively and procedurally, in dealing with these issues.

Notes

1. This point is made in summary form in Charles E. Lindblom, *The Policy-Making Process* (Englewood Cliffs, N.J.: Prentice-Hall, 1968), chapter 1. Its elaboration, from which much of the subsequent discussion is drawn, may be found in Charles E. Lindblom, *The Intelligence of Democracy* (New York: The Free Press, 1965).
2. This point is made cogently in David B. Truman, *The Governmental Process* (New York: Alfred A. Knopf, 1960), chapter 9.
3. Charles E. Lindblom, *op. cit.*, p. 26.
4. *Ibid.*, p. 27.
5. Theodore Lowi, "The Public Philosophy: Interest-Group Liberalism," *American Political Science Review*, March, 1967, p. 18.
6. Grant McConnell, *Private Power and American Democracy* (New York: Vintage Books, 1968), p. 162.
7. The role of advisory bodies in administrative decisions is usefully summarized in Harold Seidman, *Politics, Position and Power: The Dynamics*

of Federal Organization (New York: Oxford University Press, 1970), pp. 237–68; the figure cited is taken from this discussion.

8. Morton Grodzins, "The Federal System," in Aaron Wildavsky, *American Federalism in Perspective* (Boston: Little, Brown and Co., 1967), p. 257.
9. *Ibid.*, p. 260.
10. Francis E. Rourke, *Bureaucracy, Politics and Public Policy* (Boston: Little, Brown and Co., 1969), p. 103.
11. *Ibid.*, p. 113.
12. This is certainly the sense in which it is commonly discussed among academic social scientists. See, for example, Glendon Schubert, *The Public Interest* (Glencoe, Ill.: The Free Press, 1960).
13. Matthew A. Crenson, *The Un-Politics of Air Pollution* (Baltimore: The Johns Hopkins Press, 1971), p. 137.
14. This argument is suggested by Ted Caldwell and Leslie L. Roos, Jr., "Voluntary Compliance and Pollution Abatement," in Leslie L. Roos, Jr., *The Politics of Ecosuicide* (New York: Holt, Rinehart and Winston, 1971), p. 243. Federal policy guaranteeing multiple use of the national forests might be considered a case of such symbolic legislation. See chapter 7 for a discussion of this issue.
15. Marver H. Bernstein, *Regulating Business by Independent Commission* (Princeton, N.J.: Princeton University Press, 1955), p. 156.
16. *Ibid.*, p. 154.
17. Anthony Downs, *Inside Bureaucracy* (Boston: Little, Brown and Co., 1967), p. 195.
18. Council on Environmental Quality, *Environmental Quality, 1971* (Washington, D.C., 1971), p. 15.
19. Local views are nicely summarized in J. Clarence Davies, *The Politics of Pollution* (New York: Pegasus Press, 1970), pp. 130 ff.
20. Charles R. Ross, "The Federal Government as an Inadvertent Advocate of Environmental Degradation," in Harold W. Helfrich, Jr. (ed.), *The Environmental Crisis* (New Haven: Yale University Press, 1970), p. 182.
21. Joseph L. Sax, *Defending the Environment* (New York: Alfred A. Knopf, 1971), p. 55.
22. *Ibid.*, p. 53.
23. The argument for a judicial approach is most carefully presented in *Defending the Environment* by Joseph L. Sax, noted above. A summary with a slightly different emphasis may be found by the same author in "The Search for Environmental Quality: The Role of the Courts," in Harold W. Halfrich, Jr., *The Environmental Crisis* (New Haven: Yale University Press, 1970), pp. 99–114.
24. Some early results of this philosophy are analyzed in Walter A. Rosenbaum and Paul A. Roberts, "The Year of Sour Pork: Comments on the Role of the Courts as Environmental Defenders," *Law and Society Review*, Fall, 1972, pp. 33–60.
25. Public Law 91-190, January 1, 1970.
26. Council on Environmental Quality, *Environmental Quality, 1971* (Washington, D.C., 1971), p. 26.
27. See Walter A. Rosenbaum and Paul A. Roberts, *op. cit.*

5 *"You've Got to Hit Them with a Two-by-Four": Regulating Air and Water Pollution*

Numerous environmentalists who were first incensed by Walter J. Hickel's appointment as Secretary of the Interior were later angered by his dismissal. Before the President permanently benched him from the Nixon team for "personal disloyalty" in 1970, Hickel in his brief tenure had earned the respect of many ecologists for his progressively tough stand against environmental degradation, a surprise to many who initially considered him a weak conservationist. One incident that nourished Hickel's disenchantment with federal environmental regulation was the aftermath of the 1969 Santa Barbara oil spill. Convinced that the California incident arose from corporate negligence toward safety regulations and weak bureaucratic enforcement, Hickel ordered an inspection of 7,000 oil rigs in the Gulf of Mexico that revealed hundreds lacking the federally required safety chokes; immediate prosecutions were ordered. Reflecting upon that incident, the Secretary propounded what might be called Hickel's Law for dealing with pollution violaters: "You've got to hit them with a two-by-four to make them believe you."[1]

Until recently, Hickel's Law did not inspire the federal government's approach to pollution control. Past attempts were indecisive, reflecting a general weakness in federal pollution regulations that were encumbered with vague or unenforceable standards, irresolute leadership, and fragmented authority. Mounting evidence of environmental degradation and the conspicuous failure of past abatement policies have lately forced Washington to take the first tentative steps toward a more rigorous abatement policy. But the federal government's historically crabwise approach to pollution control has left in its wake a multitude of policies and precedents that impede today's more decisive efforts. We are apparently in a transitional period between an era of feeble pollution abatement and a period promising more aggressive, vigorous controls; the potency of these new policies has yet to be demonstrated.

Until the mid-1960's, the federal government's efforts at controlling air and water pollution consisted principally of encouraging the states to initiate their own programs, providing funds for air and water pollution research at federal, state, and local levels, and (in the case of water pollution) allocating funds for pollution control facilities. In addition, the Congress provided federal pollution control officials with rather restricted powers to abate air or water pollution when it was interstate and threatened public health and safety. Beginning with the 1965 Water Quality Act and the 1967 Air Quality Act, the federal government adopted the "standards-and-enforcement" approach to pollution regulation that still governs many important aspects of federal pollution policy.

Standards and Enforcement

Only a relative handful of Americans are likely to understand much about the intricacies of pollution control policy. Americans may be pardoned for their ignorance. The design of federal policy-making on air and water pollution seems extraordinarly convoluted and tortuously complex, abounding with technicalities and bristling with an esoteric vocabulary—a situation that easily confounds the layman and deflates the resolve of even the well-motivated investigator. The complexities, however, are not necessarily as forbidding as they may appear. The key to imposing order on this process is an understanding of the standards-and-enforcement approach to pollution control that underlies Washington's current attack on air and water contamination. Once one understands the architecture of this system and its technical vocabulary, both the logic and the problems inherent in federal pollution abatement are revealed.

Essentially, the standards-and-enforcement method of pollution abatement involves a series of five phases through which pollution policy must pass before it is fully operative. Leaving aside for a moment the matter of which governmental officials will make and implement the policies at each phase, we can briefly describe the system in broad outline.[2]

Goal Setting. In theory, the first step in pollution abatement begins with a determination by public officials of the ultimate objectives they seek to accomplish through air and water pollution management. In the case of water pollution, for example, this may consist of a set of different uses to be assigned various water bodies; some might be designated for recreational use, others for navigation or commercial traffic, still others for industrial purposes—many categories and combinations are possible. In the case of ambient air, the goal may be to prevent the creation or aggravation of various respiratory illnesses, to eliminate smog, or to reduce crop damage. Logically, the specification of goals is the necessary first step in pollution abatement because it establishes the target for abatement policy. In practice, goals are sometimes vague or unspecified; there may be scant information available concerning what pollution levels are compatible with various goals or, especially in air pollution matters, officials may be content to pledge themselves to achieve the maximum abatement possible with existing technology.

Criteria. Criteria are technical data, commonly supplied by research scientists, that indicate what pollutants are associated with environmental damage and how different levels and combinations of pollutants will affect the environment. The practical purpose of criteria is to give public officials some operational concept of what pollutant levels they must achieve if various "goals" for air and water purity are to be realized. If, for instance, officials are pledged to reducing the danger of respiratory illness from ambient air in industrial centers, they will need to know what effect varying levels of sulfur oxide may have on humans. In a similar vein, if officials want to protect a river for a recreational use such as fishing, they will need to know how much organic waste can be tolerated before its biochemical oxygen demand (BOD) robs sports fish of necessary oxygen; officials may also want data concerning what BOD levels are desirable for various types of sports fish. Such criteria must be established for each pollutant.

Creating criteria for major air and water contaminants is extremely slow, laborious, and costly. Until the 1960's, little such research had been conducted. Only in late 1971 did the Environmental Protection Agency begin the first large-scale survey of industrial wastes discharged into the nation's waterways; although the Council on Environmental Quality estimates that more than one hundred different indexes of environmental quality should be studied, little data have been assembled. With adequate funding (which is not always dependable), reliable data take years to accumulate, and even then may be extremely contentious. Arguments arise not only among scientists who may disagree about the reliability of the data, but also among scientists, public officials, and the principal interests affected by pollution abatement. Although criteria are supposed to be only "advisory" to public officials, once scientists create such a standard for a given pollutant it is often regarded as a final verdict; thus, if researchers advise that a given concentration of particulates seems likely to create chronic smog, officials may treat this as the particulate level to be recommended for smog control. Understandably, those interests who think they will suffer from such a decision are likely to attack the actual pollutant criteria.[3] In any case, these measures for major air and water contaminants are clearly essential for effective, rational pollution control. Although public officials have often been forced to set air and water quality standards without adequate criteria, as more refined criteria become available they should form the basis for policy decisions.

Quality Standards. Goals and criteria are a prelude to the critical business of establishing air and water quality standards—the maximum levels of various pollutants that will be tolerated in bodies of water and ambient air. As a practical matter, creating air and water quality standards amounts to defining what the public, acting through its officials, will consider pollution to be. An adequate set of quality standards should specify which contaminants will be monitored, what the maximum tolerable amounts of the contaminants will be, and what variation, if any, in levels and combinations of pollutants will be accepted if differing qualities of air or water are to be created.

An illustration of air quality standards can be drawn from the State of New York, where the Department of Environmental Conservation created four sets of air quality standards varying according to the population, industrial development, and geographic setting of communities. For the New York metropolitan area, the standards are those intended primarily "to prevent adverse health effects" and include the following specifications for some major pollutants:

Sulfur Oxides:	the level shall not exceed 0.03 ppm (parts per million) on an annual average and 24-hour averages shall not exceed 0.11 ppm more than 3 days a year.
Particulates:	concentration must not exceed 75 micrograms per cubic centimeter.
Photochemical Oxidants:	the 24-hour average should be less than 0.05 ppm and 1-hour averages should not exceed 0.15 ppm.[4]

Emission Standards. Air and water quality standards are only a statement of aspirations unless they are accompanied by appropriate emission standards that describe the acceptable level of pollutants from important sources of air and water contamination. Emission standards are the cutting edge of pollution abatement; a successful program of pollution control needs emission standards as an essential ingredient. If emission standards are to be effective, they must clearly indicate the limits of tolerable pollution from all important sources and should be devised so that they are related to the air or water quality goals set by policymakers. Because air or water quality standards are almost impotent by themselves, proponents of stringent pollution control have always insisted that tough, explicit, and thorough emission controls accompany all abatement programs.

Emission controls are often bitterly controversial. Scientists and economists have often encountered extreme difficulty in determining how much of a pollution "load" within a given body of water or air can be attributed to specific sources; this, in turn, often compounds the problem of apportioning the responsibility for pollution abatement equitably among a large number of polluters.[5] Moreover, the technology of emission measurement is still relatively primitive. Businessmen commonly balk at strict emission management, frequently arguing that they are forced to accept responsibility for sometimes severe emissions cutbacks when their actual contribution to a pollution problem remains problematical. They often assert that "premature" emission standards saddle them with a heavier burden of capital investment for pollution control equipment than more careful research would justify. Not infrequently, they argue that the technology required to achieve various emission standards is unavailable or prohibitively expensive. Public officials, exposed to the full weight of this industrial backlash, are often sorely pressed to yield ground. They not only have to contend with the ire of influential businessmen but also have to face a shortage of trained pollution abatement personnel and often a lack of sophisticated equipment for the essential monitoring of factory emissions; it is easy, as well as expedient, for them to rationalize vague or weak emission requirements or to sanction long delays in setting the requirements while "further study" is undertaken. Whatever the real or alleged obstacles of effective emission controls may be, setting quality standards for air and water without a viable emission control system will be largely an exercise in futility.

Enforcement. A great diversity of enforcement procedures might be used to assure that air and water quality standards are achieved; adequate enforcement measures, as Hickel's Law implies, must carry enough force to command the respect of those subject to pollution regulations. Satisfactory enforcement schemes have several characteristics: They enable public officials to act with reasonable speed (and very rapidly, in case of emergencies) to curb pollution, they carry sufficiently strong penalties to encourage compliance, and they do not enable public officials to evade a responsibility to act against violations when action is imperative. It is desirable, moreover, that officials have a range of enforcement options that might, at one extreme, consist of little more than gentle prodding to secure compliance, all the way to court action and criminal penalties for severe, chronic, or reckless violations. Flexible, rigorous enforcement must be a component of sound pollution abatement, but abatement—like other regulatory policies—still depends heavily on voluntary compliance. It is impossible to initiate enforcement proceedings against all suspected violators or to guarantee compliance only through the threat of enforcement proceedings. Enforcement, in short, is considered the last resort in pollution abatement, not the everyday working method for the system.

The Logic of the System. Environmentalists have been less than enthusiastic about the standards-and-enforcement approach to pollution abatement. One reason is that the system, cast from the incremental mold that has shaped most of the governmental policy process, permits too much delay and too little innovation in abatement policy. Critics assert, for example, that it takes enormous time to initiate abatement of even one pollutant: First, goals must be established, then protracted research must be conducted to create the criteria for that pollutant, then standards for that pollutant must be drafted, then the equally complicated task of emission standard-setting must be undertaken—all this before any enforcement is contemplated. This process must be repeated for *each* pollutant. Such a procedure, it is argued, not only consumes time (while pollution proceeds apace) but also requires such protracted negotiation and accommodation among so many public and private interests that a truly innovative abatement program is almost impossible.[6]

Conservationists maintain that this system indulges pollution by placing the burden of proof on the government to establish the toxicity of various pollutants and to identify the source and volume of major pollutants. This allegedly frees the polluter to contaminate the air and water until the extent and danger of his pollution can be determined—if it can—while imposing such a large burden of responsibility for proving pollution damage on the government that enforcement is extremely difficult when it leads to the courts, where rigorous rules of evidence prevail.[7] Environmentalists note that it will be, at best, many years before the technical data, skilled personnel, and technology are available to equip public officials with the resources they need for such a task; for instance, more than five hundred new or modified chemicals come onto the market each year, and any or all of these are potential pollutants that must be analyzed. It would be better, they suggest, to create an abatement system that does not impose on public officials such a formidable task of data gathering and analysis before they can act against a problem that most scientists readily admit is already serious.

Though some Congressmen and administrators agreed with these arguments, most had little effect on Washington policymakers prior to 1970. During the 1950's and 1960's, Congress created a policy framework for pollution control that rested heavily on the standards-and-enforcement philosophy and then added some additional features that largely compounded the difficulties already inherent in the approach. Although Congress came reluctantly to recognize that the system was gravely deficient and wrote new measures in the early 1970's to invigorate the old system, what resulted from grafting the new procedures on the old is a hybrid of still uncertain quality.

Water Pollution Abatement: "Limited and Cumbersome"

Water pollution results from many elements acting singly or in numerous combinations. An inventory of these pollutants would include, at a minimum, organic wastes and biological nutrients such as the phosphates in detergents that remove oxygen from the water, disease-bearing organisms, thermal pollution in the form of heated water whose discharge into cooler waterways may upset ecological balances, and an enormous variety of synthetic chemicals. This pollution comes primarily from municipal wastes, and so-called nonpoint sources (agricultural, mining, and real estate development run-off). Until the mid-1950's, the federal government confined itself largely to grants or loans to state and local governments for sewage treatment facilities and waste-treatment planning; by 1971, this federal effort at municipal waste control already amounted to a healthy contribution of $1.5 billion and has steadily increased in subsequent years; between 1971 and 1973, an additional $1.3 billion in federal construction grants for municipal waste treatment facilities is expected. While Washington's role in municipal waste management is not free of problems and controversy, ecologists have been especially concerned with the federal government's current approach to the industrial waste crisis.

Industrial Pollution. The industrial demand for water and the volume of pollutants dumped into the nation's waterways is growing. American industry, now using ten times the volume of water consumed by municipal sources, will probably require sixteen times the municipal demand by the year 2000. No complete inventory of pollutants discharged into the nation's waterways is yet available; when the inventory is complete, the volume and variety of contaminants from major industry will be extremely large. Some idea of the water contaminants from industrial sources can be gained from the steel industry, which is, as one recent study notes, "the king of the manufacturing consumers":

> The steel industry [uses] upward of four trillion gallons of this precious fluid a year. Steelmakers need water to cool and condense hot metal . . . and to "scrub" bases before using them for fuel; they also blast finished sheets of steel with a high-velocity water spray to knock off the waste scale clinging to the steel surface. The average steel plant produces one million ingot tons of steel each year. For each ingot ton a plant puts out, it also generates 125 pounds of suspended solids, 2.7 pounds of lubrication oils, 3.5 pounds of free acids (like sulfuric acid), 12.3 pounds of combined acids (like metal sulfates), eight ounces of emulsions, and between one and two ounces of such poisons as phenol, flouride, ammonia and cyanide. Each ingot ton produced raises the temperature of the water used for cooling by 10°.[8]

By far the largest portion of pollutants currently found in the nation's waterways comes from industry. More than 80 per cent of the water pollutants, measured by their biological oxygen demand, originates in industry; among its many environmental hazards, this organic waste is responsible for the "dying" (eutrophication) of lakes and streams when it reaches a concentration that robs higher life forms, such as fish and shellfish, of dissolved oxygen, thus suffocating them. This organic waste is seldom treated; practically all the industrial wastewater containing more than three-quarters of the biochemical oxygen demand is directly emptied into streams, rivers, or lakes in its raw condition.

In recent years, scientists have become increasingly apprehensive about two other sources of water pollution closely related to industrial processes: oil spillage and thermal pollution. Oil discharges in the Santa Barbara channel in February, 1969, which released 235,000 gallons of crude oil into the Santa Barbara harbor, and a year later in Tampa Bay (10,000 gallons of crude oil from a grounded Greek tanker) dramatized the urgency of the oil pollution issue. More than one thousand oil spills involving more than one hundred barrels of crude oil were reported in the United States in 1969; these discharges contaminate sea water and nearby estuaries and often mar beaches, causing considerable cost to public officials for clean-up. Thermal pollution is caused when water, heated from use as a coolant for industrial equipment, is released in large volume into cooler waterways; the subsequent alteration in water temperature can extend for many miles from the source and may drastically transform the ecology of the water bodies it affects. The major cause of this pollution is electric power generation, which produces more than 80 per cent of thermal heat released into the nation's waterways. With the great expansion in electric power generation anticipated in the next decades and the growing use of nuclear power equipment (which produces 50 per cent more thermal pollution per unit of power than conventional generators), the thermal pollution problem threatens to become increasingly severe.[9]

The Congressional architects of federal water pollution policy, reluctant to give Washington a vigorous role in water pollution control and extremely deferential to the concerns of the regulated industries, created a policy process that the Council on Environmental Quality has called, with delicate understatement, "limited and cumbersome." In many respects it is the quintessence of a decentralized, incremental policy process that virtually ensures that decisions will evolve sluggishly and conservatively. So unwieldy has this system proved in the face of growing water pollution that circumstances have forced Congress to amend it in the search for a stronger tool.

The Water Pollution Control Act (1956). The first significant Congressional effort to define an explicit role for the federal government in dealing with water pollution is contained in the 1956

Water Pollution Control Act, the key provisions of which illustrate Congress's conservative approach to the federal control of water pollution.[10] The most important of these provisions are (1) the definition of the respective federal and state responsibilities for pollution management, (2) the enforcement powers granted the federal government in abating pollution control, and (3) the freedom of choice bestowed upon federal officials when dealing with alleged pollution incidents.

The underlying philosophy of the act is summarized in its declaration that water pollution abatement is "a uniquely local problem." Advocating "partnership" between federal and state governments in attacking water pollution, the act left the responsibility for setting and enforcing water pollution standards almost entirely to the states; no federal power to establish water pollution standards or to goad the states into doing so was provided. Aside from a modest appropriation for water pollution research and a largely empty admonition to the states to set up water pollution control, the act placed no pressure on state officials to control water contamination. Advocates of strong pollution control argued that this was a directive for inaction because few states would voluntarily write or enforce stringent water pollution controls; quite the contrary, the states, anxious to lure industry and vulnerable to industrial threats to move elsewhere, would engage in a tacit competition to avoid pollution policies that might alienate major industry.

The most important, enduring features of this legislation are those defining the power of federal officials to act against existing water pollution and outlining the procedures to be used. A superficial reading might suggest that the responsible federal official (now the administrator of the EPA) has rather ample powers to act; the legislation gives him the following authority:[11]

1. He is *compelled* to act against alleged pollution when interstate waters are involved and the governor of a state requests it.
2. He *may* initiate action against alleged pollution if (*a*) he has "reason to believe" it has occurred in interstate waters; (*b*) the interstate sale or marketing of shellfish is allegedly ham-

pered by pollution and a governor requests intervention; or (*c*) when a governor requests intervention in an intrastate water pollution case.

A close reading of these provisions, however, reveals numerous deficiencies. In most instances—and often in cases where the most serious water pollution may occur—the federal government has no power to *initiate* abatement action unless requested to do so by a governor or other state authority. No intrastate pollution or shellfish damage, for instance, can be investigated unless state officials first request federal action. Moreover, in cases where Washington *may* initiate proceedings, federal officials are not compelled to do so (with the one exception noted above); this freedom of action, as many observers have pointed out, makes the decision to act against water pollution a "political" one in which important private interests can exert their influence to forestall Washington's intervention in a pollution case. For these reasons, among others, the legislation, far from stimulating a vigorous federal effort at water pollution control, seems inspired to discourage it.

If, despite these deterrents to action, federal officials are prompted or forced to start proceedings against an alleged water polluter, the "conference system" for abatement will almost certainly assure delay, if not failure, in the attempt. The conference system, later written into air pollution measures, still remains one major tool that federal officials have been provided with to fight water pollution. Assuming that federal officials have "reason to believe" serious water pollution is occurring and that they have decided to initiate proceedings against the polluter, the following procedures are observed:

Step 1: A "conference" is held. Washington may speedily order the conference or delay it. The conference brings together representatives of all federal, state, and interstate agencies with jurisdiction over the matter, who then join with concerned legislators to discuss the problem. After these deliberations—which may be prolonged—a set of "recommendations" is made to federal officials to suggest how they might attack the problem (if it is still considered a problem).

Step 2: Federal officials ponder the recommendations. After reviewing the conference recommendations, the administrator of the EPA may create a list of "official" recommendations that prescribe the steps to be taken to clean up the pollution—steps with which the polluter is expected to comply. The administrator may also ignore the conference recommendations and do nothing further.

Step 3: A "hearing" may be convened. If the EPA administrator believes that pollution abatement is too dilatory, he can now order a formal "hearing" involving the concerned parties. He must, however, wait at least six months after issuing his initial recommendations before ordering a hearing. He may wait considerably longer. He may decide, as well, to cancel a proposed hearing if the guilty party seems ready to stop his polluting.

Step 4: The hearing. This is a formal, quasi-judicial meeting before a panel of examiners representing federal, state, and "public" interests; adversary proceedings are followed with the taking of evidence and testimony. At the end of a hearing, another set of recommendations is proposed to the EPA administrator, who may, if he chooses, order the polluter to comply with them.

Step 5: Court action might be initiated. After waiting at least six months following orders he has issued as a result of the hearing, the EPA administrator *may* ask the Attorney General to begin civil proceedings against the polluter. The Attorney General *may* comply if he believes it advisable.

Step 6: An abatement order might come from the bench. An extended judicial battle is almost certain. Since judicial rules of evidence and the large burden of proof on the government often work to the advantage of the alleged polluter, a judgment in favor of the government is always problematical. In case a polluter does lose his case, the penalties imposed are largely at the court's discretion.

While this procedure may seem tortuously long, a summary understates its difficulty. A "conference" may be repeatedly adjourned and reconvened for years; officials may take months to reflect on recommendations from a conference or hearing before issuing orders (if they do); the mandatory six-month wait before a hearing can be ordered, or before a court action can be initiated after a hearing, can easily extend into years. When these numerous opportunities for delay are coupled with the great discretion given federal officials to avoid enforcement proceedings, it is not surprising that enforcement records have been lackluster.[12] From 1956 through 1971, only fifty-one conferences were ordered, only four reached the hearing stage, and only one ended in court. (The one judicial incident has, by perverse logic, become a tribute to the ability of polluters to resist abatement proceedings. In 1957, the government initiated a conference to goad the city of St. Joseph, Missouri, into treating its heavily fouled municipal waters; when little was done and a subsequent hearing failed to produce results, the Attorney General went to court in 1960. Due to delay by local officials and the failure of several local referenda for water treatment bonds, the city was not expected to comply with the original hearing orders until 1972, fifteen years after the abatement proceedings started.)

There is other evidence of the system's defects. Of ninety major pollution areas in the nation designated by federal officials in 1963, only twenty-two had experienced any enforcement conferences by the early 1970's; despite the 1963 addition of the "shellfish" clause to the original legislation—a change enabling federal officials to initiate action against pollution endangering commercial shellfish—federal officials initiated conferences in only five of the 427 areas designated by the Public Health Service as examples of serious shellfish blight.

The 1965 Water Quality Act. By the early 1960's, it was clear that the states were taking few significant steps to abate pollution and that Washington's cumbersome enforcement procedures accomplished little more. After considerable deliberation, Congress created a number of important amendments to the 1956 legislation that became known collectively as the Water Quality Act of 1965.[13] Essentially, the purpose of the new bill was to prod the states into taking firmer measures against water pollution by giving the federal government new powers to hasten state activity.

This legislation created the policy-making procedures still

used nationally for water pollution abatement. The major features of this legislation were (1) a requirement that the states set "water quality standards" defining the outer limits of permissible pollution for interstate and intrastate water bodies in their jurisdiction; (2) a requirement that the states accompany these standards with "implementation plans" indicating the procedures they would use to keep a polluter's emission standards within levels compatible with the quality standards; and (3) a new, quick 180-day enforcement procedure that Washington might use, as an alternative to the older conference procedure, to abate pollution. A deadline of June, 1967, was set for state submission of water quality standards and implementation plans to Washington, where federal officials could approve them, order their revision, or substitute their own abatement plans if state ones were unsatisfactory. Once created and approved, state plans were theoretically enforceable by federal or state agencies. With this new legislation, Congress had committed the federal government to the standards-and-enforcement approach to pollution control and had seemingly given Washington a more incisive, effective part in the anti-pollution battle.

Since its inception, however, numerous problems have arisen in the application of the 1965 legislation; its merits have yet to be convincingly demonstrated. Environmentalists have objected to the legislation because it takes as given that pollution must exist and confines itself to formulating schemes for defining acceptable levels of water degradation; this concession, they assert, is a major victory for polluters. Several difficulties have arisen in the formulation of state water quality standards and implementation plans. The states were extremely slow in formulating these plans; by late 1971, less than thirty states had plans that met Washington's minimum standards, and many were not wholly satisfactory. More importantly, state officials were hesitant to take a firm stance against pollution. Most states, for instance, made little or no effort to write an enforceable scheme of careful emission controls against major pollution sources; most states, additionally, permitted some deterioration of existing clean water bodies when writing quality standards for them. Washington seemed equally reluctant to take a hard line. For example, federal officials did not stick to a strong "nondegradation" policy that would prevent the states from setting water quality standards for clean water bodies that were lower than the existing quality of the water. Instead, federal officials insisted that the states include a nondegradation provision in their plans, but Washington still permitted a lowering of standards for clean water when "such change is justifiable as a result of necessary economic and social development."[14] Moreover, federal officials did not press the states to create emission standards for individual pollution sources—a procedure that seemed possible, and many experts believed extremely desirable, under the law. Washington, additionally, required no state implementation plans for pollution control from so-called nonpoint sources such as urban stormwater, feedlot run-off, and construction site run-off, which contribute heavily to water contamination. Enforcing a nondegradation policy, controlling nonpoint pollution, and other stringent pollution measures are no easy feats technically, nor can impressive results be predicted with the most diligent efforts; in these respects, pollution control officials have many justifiable reasons for reservations about the effectiveness of such policy. However, environmentalists have asserted that there was, in any case, little enthusiasm for undertaking the task.

The enforcement procedure in the new legislation was its major weakness. The legislation appeared to empower federal officials to give a polluter in violation of state water quality standards a 180-day notice to meet state standards or face court action —this in addition to the older conference procedure still available. However, this enforcement scheme applied only in case of pollution to *interstate* water, not to all navigable waterways. Since only 4,000 of the 26,000 navigable water bodies in the United States are interstate and many of these are inconsequential, such a law severely restricted the government's ability to use the 180-day procedure against a polluter of intrastate waters; the burden of proof on the government was extraordinary, in some ways even more troublesome than under the older enforcement system, so that effective prosecution in the courtroom seemed difficult indeed.

As federal and state efforts to implement the 1965 legislation have unfolded in the 1960's and early 1970's, the combined governmental attack on national water pollution has seemed sluggish, vacillating, and very ambiguous. While the states and Washington labored to enforce the legislation, with unpredictable results, a new, unexpected direction was imparted to federal water pollution policy by the rise of an obscure law to a place of major importance.

The 1899 Refuse Act. The Refuse Act of 1899 is a curiosity in water pollution politics. Plucked from the limbo of forgotten legislation by alert environmentalists in the late 1960's, the act may provide the most uncomplicated, effective approach to water pollution control now available to the federal government. The most significant provision of the act is its clear, straightforward order that "It shall not be lawful to throw, discharge or deposit . . . any refuse matter of any kind or description whatever . . . into any navigable water of the United States" without permission from the Army Corps of Engineers; violators of the law, subject to civil and criminal action, could be sued by the government or private citizens if public agencies refused to act.[15] In 1966, the U.S. Supreme Court declared that "refuse matter" included industrial pollutants and, thus, brought virtually all the nation's 44,000 industrial polluters within the ambit of the legislation.

Until the early 1970's, federal officials showed little enthusiasm for using this legislation as a device for water pollution abatement. However, in December, 1971, President Nixon announced the creation of a new "permit system" based on the Refuse Act as a major new approach to water pollution control. Drawing upon the authority conferred by the Refuse Act, the President announced that henceforth all industries discharging effluents into navigable waters would have to obtain a federal permit; obtaining this permit would require the polluter, among other things, to indicate the nature and volume of pollutant he intended to discharge. Once this data became available, the Corps of Engineers, depending heavily on the judgment of the Environmental Protection Agency, would decide whether a permit would be issued and what emission levels would be allowed.[16] In theory, such an approach seemed a major improvement over previous methods created by Washington. Unlike other current Congressional water pollution bills, the Refuse Act did not confine federal authority to interstate waters but categorically gave Washington permit power over all navigable waters. A means of direct enforcement totally in federal control was also provided: Failure to comply with the law could lead to civil or criminal prosecution without any protracted conference system or waiting period for action. Another desirable feature was that it gave Washington the power to obtain accurate information about the volume and composition of effluents discharged by industry in the nation's waters and permitted direct emission controls. Since the President further declared that industrial violators of federal or state water quality standards would be denied permits, the Refuse Act also seemed to be a useful weapon to stimulate compliance with water quality standards.

During 1971 and 1972, both federal and private interests seized upon the opportunities in the Refuse Act to accelerate judicial action against alleged violators even before the President's permit system was fully in operation (the President, in any event, had declared no moratorium on violators while the permit system was being implemented). In 1970 and 1971, federal officials initiated more than 250 criminal actions against industrial polluters, and a number of significant private suits were successfully prosecuted; in the state of Washington, for instance, a private suit under the Refuse Act produced an agreement from an ITT-Rayonier pulp processing plant to construct a $22 million waste treatment facility. By late 1972, the first phase of Nixon's permit system had resulted in permit applications from 18,000 industrial establishments representing about 90 per cent of the effluents discharged into national waterways.

Despite its great possibilities and the President's initiation of his permit program, the long-range impact of the Refuse Act remained cloudy until the strength of the Environmental Protection Agency's commitment to the program could be tested and many complex issues resolved. The permit system's effectiveness, furthermore, depended heavily upon voluntary reports of effluent discharges from industry; how carefully these would be checked and the subsequent emission limitations enforced remained unknown. When the Environmental Protection Agency indicated in 1972 that it would generally defer to the states in determining whether permits for discharge into intrastate waters carried adequate pollution controls—a decision not required by the Refuse Act—it seemed as if the permit program would revert, like other water pollution measures, to state initiative; this, in the view of most environmentalists, had already proven a sure deterrent to effective pollution control when practiced in other water pollution programs. Thus, the Refuse Act seemed in danger of the emasculation so often the fate of other pollution abatement programs, and environmentalists turned increasingly toward promoting legislation that would entirely abolish the standards and enforcement approach together with state-formulated quality standards. After a prolonged struggle, they finally succeeded in convincing Congress to pass the Water Pollution Control Act of 1972, the most radical, expensive and comprehensive attack on water pollution yet attempted in the nation.

The Water Pollution Control Act of 1972. By late 1971, it was apparent that numerous congressmen, disillusioned with existing federal pollution programs, wanted stronger measures. In 1971, Senator Edmund Muskie, once a major proponent of the standards-and-enforcement system adopted by Congress in 1965, concluded that the approach was unsatisfactory; working through the Senate Subcommittee on Air and Water Pollution of which he was the chairman, Muskie and his collaborators wrote a new water pollution bill that marked a major departure from previous Congressional philosophies of water pollution abatement. In late 1971, the bill was passed unanimously by the Senate and sent to the House where a slightly different bill had passed that chamber. After considerable further discussion, interrupted by the 1972 presidential campaign, the two houses agreed upon a compromise bill that generally followed the Muskie plan and became the Water Pollution Control Act of 1972, passed by Congress in October, 1972.

The new legislation, vigorously supported by most environmental groups, marked a new direction in federal water pollution policy. It abolished the standards-and-enforcement method of pollution control, abandoned a tolerance for limited pollution in favor of complete pollution abatement, and gave Washington a decisive role in enforcing strict pollution controls, to be accomplished in a relatively short period. Specifically, the bill included the following major provisions.

1. *Congress set a goal of ending all water pollution by 1985.* Although this deadline was a "goal" rather than a strict mandate that must be accomplished, it appeared vastly to accelerate the pace of pollution abatement and, for the first time, placed Congress on record as favoring the elimination of *all* water pollution.

2. *All industry discharging effluents into waterways must use the "best practicable" technology to control pollution by 1977 and the "best available" technology by 1983.* Not only did this provision set firm dates by which industrial polluters must install pollution control equipment, but it required that by 1983 they must, in effect, control their pollution by whatever means would do the job best. This procedure abolished the standards-and-enforcement approach to pollution control by insisting, instead, that industrial polluters must clean their discharge to the maximum feasible limit.

3. *During the period between 1972 and 1983, a permit system for industrial discharges will exist, enforced by the states according to guidelines established by Washington.* The permit system is to be only an interim measure, serving as a means to control water pollution until the deadline for abatement ocurrs in 1983. Under this provision, the federal government will establish broad guidelines which the states must follow when issuing permits for industry to discharge pollutants into waterways. If state guidelines prove unacceptable or the states fail to establish a permit system, the Environmental Protection Agency is authorized to assume control of state permit systems.

4. *Standards for permits will be industrywide.* Even though the permit system will be only temporary, the new legislation orders that the state-by-state approach to permit standards be abolished and replaced by standards applicable to whole indus-

tries on a nationwide basis. This eliminates the states' discretion in setting standards for one industry differently and imposes firm federal control over minimum standards.

5. *Congress authorized $24.6 billion dollars to be allocated over three years to assist municipalities in creating sewage treatment plants and other water purification systems.* This was the most massive appropriation for sewage treatment facilities ever authorized by Congress and would be a major step toward eliminating the frequently ineffective treatment of water by local government. Since the federal government's share of treatment facility costs was also increased from 50 per cent to 75 per cent, it seemed likely that a new surge of treatment facility construction would soon begin.

Congress's commitment to this new approach was demonstrated in late 1972 when both houses overrode President Nixon's veto of the bill (he had objected primarily to the huge grant for sewage treatment facilities which he regarded as too inflationary); the new legislation would undoubtedly be the framework for federal water pollution policy for several decades.

Since the ink is scarcely dry on this new legislation, it is far too early to assess its importance. Clearly, important issues remained to be settled. How strict would be the EPA's interim permit standards? Would the EPA really hold industry to creating the "best available" controls on its pollution by 1983? Would the federal government prosecute violators vigorously and consistently? Once again, the critical questions dealt with the administrative implementation of environmental legislation. What did seem clear in the early days of the new legislation was that Washington had created at least the opportunity for the most far-ranging, incisive, and effective attack on water pollution ever experienced in the nation. Environmentalists could only wait and hope.

Air Pollution Abatement: An Unexpected Turn

Given Washington's irresolute approach to water pollution, one would expect similar conditions to prevail in air pollution control. This has fortunately not been the case. Although Congress began its approach to air pollution inspired by the same peculiar logic that fashioned water pollution policy, the attack on air pollution took a turn in the late 1960's and early 1970's that surprised many observers by its apparently greater toughness and consistency. The sharpened federal air pollution policy is especially noteworthy because the interests affected by the policy, as well as the long-range implications of control, are as substantial politically and economically as they are in water pollution.

The Regulated

The weight of federal air pollution policy rests heavily on three sectors of the American economy. Almost half (42 per cent) the total volume of air pollutants comes from automobiles and trucks, a fifth (21 per cent) from electric generating sites, and a substantial remainder (14 per cent) from industry; together, these sources pour more than three-fourths of the yearly pollution load into the nation's atmosphere. The volume of the five most significant pollutants created by these sources is indicated in Table 2.

The Electric Power Industry. The electric wire has become the umbilical cord of American society. We depend heavily on electric power: Industry consumes about 41 per cent of the available power, residential users about 32 per cent, and commercial enterprise an additional 23 per cent. The demand for electric power in the United States—power without which almost all industrial, scientific, domestic, and commercial activities would cease—is escalating rapidly; projections indicate that national demands will quadruple between 1970 and 2000. The present 3,400 generating plants in the country must be supplemented by at least 255 additional plants to meet this demand; not surprisingly, the electric utilities are the fastest growing major industry in the United States.

This insatiable appetite for electricity is ominous because electric generating plants are extremely "dirty" environmentally. Particulate matter and nitrogen oxides are two hazards, but the most dangerous emission is sulfur oxides—an acrid yellow gas emitted in great volume from plants burning fossil fuels (oil, gas,

TABLE 2
Sources of Air Pollution in the U.S., 1968
(Percentages by Weight)

Source	Carbon Monoxide (100 million tons)	Sulfur Oxides (33 million tons)	Hydro-carbons (32 million tons)	Nitrogen Oxides (21 million tons)	Particulates (28 million tons)
Fuel Burning for Transportation	63.8%	2.4%	51.9%	39.3%	4.3%
Fuel Burning in Stationary Sources	1.9	73.5	2.2	48.5	31.4
Industrial Processes Other Than Fuel Burning	9.6	22.0	14.4	1.0	26.5
Solid Waste Disposal	7.8	0.3	5.0	2.9	3.9
Miscellaneous*	16.9	1.8	26.5	8.3	33.9

* Includes forest fires, agricultural burning, coal waste fires, and gasoline marketing.

SOURCE: John Holdren & Philip Herrera, *Energy* (San Francisco: The Sierra Club, 1971), p. 145.

and coal) and responsible for most of the reported respiratory ills associated with the presence of electric generating plants. Large plants disgorge huge quantities of this potentially lethal gas: Chicago's Consolidated Edison produces 420,000 tons of sulfur oxides annually. However, this is only a sniff alongside the volume that will arise from the controversial "Four Corners" project currently under way in the open desert where New Mexico, Arizona, Utah, and Colorado meet; only partially complete, the project when constructed will be the largest power generation complex in the United States, daily producing 1,280 tons of nitrogen oxides, 240 tons of fly ash, and 1,970 tons of sulfur oxides; existing generators at the site produce a thick smoke trail 215 miles long—big enough to be observed from Gemini 12 more than 170 miles away from earth. At the moment, controlling these emissions is difficult and expensive. The most effective approach is to reduce the sulfur content in the fossil fuels used by the generators by switching to low-sulfur fossil fuels; limited success has been achieved through the utilization of expensive hydrostatic "scrubbers" and electrostatic devices that remove some sulfur oxides before they leave the stacks. Such techniques are still experimental and do not guarantee the removal of all dangerous sulfur oxide emissions.

Automobiles and the Fuel Complex. Automobiles and trucks pour 180 billion pounds of contaminants into the air annually; almost two-thirds of the carbon monoxide and half of the hydrocarbons released are traceable to internal combustion engines, which also cause the chronic smog found in Los Angeles, New York, and other metropolitan areas. Spurred by massive governmental expenditures for highways and encouraged by automakers' pervasive advertising, Americans have fully embraced the automobile as a fundamental of their life style and show no inclination to change their ways. Almost 100 million automobiles and trucks now exist in the United States, supplemented annually by 10 million new vehicles.

It would be difficult to overstate the economic and political importance of the automotive industry in the United States. General Motors, the largest industrial corporation in the world, currently has an annual sales volume approaching $20 billion, which exceeds the gross national product of all but a few nations. The automobile industry employs about 810,000 individuals, sustains numerous service industries, and consumes many raw and manufactured products, including steel and other metals, crude rubber and finished rubber products, and a great diversity of other materials. Any significant change in the technology or economic structure of the automobile industry brought about by governmental controls on air pollution is bound to have enormous direct and indirect effects on this most important sector of the economy. The intense political involvement of the industry's leaders and lobbyists in air pollution policy has brought the weight of one of the world's most powerful corporate structures to bear upon this issue.

In good part, air pollution policy must be fuel policy. Any effort to control air contamination affects the volume and content of fuel used for energy production in all sectors of American society. The nation's coal, gas, and petroleum industries have a substantial stake in air pollution policy and have been deeply implicated in the policy process associated with air pollution abatement.

The fuel industry is interlocked with the power and automobile industries technologically, financially, and structurally. The link between petroleum and the automobile is rather obvious: The internal combustion engine is the principal consumer of gasoline, the most expensive of fuels distilled from crude oil and the backbone of the petroleum market (about 80 billion gallons of gasoline are annually poured into America's automobiles). A less familiar but instructive example of interdependence between fuel producer and consumer is the relationship between coal producers and the electric power industry. This relationship stands out in sharp relief when the problem of sulfur oxides is raised.[17] Currently, more than half the electric power generated in the United States is produced by medium- to high-sulfur coal, which will probably cease to be a generally acceptable fuel when federal and state sulfur-oxide emission standards are firmly established. Although there are, or may soon be, some alternative methods of converting high-sulfur coal into a form more acceptable for use when sulfur-oxide emission standards are enforced, the coal industry is understandably concerned with how severely the emission standards will limit the present market for existing high-sulfur coal. Many of the coal companies own large reserves of high-sulfur fuels; clearly, the strength of the market and its potential income will depend on the sulfur emission standards. Moreover, many coal companies, having negotiated thirty-year contracts with electric companies, are heavily committed to specific electric utilities. In some instances, electric utilities (such as the General Public Utilities Corporation, a large eastern holding company) have built "mine mouth" generating stations on the coal mining sites as an alternative to transporting the coal long distances to generating plants; such companies, dependent in the most fundamental manner on existing coal sources, cannot easily find new coal supplies. Further, many electric plants would have to convert boilers and accept higher fuel costs in order to switch to low-sulfur coal. None of these is an insurmountable problem—in fact, many East Coast utilities have

TABLE 3
Leading Industries and Their Principal Pollutants

Industry	Principal Pollutants	Annual Average Volume, in Billion Pounds
Petroleum refining	Particulates, sulfur oxides, hydrocarbons, carbon monoxide	8.4
Smelters (aluminum, copper, lead, zinc)	Particulates, sulfur oxides	8.3
Iron foundries	Particulates, carbon monoxide	7.4
Kraft pulp and paper mills	Particulates, carbon monoxide, sulfur oxides	6.6
Coal cleaning and refuse	Particulates, sulfur oxides, carbon monoxide	4.7

SOURCE: John C. Esposito, *Vanishing Air* (New York: Grossman Publishers, 1970), p. 70.

already turned to new low-sulfur coal sources or have converted to other fossil fuels with moderate sulfur content—but the economies of electric power and coal, like the economies of other fuel users and fuel producers, are so intertwined that both will be vitally affected by air pollution policy. In many cases, any change in fuel use can only be accomplished by rather massive changes in both consumer and producer relationships.

Heavy Industry. Although the nation's heavy industry ranks third among the leading producers of air pollution, this still amounts to 85 billion tons of pollutants contributed to the atmosphere annually—about 300 pounds for every citizen. No major industry in the nation is innocent of air pollution; Table 3 lists the leading industries and their principal pollutants. The greatest volume of these pollutants is discharged in the Northwest and in the Great Lakes region of the Midwest, around large cities generally, and in the Southwest; in recent years, however, the spread of heavy industry across the United States and increasing urbanization have almost done away with areas free of significant air contamination. Since American heavy industry produces almost half of the nation's gross national product, the economy is very dependent on its continuing operation and profitability.

Washington's approach to air pollution began as a carbon copy of water pollution procedures. The first two important air pollution bills created by Congress in the 1960's—the Clean Air Act of 1963 and the Air Quality Act of 1967—adopted the same standards-and-enforcement scheme and deference to the states in setting policy guidelines that were found in water pollution legislation. The impotence of this approach convinced Congress that much stronger measures were necessary. In the early 1970's, air pollution policy took an abrupt turn away from the existing hesitant, incremental philosophy, toward a decisive, unprecedentedly tough attack on the problem.

The 1963 Clean Air Act. The purpose of the 1963 Clean Air Act, the first significant federal involvement in air pollution control, was to nudge the states into some air pollution abatement and to give Washington very limited means to encourage this effort. While the legislation did give federal officials limited funds for air pollution research, the most important provision of the act was its creation of a pollution abatement procedure that was practically identical to that used in water pollution control. Thus, Washington for the first time—but not very impressively—asserted some authority over air pollution abatement.

Adhering to the philosophy that the states should take the principal responsibility for air pollution control, Congress permitted federal officials to intervene in air pollution problems only at the request of state authorities. Upon receiving such a request, the responsible federal official (then the Secretary of Health, Education, and Welfare) would initiate the cumbersome, tedious abatement procedures already familiar from water pollution legislation: (1) a conference, which might be followed by (2) a formal hearing, which might lead to (3) legal action, which might produce conviction of the alleged polluter. Since all the mandatory delays and discretionary opitions found in water pollution abatement were reproduced in the air pollution abatement system, federal officials—facing the same legal and political obstacles found in water pollution abatement—produced a similarly lackluster enforcement record. Indeed, only eleven abatement actions were initiated between 1965 and 1970, and only one went so far as a judicial test.[18] This single judicial action, against a small chicken-rendering plant in Bishop, Maryland, whose air contamination was so foul it sickened investigating officials, took five years to complete; given the long time and the relative unimportance of the polluter against whom it was directed, the enforcement scheme's sole judicial triumph seemed an empty victory.

The Air Quality Act of 1967. Having failed to move the states with gentle prodding, Congress in 1967 turned on slightly greater pressure by creating the Air Quality Act, actually a set of amendments to the earlier 1963 legislation.[19] The new legislation, fully embracing the standards-and-enforcement logic, still left the states with the primary responsibility for air pollution control, albeit modestly strengthening Washington's authority. Under the new act, national air pollution control was supposed to proceed as follows:

1. The Secretary of HEW would designate "air quality regions" that might embrace whole states, intrastate regions, or interstate areas.

2. Once these "air quality regions" were created, the states within the regions were given three months to indicate an intention to establish air quality standards for the region; if the states failed to establish the standards or they proved unsatisfactory, the Secretary could substitute his own standards.

3. The Secretary was expected to conduct research leading to the publication of criteria on the effects of *each* major air pollutant; information was also to be available on current control technologies for each pollutant.

4. Once the information on criteria and technology was available to the states, they were expected to establish emission standards for each pollutant and to indicate how they would maintain their standards.

5. In addition to the older conference procedure, the federal government could proceed against a violator of state emission plans by giving him a 180-day abatement notice and then initiating court action if abatement proved unsatisfactory. Immediate abatement action was permitted only if Washington found air pollution "an imminent and substantial endangerment" to life or health.

This proved to be a ponderous and convoluted procedure; three years after its inception, only a modest beginning on the first essential steps had been achieved. The states had to wait for Washington to create "air quality regions" and to publish criteria for each pollutant, together with data on its control technology, before they were responsible for creating their air quality standards and abatement plans. In early 1970, only twenty-five of the projected ninety-one air quality regions had been designated by the Secretary of HEW. Further, by placing full responsibility upon Washington for investigating the hazards and control technologies for each of thirty major air pollutants, the act made it inevitable that action against the pollutants would proceed sluggishly. By early 1970, criteria and control information were available for only two pollutants—particulates and sulfur oxides—and most of the nineteen states then within an air quality region were still in the process of creating their quality standards and abatement plans for these two pollutants. (From the time the federal information became available to the states, the act gave the states at least fifteen months to complete this job.) At this point, federal officials had only begun to evaluate the few state implementation plans then available—a slow procedure that had to be repeated with each new pollutant once Washington created criteria and control information for it.

In practical terms, three years after Congress had attempted to stiffen the governmental attack on air pollution, the bare policy-making framework it had ordained was still incomplete; no enforcement procedures under the act had been accomplished—understandably, for no complete and approved standards-and-enforcement scheme had yet been created by state and federal policy-makers. It was increasingly apparent, even to many early advocates of standards and enforcement, that the procedure had become an exercise in slow motion.

The Motor Pollution Control Act (1965). In the early 1970's the average American buying a new car paid about fifty dollars for its pollution control equipment—a modest penance, indirectly ordained by Congress, for the privilege of owning the nation's most proficient air polluter. Since almost two-thirds of the total volume of air pollutants released yearly results from internal combustion engines, advocates of federal pollution control had long pressed Congress to legislate on emission controls on trucks and automobiles. While Congress was pursuing its extremely oblique attack on other forms of air pollution, it wrote the Motor Pollution Control Act of 1965, which produced a more direct approach to auto emission controls and resulted in the mandatory equipment on new cars in the early 1970's.[20] The legislation ordered the Secretary of HEW to establish emission standards for new motor vehicles; the first regulations, to apply to new vehicles in the 1968 model year, was intended to reduce hydrocarbon and carbon monoxide emissions by 90 per cent each. Beginning in 1968, manufacturers were expected to secure a "certificate" from Washington, indicating that new models complied with the federal emission standards, before the vehicles could be sold; uncertified vehicles would not be marketed.

The auto emission program has been controversial among environmentalists and enforcement officials principally because of the manner in which "certification" has been achieved. The usual procedure is for federal officials to test only prototypes of each major production-line engine; if the prototype meets emission standards, all production models are deemed to comply with federal regulations, which also dictated that emission controls should meet the minimum standards for 50,000 miles with one 25,000-mile tune-up. Critics charge that the prototype engines, far from representing production-line models, are carefully tuned and coddled machines selected to camouflage the imperfections in the average models; the 50,000-mile test, it is further asserted, is conducted on the prototypes under conditions far less severe than the average automobile would experience during a similar period. Since only a minuscule sample of all production-line cars is represented by the prototypes (one study indicates that 1.2 million cars may be certified on the basis of tests on four prototypes), the critics charge that the tests, under the best circumstances, are still unreliable. A number of tests conducted on average production vehicles would seem to confirm these assertions. One study, conducted by federal officials on 333 new vehicles produced in 1968, indicated that the average car was near failing its emission standards by 11,000 miles; after reviewing the results of another

California test on more than 4,000 vehicles, the head of the federal air pollution control effort reluctantly admitted to Congressional investigators in March, 1970, that "very often 75 to 80 per cent of the cars failed to meet" federal emission standards.

In any case, arguments over certification standards may prove academic. Data suggest that even stringent, careful regulations of emissions on new automobiles will, under the best conditions, only reduce air pollution from vehicles for a short time. Eventually, new vehicles will appear in such numbers that their total emissions will create a pollution load far exceeding the current one, even though each car may be releasing less air pollution than presently.[21]

The End of Indulgence. By 1970 it was obvious to observers that federal air pollution control had failed to produce positive results. In a dramatic departure from its previously timid attack on the problem, Congress in that year enacted legislation amounting to the strongest pollution bill yet passed in Washington —legislation, passed with great unanimity despite opposition from the Nixon administration and most major industries, giving the federal government a firm, potentially decisive role in shaping pollution policy.

The major features of the legislation, known as the Clean Air Amendments of 1970, suggest how it departed from past policies.[22]

1. *National air quality standards.* Turning away from reliance on the states to set air quality standards on a region-by-region basis, the new law ordered the administrator of the EPA to establish *national* air quality standards for all the major pollutants already designated.

2. *The burden of proof on the polluter.* The legislation removes the troublesome burden of proof on federal officials to establish the danger of pollutants. Henceforth, when the EPA's administrator labels a pollutant hazardous, it was to be assumed so unless industry or other dissenting interests could demonstrate "that such pollution clearly is not a hazardous air pollutant."

3. *The states to establish emission controls.* Each state is responsible, after a public hearing, for implementing national air

quality standards through emission controls on major pollutants. If the plan can be implemented in three years and proves otherwise satisfactory to the EPA, it may be approved; the EPA administrator may also substitute his implementation plan if state programs prove unsatisfactory.

4. *A deadline for control of new auto emissions.* The act requires auto manufacturers to reduce their carbon monoxide and hydrocarbon emissions by 90 per cent of the 1970 levels by 1975; a 90 per cent reduction in nitrogen oxide emissions (by 1970 standards) must be accomplished by 1976.

5. *New enforcement procedures and penalties.* Once air quality standards and state emission controls are created, the federal government may notify a violator and require compliance; if compliance is not obtained, the federal government can either order compliance or initiate a civil suit against the violator. A fine of $25,000 per day and a year in prison is provided; additional violations can result in $50,000-per-day fines.

6. *Controls on fuel.* The EPA is given the power to control or prohibit the sale of fuel or fuel additives if their emissions interfere with public health or obstruct the operation of auto emission control devices.

Essentially, these provisions did away with the ineffectual state-by-state process for establishing air quality standards and substituted a strong, comprehensive federal authority to create national air pollution standards. Gone is Congressional deference to the states and, apparently, legislative patience with the regulated industries. The new requirements for state emission standards and the new enforcement scheme—a promising alternative to the moribund conference system—promise a direct, stringent enforcement of controls on effluents where none had previously existed. The automobile and petroleum industries, especially, were treated with uncommon toughness. The new requirements for almost complete control of major auto emissions by 1976 are intensely unpopular among automakers, who argue that the goals are unattainable in such a short period. The EPA's new authority to regulate fuels appears to be a prelude to a concerted federal effort to discourage leaded gasoline from the American market—an assumption confirmed when President Nixon requested in 1971 that Congress permit a new tax on leaded gasolines that would probably diminish their use greatly. Many observers sensed that Congress has possibly reached the end of a decade's indulgence of air polluters and might soon turn to water pollution problems with similar incisiveness. However, the effectiveness of this legislation will ultimately depend on how strictly and consistently it is enforced.

The First Test. In mid-1972, the EPA issued the first national air quality standards for four major air contaminants: sulfur oxides, carbon monoxide, photochemical oxidants, and nitrogen oxides. The states then had nine months in which to create their implementation plans (including the essential emission standards). While these plans will be incomplete for some time, early evidence indicates that the EPA will take a hard line on stringent emission controls.[23] The most notable test to date of the EPA's attitude toward the new legislation came when major domestic and foreign automakers requested the EPA to grant a year's delay in enforcing the new emission controls, a delay permitted by the legislation if the administrator felt it necessary. Regulated interests followed the events with a keen eye. Intense pressure on the EPA was generated by auto industry spokesmen, lobbyists, and Congressional allies; public statements were made by auto industry leaders suggesting that they could not meet the deadlines and might have to cease production as a result. Nonetheless, after extensive hearings, the EPA administrator, William Ruckelshaus, announced in March, 1972, that the manufacturers had failed to substantiate their claim that the technology was unavailable to meet the original emission deadlines. A high official in the EPA, predicting that the auto emission issue would be a crucible for the agency, felt it had to stand firm if the regulated industries were to respect the new legislation. It was, he observed, a case where the "credibility of the agency" was at issue.[24] The EPA's strong stand in the face of formidable opposition seemed to suggest that federal administrators were finally taking the hard line against air pollution.

Business and Regulation

In their attitude toward pollution policy, American business has seemed akin to the man who loves humanity but isn't especially fond of anyone in particular. Although endorsing pollution abatement and governmental regulation in principle, American business has demonstrated scant enthusiasm for the details. Pollution abatement depends heavily on the voluntary cooperation of American corporations, to such an extent that business attitudes can materially hinder or advance the fight against air and water contamination.

Businessmen have many reasonable grounds for concern with pollution policy. The capital investment for installing and maintaining emission control equipment, which may total several million dollars in some industries, is a cost factor that may alter the internal economics and market position of many corporations. Long-range industrial growth may be affected by pollution control costs, as may the relative market position of one industry vis-à-vis its competitors. The ramifications of cost impacts on particular industries may ultimately lead to changes in the rate and direction of growth in the gross national product.

Corporate leaders have echoed some common apprehensions about pollution abatement. One frequent assertion is that government is overreacting to pollution problems by creating a too stringent and costly pollution policy. When the senior vice-president of Texaco, Inc., decried "the regulatory overkill with respect to environmental problems" and the president of the National Coal Association warned against a "political overreaction" that is "frustrating the domestic production of essential fuels," they spoke for numerous kindred minds in corporate boardrooms who also believe environmental ills are being exaggerated. Additionally, business leaders—affecting an ominous tone that might unsettle most Americans—have peppered their discussion of pollution policy with allegations that the cost of pollution abatement will have grave effects on the economy. "The nation's pollution control bill will be staggering," predicted a petroleum company leader. In September, 1971, the U.S. Chamber of Commerce warned, "All existing firms will be adversely affected, but in some cases the economic impact will be severe." When Secretary of Commerce Maurice Stans observed darkly in mid-1972 that pollution control costs "might throw thousands out of work" and "cause whole communities to be run through the economic wringer," it became clear why many businessmen should be apprehensive on regulation.

This corporate ambivalence, common at all levels of the economy, often represents a genuine confusion among business leaders, who have difficulty reconciling the traditional doctrines of economic growth and satisfaction of consumer demands with the new imperatives for economic controls to assure environmental protection. Typical of this attitude is the electric power industry's handling of public advertising. Private utilities, in areas where there is little surplus generating capacity, have reduced or entirely abandoned promotional advertising that might increase power demands, while many other utilities have urged consumers to conserve power. Still, the seventy-three private utilities supporting the Electric Companies Advertising program, the largest single industry promotion campaign, rejected a proposal in 1972 to initiate a national effort to decrease power demands on the grounds that it had an obligation to encourage economic prosperity.

Clearly, a major issue is the actual cost of pollution control; all estimates remain tentative, but some information is available to shed light on the impact of pollution control on the economy and on industry itself.

Pollution Control and the Economy

The most grievous predictions about the depressant effect of control costs on the economy appear to be premature. The Council on Environmental Quality has estimated that controls might produce a slight decrease in the production of finished goods and a slight increase in the price of goods requiring environmental controls, yet there will be little effect on employment or the gross national product. Another joint study by the EPA, the Council on Environmental Quality, and the Department of Commerce indicates that some small businesses may indeed be forced to close because they cannot run profitably with additional pollution control costs; in such cases, communities depending on these corporations for employment are likely to face a major recession. However, careful studies show that the plants that will have to shut down because of pollution abatement costs are already marginal operations in which obsolescent equipment and aging technologies are most often the cause of failure. Unemployment attributable to pollution control expense, directly or indirectly, was estimated at only 1,500 nationally in 1971–72. While some businessmen have warned that consumers will pay for ecology in the form of significant price increases for goods and services, projections suggest that by 1977 consumer prices will increase by only 0.7 per cent as a result of industry's pollution control investment; almost all this amount is attributable to the one major price increase clearly linked to pollution controls—a healthy 10 per cent rise in new car costs.

Industry and Pollution Control Costs. Though pollution abatement may put a small dent in the national economy, it will represent considerable industrial investment. The best current estimates are that industry will need to spend about $42 billion between 1973 and 1977 for air pollution control equipment and an additional $13.5 billion in water pollution costs (most of the water pollution costs are absorbed by municipalities).[25] This large investment nonetheless represents a small proportion of total capital expenditures or sales volume of most major industries—two useful indicators of the burden such control places upon industrial economies. Some idea of the actual control costs to various industries can be found in Table 4, which projects the cost of air pollution abatement in major national industries as a percentage of their value of shipments; while this estimate appears to be somewhat conservative, later calculations are not likely to increase the cost estimates very greatly.

Roughly, these figures indicate that a relatively small portion (7 per cent) of all capital expenditures will be needed by industry for air pollution control through 1976. A similarly modest amount of capital expenditures will be required for water pollution abatement. The social value of these expenditures should be assessed not only by figuring the cost to industry but also by paying careful attention to the cost of pollution damage in the

TABLE 4
Impact of Air Pollution Control Costs on Selected Industries, 1976
(Dollars in Millions)

Industry	1967 Value of Shipments	Total Control Costs	5 Per Cent Increase in Wages	Control Costs As Per Cent of 1967 Value of Shipments	5 Per Cent Increase in Wages As Per Cent of 1967 Value of Shipments
Food and kindred products	$84,062	$296	$506	.4%	.6%
Paper	20,740	43	221	.2	1.1
Chemicals	42,470	60	325	.1	.8
Petroleum	22,042	23	61	.1	.3
Rubber and plastics	12,789	1	165	.01	1.3
Stone, clay, and glass	14,604	76	192	.5	1.3
Primary metals	46,550	875	492	1.9	1.1

SOURCE: Council on Environmental Quality, *Environmental Quality, 1971* (Washington, D.C., 1971), p. 124.

United States. Air pollution damage alone probably exceeds $25 billion yearly; accurate estimates of water pollution costs are still unavailable. If corporate investment in pollution control is viewed as a "trade-off" to reduce the nation's annual pollution toll, the investment can be seen as a valuable national effort to reduce the social costs of ecological damage.

Unlike industry generally, auto manufacturers and their satellite concerns can expect a major market impact from emission control equipment. When the stringent new emission controls ordained by the Clean Air Amendments of 1970 finally come into effect in 1975 and 1976, the cost of new automobiles will increase by at least two hundred dollars a year, and average auto prices may go up as much as 10 per cent.[26] Whether this substantial cost increase will continue in subsequent model years and what effect it is apt to have on the new-car market remain problematical; major domestic and foreign automobile manufacturers, however, have been uneasy lest the sudden price surge depress the demand for new automobiles.

Private Efforts

With the blossoming of ecology into national prominence came the painful recognition among industrial leaders that the public often regarded them as the nation's principal polluters. Major corporations felt an acute need to demonstrate their pollution consciousness and, at the same time, to displace some of the responsibility for environmental clean-up from themselves. Part of this strategy took the form of advertising that urged citizens to participate in the drive for pollution abatement. Corporate advertising also focused on industry's alleged efforts to stop air and water pollution, as well as the victories won. A major private investment would be desirable as a valuable supplement to governmental and academic studies. Indeed, significant private research might hasten the end of serious pollution problems, especially if it produced new, less polluting products or technologies that diminish environmental degradation. Not least important, a serious corporate commitment to such research would be an encouraging demonstration of sincerity regarding environmental protection—a hopeful portent, because much pollution abatement must ultimately depend on the voluntary efforts of major polluters.

One indicator of industrial research is the amount of their total capital expenditures which major corporations are investing in pollution research and control. According to estimates by the Council on Environmental Quality, the record is very uneven. A few major polluters, including the iron, steel, and paper industries, had approached 10 per cent of capital investment in pollution control research, but most major polluters were investing rather miserly amounts in comparison to the problem's gravity; electric utilities (3.8 per cent), mining (6.1 per cent), and auto manufacturing (4.2 per cent) are the industries most often accused of underinvestment in pollution abatement. Among most electric utilities, for instance, tight-fisted research spending stands in sharp contrast to generous promotional advertising, which, according to one recent study, accounts for six times the dollar expenditure for research among fifteen of the nation's largest firms.[27] The Council on Environmental Quality has predicted that most major industries will meet the required research investment levels by the mid-1970's, yet it warns that "higher rates of spending will be required of some industries" than they appear willing to invest. Despite the council's guarded optimism, numerous major industries were slow to take the initiative in research, let alone to compete for leadership in the field. Much of industry, for instance, has traditionally relied on municipal treatment plants to handle their effluents and still supports increased expenditures for municipal treatment in preference to strict emission controls—a system, in effect, that results in the taxpayer's subsidizing much of industry's pollution treatment. In managing air pollution, most industries seemed reluctant to go where they weren't led, usually investing little more than what seemed required to meet federal and state air quality standards. In the 1970's, it is not inconceivable that industry will gradually make a greater effort to develop its own research capabilities for pollution control, but the prognosis at this time is not very promising.

Summary: The Battle Has Just Begun

In the span of the last two decades, we have passed through three phases in pollution abatement. Phase one, lasting until the mid-1960's, consisted of largely symbolic, minimal gestures at air and water pollution control by government, with virtually no industrial contribution of consequence. Phase two, beginning in the mid-1960's, represented an attempt to attack the pollution problem through the incremental, decentralized, interest-group-based policy system epitomized by the standards-and-enforcement procedure. This approach, inspired by the customary logic of public policy in the United States, has proved an almost complete failure, leading to phase three, which has only just begun. Phase three, symbolized by the Clean Air Amendments of 1970, produced a new centralization of pollution control authority in Washington, a rejection of decentralized, state-by-state pollution control planning, and the abandonment of Washington's previous indulgent attitude toward the regulated industries. So far confined to air pollution and yet to prove itself, this strategy is nevertheless a major departure from the logic that has dominated public policy, and, if successful, it will mark the first incisive federal effort to control pollution.

Despite industry's desire to establish its credibility as an environmental protector, the record of the private sector has been, at best, indifferent and often negligent with regard to pollution control. Seldom leading in the fight but often led, more responsive to governmental coercion than to admonitions, the nation's corporate interests have yet to establish a record of pollution abatement commensurate with the public image they have concocted for themselves in their own advertising.

Notes

1. Walter J. Hickel, *Who Owns America?* (Englewood Cliffs, N.J.: Prentice-Hall, 1971), p. 110.
2. The standards-and-enforcement procedure is more completely analyzed in J. Clarence Davies, *The Politics of Pollution* (New York: Pegasus Press, 1970), chapters 7 and 8; and in John C. Esposito, *Vanishing Air* (New York: Grossman Publishers, 1970), chapter 7.
3. An example of such a battle is the one that erupted over sulfur oxide criteria initially formulated by federal officials in the early 1970's. This is fully described in J. Clarence Davies, *op. cit.*, pp. 163–69; and in John C. Esposito, *op. cit.*, chapter 10.
4. Neil Fabricant and Robert M. Hallman, *Toward a Rational Power Policy* (New York: George Braziller, 1971), pp. 23 and 24.
5. Many of the problems arising from emission controls, together with a comparison of other pollution abatement methods, may be found usefully summarized in George Hagevik, "Legislating for Air Quality Management: Reducing Theory to Practice," in Leslie L. Roos, Jr., *The Politics of Ecosuicide* (New York: Holt, Rinehart and Winston, 1971), pp. 311–45.
6. Indeed, even the Council on Environmental Quality has been critical of the standards-and-enforcement system. See Council on Environmental Quality, *Environmental Quality, 1971* (Washington, D.C., 1971), p. 4. An extended analysis of the problems associated with standards and enforcement may be found in Earl Finbar Murphy, *Governing Nature* (Chicago: Quadrangle Books, 1967), pp. 218 ff.
7. This point is argued most forcefully in David Zwick and Marcy Benstock, *Water Wasteland* (New York: Grossman Publishers, 1971), chapter 14.
8. David Zwick and Marcy Benstock, *op. cit.*, p. 44.
9. The thermal pollution problem is analyzed most informatively in Richard Curtis and Elizabeth Hogan, *Perils of the Peaceful Atom* (New York: Ballentine Books, 1969), chapter 8.
10. Public Law 84-660.
11. The 1965 legislation is fully discussed in David Zwick and Marcy Benstock,

op. cit., chapter 6; while the more general problems of securing compliance are analyzed in J. Clarence Davies, *op. cit.*, chapter 8.

12. There is little debate over the adequacy of enforcement procedures; even responsible federal officials recognize the weakness. See, for instance, the assessment of the Council on Environmental Quality, *Environmental Quality, 1971,* pp. 12–13. The most critical examinations are found in John C. Esposito, *op. cit.*, chapter 6, and David Zwick and Marcy Benstock, *op. cit.*, chapter 6. One of the few case studies of voluntary compliance problems is found in Ted Caldwell and Leslie L. Roos, Jr., "Voluntary Compliance and Pollution Abatement," in Leslie L. Roos, Jr., *The Politics of Ecosuicide* (New York: Holt, Rinehart and Winston, 1971), pp. 236–67.
13. Public Law 89-234.
14. David Zwick and Marcy Benstock, *op. cit.*, p. 271. In mid-1972, a federal district court prohibited the EPA from approving any state air quality plan that permitted "degradation" of air quality. The EPA, however, has appealed the decisions and maintains that the matter, in any case, affects only a small number of states. See the statement of EPA administrator William D. Ruckelshaus in the *New York Times,* June 1, 1972.
15. This act (33 U.S.C. 407) is contained in the Rivers and Harbors Act of 1899.
16. Executive Order No. 11574, 3 C.F.R. 188 (1970).
17. This interlock is discussed in Esposito, *op. cit.*, chapter 5.
18. See John C. Esposito, *op. cit.*, chapter 6, for a discussion of abatement proceedings under the law.
19. Public Law 90-148.
20. Public Law 89-232.
21. On the obsolescence of emission controls, see Council on Environmental Quality, *Environmental Quality, 1970* (Washington, D.C., 1970), pp. 77–78.
22. Public Law 91-604. These provisions are summarized in *Congressional Quarterly Weekly Report,* January 1, 1971, pp. 14–15.
23. Evidence of the EPA's firmness came in mid-1972, when the administrator upheld Montana's high-sulfur-oxide emission controls requirements over the vigorous objection of Anaconda Copper and American Smelting and Refining, both economic powers in the state. The EPA held its ground despite pressure from the White House and influential Montana public officials. See *New York Times,* August 5, 1971.
24. George Allen, deputy assistant administrator of the EPA, quoted in *New York Times,* April 10, 1972.
25. Estimates for air pollution control found in U.S. Environmental Protection Agency, *The Economics of Clean Air* (Washington, D.C., March, 1972), p. 1–1; water pollution costs estimated by Council on Environmental Quality, *Environmental Quality, 1971* (Washington, D.C., 1971), p. 111.
26. This is a very conservative estimate, made by the Council on Environmental Quality, *Environmental Quality, 1971, op. cit.*, p. 125. A private group of experts, consulted by the EPA, suggests the cost might approach $755 (*New York Times,* April 10, 1972).
27. According to the Council of Economic Priorities, the fifteen power companies generating a quarter of all the nation's electric output spent $126.9 million for advertising compared with only $21.4 million for research and development in 1970.

6 *Earmuffs for Alligators: The Politics of Water Resources*

Alan C. Stewart was a dedicated man, candid to the point of indiscretion, quick-tempered and vastly impatient with the environmentalists who disliked his airport. For a quarter century, as director of the Dade County Port Authority, he had tenaciously campaigned for big aviation in Miami. But for the environmentalists, he would have succeeded. In 1968, the Federal Aviation Agency announced the first planning grants for one of the world's largest jetports to be located near Miami. Rising in the green wilderness forty-five miles from the city, embracing an area larger than Miami itself, the runways alone would have exceeded the total size of the four largest ones existing in the nation; two six-mile runways, the site showpieces, would launch more than 200,000 commercial flights yearly. "It's not fantasy," Stewart had burbled. "No matter how big they build the monsters of the airlines, we'll have space for them."[1]

But conservation killed the Great Miami Jetport. A broad alliance of environmental groups launched a furious campaign against the project because it appeared to threaten the ecology of the vast Everglades National Park adjacent to the future runways. Skillfully using the media, ecologists cited expert evidence indicating that aircraft noise and airport congestion would drive rare birds from their nesting, that a continual drizzle of jet fuel would drive away or poison numerous park animals, and that the combined inroads of aviation and commerce might eventually despoil one of the nation's great natural adornments.

Finally, in January, 1969, government officials agreed to seek an alternate site less menacing to the unique Everglades wilderness.

Seldom indulgent toward conservationists, Stewart grew bitterly caustic as his jetport evaporated. In his lexicon, they had always been "butterfly chasers"; now he suggested to the press that all conservationists protected were "yellow bellied sapsuckers." Why not, he asked, build an astrodome next to the runways where the conservationists could chase their butterflies unmolested? When told that conservationists expected the jet noise to disturb the Everglades alligators, he reportedly quipped that he would buy the alligators earmuffs. All this further mobilized environmentalists and brought many previously disinterested citizens into the fray on the side of the butterflies. Alan Stewart, in the end, contributed in no small measure to a significant environmental victory.

In retrospect, most of Stewart's remarks were counterproductive and silly. To many ecologists, however, he was the incarnation of a resource ethic that had dominated American government for more than a century. Earmuffs for alligators and a stadium for butterfly chasers could be dismissed as the indiscretions of an embittered man, yet such flippancy also betrayed a callousness toward environmental values that conservationists had long perceived, less crudely stated, among other public officials with resource responsibilities. To many conservationists, the airport battle became one of those rare occasions in which the traditional official indifference toward environmental values had been blatantly declared and publicly exposed. In sparing the alligators their earmuffs, many conservationists believed they had achieved both a material and a symbolic triumph over a longstanding resource ethic in official circles.

Despite the jetport decision, altering governmental attitudes toward natural resources is still a difficult task. To begin, it requires a transformation in a pervasive attitude found among most governmental officials and policy-makers with resource responsibilities. Federal officials have frequently genuflected to environmental protection in the past, but environmental values customarily took second place in their approach to resource use. Washington adopted two methods for dealing with major resources. In some cases, it has used a *laissez-faire* philosophy, leaving many resources largely open to appropriation by private interests without significant federal opposition. In the case of most resources now considered nationally important, Washington asserted control over resource use, but the policy-making process has been organized in a manner very responsive to the interests of those using the resources for personal or corporate gain. Grant McConnell's description of federal land policy generally characterizes Washington's past resource policy: "The persistent success of demands for private exploitation has become a tradition, conferring a degree of legitimacy on a wide variety of actions that give control of land and land policy to limited groups, within the general population."[2] Such a procedure amounted to promoting resource use with little concern for environmental consequences.

Once corporate interests gained their access, they customarily created a strong, resistant political structure to protect and enhance their objectives, usually with considerable indifference to environmental amenities. Commonly, large national trade associations representing the major corporate users, formed in conjunction with state and local counterparts, gained entrée and influence among Washington officials charged with resource regulation. Eventually these interests became the clientele groups for their regulatory agencies, and the pattern of cooperative accommodation between regulated interests and their governmental regulators developed, as it did in other areas of federal regulation. Thus, environmentalists who are determined to introduce a larger measure of concern into deliberations on resource use must confront both an official inattention to environmental values and a sturdy political structure resistant to major policy change. The problems these institutionalized obstacles pose for environmentalists can be illuminated by examining recent federal policy affecting water development.

Water Resource Politics

The federal government has promoted water resource development since George Washington's first administration, but the great expansion of federal effort, authority, and investment in these projects did not occur until the twentieth century. Congress set the administrative design for federal water resource development in the Federal Power Act of 1920. This legislation divided authority over water resource projects among the Army Corps of Engineers, the Interior Department's Bureau of Reclamation, and the Agriculture Department's Soil Conservation Service. Intense infighting had erupted between private groups and public officials partisan to each agency, in their struggle to assure a major policy role for their respective administrative favorites, and Congress ended the conflict without resolving it. Each agency was given essentially similar responsibilities, although on different scales, a decision that precluded the possibility of a coherent, carefully planned national water resource policy and assured that the agencies would be chronic competitors for control of water resource policy and projects. Further, various Congressional committees exercised jurisdiction over the water agencies to further confound systematic planning. However, this situation conformed to the political realities of water resource planning: It assured that client groups of each major agency would have some voice in water resource decisions. In general, water resource development has more often responded to the field of political forces surrounding it than to good principles of administrative or environmental management.

Among the three water resource agencies, the Bureau of Reclamation and the Army Corps of Engineers are clearly dominant in size, responsibilities, appropriations, and political influence. Since its major reorganization in 1923, the Bureau of Reclamation has operated exclusively in the seventeen western states, Alaska, and Hawaii. Originally given development of irrigation projects as its principal responsibility, it has now broadened its work to include flood and navigation control, recreation development, power generation, and most other enterprises associated with water resource development. With 11,000 workers and appropriations averaging almost $500 million per fiscal year, the bureau controls 252 dams in the West, together with forty-eight power plants, 344 canals with a combined length of 6,781 miles, and impounds enough water to cover New York State to a depth of four feet.[3] Within its western dominion, the bureau is a major force in shaping water use but is still eclipsed by the Army Corps of Engineers as a water resource planner for the nation. The Corps is, and has been, the nation's major administrative agent in the politics and planning of water resources; it has been the focus of persistent, intense conflicts between federal water resource planners and conservationists. Most of the environmental problems inherent in current water resource planning can be identified by examining the relationship of the Corps and its political associates and the environmentalists.

The Corps and Pork-Barrel Politics

Few federal agencies boast a longer, more impressive, or more successful history than the Army Corps of Engineers. Created by Congress in 1802 with both civil and military responsibilities, it was to be the principal engineering consultant and agent of Congress in the creation, operation, and maintenance of national navigation and flood control projects, together with related work.[4] During its history, unblemished by major scandal and adorned with praise for its professional competence, the Corps has compiled an honorable record of military accomplishments, but almost from its inception its greatest effort has been devoted to carrying out its civilian responsibilities; while it has eight operational sections (including those responsible for nuclear activities, the space program, civil defense, and missile site construction), the bulk of its appropriations and personnel are devoted to civil projects. Employing about 32,000 civilians directed by 200 military engineers who are among the army's political and intellectual elite, the Corps has amassed an impressive catalogue of achievements. By mid-1972, it had completed 3,219 projects costing $10.1 billion; 275 additional ones were under way for $13.5 billion more, and 452, still on the drawing boards, will cost $9.6 billion. The finished work amounts to 22,000 miles of navigable waterways, 350 reservoirs, 9,000 miles of levees and flood walls, and 7,500 miles of improved channels. The Corps' civil works absorb three-quarter's of all federal money allocated yearly for water resource development—an average of about $1.6 billion. Accompanying such prosperity in appropriations and projects has been an administrative and political status almost unique among federal agencies. The Corps has been virtually autonomous within the federal administrative structure, free of most supervision or control by the President, the Secretary of Defense, and the Secretary of the Army, all of whom are administrative overseers of the Corps according to the organization charts. This autonomy is further enhanced by the great favoritism and protectiveness with which Congress treats the Corps. In short, the Corps has reigned among that tiny pantheon of administrative agencies headed by the FBI, almost untouched by the political hazards faced by other bureaus.

There are several circumstances that have both contributed to the Corps' favored status and, directly and indirectly, led to its conflict with conservationists; among these are the pork-barrel system in Congress, the Corps' own political astuteness, and the phalanx of private interests associated with the Corps.

Pork-barrel Politics. To their critics, the Engineers are mercenary pork-barrel soldiers, a simplification that nonetheless recognizes that the Corps is one popular conduit for the heavy flow of pork-barrel appropriations that annually emerge from Congress.[5] Pork-barrel funds are moneys allocated by Congress for federal works at the state and local level—rivers and harbors projects, interstate highways, military bases, space installations, and other enterprises. Pork-barrel projects are extremely important to virtually all congressmen. In American political culture, senators and representatives are expected to produce a reasonable flow of pork-barrel appropriations for their constituents if they are to retain the favor of local political influentials. Pork-barrel projects infuse new federal money into constituencies, creating construction and service jobs, often producing large, continuing employment and payrolls, and frequently enhancing the civic ambience of communities; in depressed areas, pork-barrel spending may be the customary remedy for a sagging economy.

It is understandable that legislators, anxious to discover and maintain projects in their districts for which pork-barrel appropriations can be made, should look toward flood control, water recreation development, hydroelectric sites, reservoirs, canals, and other projects under the authority of water resource agencies such as the Corps. Thus, political realities create a community of interest between Congress, with its appetite for political pork, and the Corps, with its aptitude for public works. This affinity has obvious benefits for the Corps. It disposes Congress to appropriate handsomely for the Corps' projects and to protect the Corps' autonomy within the administrative branch so that it will continue to be responsive to Congress without serious obstruction from administrative superiors less addicted to the pork barrel. But the Corps' unchallenged ascendancy among water resource agencies results, in addition, from almost a century's lead over its administrative competitors in building strong Congressional relations and its virtuosity at cultivating Congressional favor.

"An Uncommonly Cordial Relationship." The traditional working relationship between Congress and the Corps can best be shown by examining briefly the planning procedures for water resource projects entrusted to the Corps. This planning involves five steps:[6]

1. Local interests request a member of Congress to propose a project. The legislator seeks, and commonly obtains, authorization for the Corps to undertake the study from the appropriate Congressional committee.
2. The Corps makes a preliminary examination to determine the project's economic feasibility.
3. If the preliminary study is favorable, a detailed engineering and economic study is made.
4. If detailed studies still justify the project, it is customarily authorized by Congress.
5. Congress appropriates funds for the project; contracts are let out and actual construction begins.

The procedure is extremely sensitive and responsive to congressmen and their constituencies. Legislators, in collaboration with local partisans of a project, initiate all Corps studies. While the Corps does not report favorably on all projects, its planning arrangements provide project promoters with many opportunities to influence agency planners and to advance their arguments effectively. During the early planning stages, for example, the

Corps routinely arranges public hearings within the area affected by a proposal. Enthusiasts for the enterprise customarily appear in force to testify to its virtues, while the hearings often generate additional local mobilization for the project and further publicize it. According to one careful estimate, there are at least thirty-two points in this planning process at which groups may voice their views to the Corps or to Congress.[7] In cases where projects are unfavorably reported, an elaborate review and appeals system exists within the Corps structure, offering project promoters a chance to urge reconsideration and further study of a project's feasibility. In short, planning has been in good measure a system for representing and adjusting local group and Congressional sentiments on proposed water resource projects. Indeed, "the planning process appears to be specifically organized in response to the need for an adjustment of group interests at the several levels at which these interests may become articulate."[8] This orientation within the Corps not only provides numerous opportunities for the expression of group opinion but also—whether intentionally or not—gives prominent voice to those most likely to promote public works in the constituency.

This planning method also means that individual projects are normally considered in isolation from one another. With its bias toward local interests and their Congressional spokesmen, the Corps concentrates on solving the engineering and economic problems associated with the specific projects advanced by such interests, and it gives comparatively little attention to the cumulative effect of individual work on large areas or whole river basins. Such an approach allows the Corps great freedom to evaluate and respond to proposals for particular projects without the constraints imposed by a comprehensive water development plan into which individual projects would have to fit or perish.

In all its planning and project investigations, the Corps insists that it is merely the administrative arm of Congress, responsible for evaluating and implementing such projects as Congress may entrust to it and offering its professional opinion when solicited. The Corps has steadfastly refused to take significant responsibility for creating and recommending to Congress any comprehensive plans for national water development. It will neither initiate comprehensive national water resource planning nor advise Congress about how such planning might proceed. In holding to this philosophy, the Corps has resolutely resisted repeated efforts to bring it within the control of a comprehensive water resource planning agency in the executive branch. As a result, the Corps can continue to encourage and respond to individual Congressional proposals without the shackles of a comprehensive plan to impede the input. Such a passive stance prevents the inevitable conflict—with the loss of Congressional grace—that would develop between the Corps and Congress if the Corps had to reject proposals on the grounds of good planning principles.

This is not to suggest that the Corps' passiveness extends to those Congressional proposals it might initially reject on engineering or economic grounds. Rather, these projects are frequently restudied until the Corps believes it has solved the original problems and can recommend the development to Congress. Sometimes a project, approved by the Engineers, may lie dormant because of the lack of Congressional funding or because the Corps has other projects to which it has assigned higher priorities. Such proposals seldom languish long, because the Corps will usually take the initiative in soliciting Congressional action upon them. In short, the Corps extends itself considerably to make projects feasible, and, notwithstanding its rejection of many projects, its working bias has been to find a way to get a project under way if at all possible.

The Corps' accommodation to Congress is mirrored in Congressional protection and promotion of the group. Congress has vigorously and successfully fought to maintain or improve the conditions enabling the Corps to work diligently at public works. The most conspicuous example is the repeated Congressional efforts to protect the Corps from the control of any executive agency or the President himself. At various times, Presidents Hoover, Roosevelt, Truman, and Eisenhower attempted to reassign the Corps' civil functions to other agencies, to impose greater White House control over the Corps, or to bring the Corps within the influence of a comprehensive water resource planning agency.[9] In all instances, Congress was instrumental in preserving the Corps' independence. During one period, between

1934 and 1942, twelve major efforts by President Roosevelt to alter the Corps' administrative autonomy were rebuffed. As a result, the Corps' formal position as a subordinate agency in the Defense Department is largely fictional. In theory responsible to the Secretary of the Army and the Secretary of Defense and, finally, to the President, the Engineers have reported directly to Congress, from whence come their marching orders.

Congress has looked after the Corps in other ways. The Engineers have a blanket authorization to initiate projects costing less than $1 million without specific Congressional approval, as well as permission to spend up to $10 million by committee resolution alone, a situation enabling the Corps to construct a continual array of small projects and giving it considerable bargaining power with congressmen who covet many modest developments in their districts.[10] Once Congress has authorized a project study, the Engineers are free to continue it indefinitely and, should they find the project feasible, to then propose it for funding. Congressional hearings on Corps appropriations and favorable study reports have been predictably amiable and complimentary. A few legislators have frequently voiced disenchantment with the Corps and proposed its reorganization in the name of better resource planning, but they are a distinct minority, impotent to ruffle seriously what one representative observer has called the "uncommonly cordial" understanding between the Corps and Congress.

Group Support. The Corps' legislative support is augmented by vigorous promotion of its programs by a great diversity of public and private groups with a stake in the Corps' endeavors. The Corps awards contracts to private firms for almost all its construction and service needs on individual projects; more than half a billion dollars in such contracts is annually dispensed to dredge-and-fill companies, concrete producers and purveyors of other building materials, land clearing enterprises, general contractors, electric contractors, equipment manufacturers, and a host of other firms. Past recipients of such largess and those with hope of future reward are customarily sympathetic to the Corps programs. So, too, are the local chambers of commerce, small businessmen, tourist industries, hotel and restaurant proprietors, land developers, and recreational interests, all of whom expect an economic boost or new amenities from various developments. State and local governmental officials, equally impressed by the aura of prosperity and growth that customarily surrounds major Corps programs, are also frequent partisans for the Corps.[11]

The most effective national pressure group allied with the Corps is the 7,000-member National Rivers and Harbors Congress (NRHC), founded in 1901 to promote national water resource projects. A group embracing in its membership the U.S. Congress (all of whom are honorary members) and all the Corps personnel engaged in rivers and harbors works (as *ex officio* members), it also has fifty state organizations and additional affiliations from state, city, and county governmental agencies, water and land development associations, business firms, and other groups. Members of Congress and the Corps take an active part in the NRHC, serving as officers, workers, and—on several occasions—presidents of the association.[12] This produces an unusual situation in which members of the legislative and executive branches with responsibility for formulating water resource policy are themselves members of a major pressure group in water resource politics; although some congressmen, Corps officials, and many conservationists have objected to what they consider the impropriety of this arrangement, it has not been significantly challenged or widely exposed and debated. The NRHC actively promotes a variety of river and harbor projects through its annual hearings and studies at its national meetings, organizes and coordinates the work of groups lobbying for such projects, and brings together within one organizational roof public policy-makers and private project promoters in a traditionally cordial atmosphere. The work of the NRHC fosters a common outlook and amiable working relations between public officials and lobbyists in water resource matters and further contributes to the Corps' high standing among interest groups concerned with its work. Besides the NRHC, a variety of regional water resource organizations also exist that usually concentrate on promoting government water development within their own geographic boundaries; among these, the Atlantic Deeper Waterways Association and the Ohio Valley Conservation and Flood Control Congress are also influential in the deliberations of Congress and the Corps on policies affecting them.

The Corps' group support rounds out the political profile of an agency that has successfully combined a remarkable degree of administrative autonomy with great finesse in Congressional policies to establish a control over national water resource development that pales its administrative rivals. Such a lofty position makes it logical and inevitable that environmentalists concerned with water resource policy should focus on the Corps.

Conservationists and the Corps

"In the view of conservationists," writes John McPhee, "there is something special about dams, something—as conservation problems go—that is disproportionately and metaphysically sinister." To many, dams are the conservationist's evil incarnate:

> The outermost circle of the Devil's world seems to be a moat filled mainly with DDT. Next to it is a moat of burning gasoline. Within this is a ring of pinheads each covered with a million people—and so on past phalanxed bulldozers and bicuspid chain saws into the absolute epicenter of Hell on earth, where stands a dam.[13]

It is a rare conservationist, in any case, who does not consider many dams and other federal water resource developments to be among Washington's most objectionable creations. Environmentalists have not been unappreciative of the valuable water resource projects sponsored by Washington, but they believe such benefits are increasingly overshadowed by the indiscriminate planning and building of federal projects with little intrinsic merit and enormous environmental cost—of which dams are the most obvious examples.

The "Engineering Mentality." The conservationist's most fundamental criticism of the Corps is that it is insensitive to the environmental degradation it creates. Supreme Court Justice William O. Douglas, an arch-conservationist, has complained: "The Corps has no conservation, no ecological standards. It operates as an engineer—digging, filling, damming the waterways."[14] Conservationists argue that the Corps is captive to an "engineering mentality" that leads it to approach a project without regard to environmental amenities, aesthetics, or long-term ecological consequences; only technical problems and solutions matter. One indication of this, suggest the critics, is the Corps' "straight-line syndrome"; it seems compelled to straighten out the pleasing bends and curves in waterways and, in so doing, systematically obliterates a river's natural beauty and much of its original ecology. Moreover, the argument continues, the Corps has an aversion to free-flowing water; it must be damned and impounded. "A free-flowing river is to any Army engineer what an unlicensed dog is to a dog-catcher," runs a variation of the complaint; "his first duty is to impound it or otherwise prevent it from running wild."[15] This environmental indifference often produces grave environmental degradation in the wake of Corps projects: Continual dredging and filling of estuaries destroy irreplaceable habitats, with their valuable wildlife and commercial fishing resources; deepening or widening rivers and constructing canals increase siltation to dangerous levels and often produce pollution of waterbodies into which the streams and rivers flow.

Environmentalists have joined many resource planners and public administration experts in indicting the Corps for its failure to practice comprehensive water development planning and for its tendency to view individual projects in isolation from one another. This myopia, they maintain, prevents the Corps from using a sounder approach in which comprehensive development plans for whole river basins or watersheds would come first; then the utility and impact of individual projects could be better evaluated and, if necessary, the projects abandoned. Under the more or less piecemeal planning system used by the Corps, suggest these observers, there is too much duplication of, or counterproductivity among, projects and unanticipated environmental damage that might be avoided by more deliberate, area-wide thinking. Conservationists have pointed to many specific projects to illustrate their charges against the engineering mentality; among them are the following:

- *The Cross Florida Barge Canal.* When it was to be completed in 1974, the east-west canal through the upper Florida peninsula would have destroyed twenty miles of the Oklawaha

River by straightening and dredging. The Oklawaha, one of the few "wild rivers" remaining in the United States, was then being considered for governmental protection. Moreover, the canal, by cutting into the Florida aquifer, the ground water system supplying all of southern Florida, was likely to alter its composition, possibly polluting it and changing major underground springs farther south.

• *The Libby Dam (Montana).* To be completed in 1972 at a cost of $428 million, the dam across Montana's Kootenai River has begun backing up water to an eventual length of ninety miles, creating a gigantic new lake. Erected to control flooding from the Columbia River, it has ended the popular cut-throat trout fishing in the Kootenai. Quite unexpectedly, the dam produced an infusion of so much dissolved nitrogen in water below the dam that major fish kills have occurred.

• *The Tennessee-Tombigbee Canal.* Begun in 1971, the waterway would be a 170-mile canal, dam, and lock project linking the Tennessee River at its southern end; estimated costs were $386.6 million. Conservationists assert that little study was given to the consequence of linking two rivers with different ecologies, that large tracts of prime forest and agricultural land would be inundated with a great loss of fish and game habitat—a consideration that did not appear to trouble the Corps.

In these instances, which environmentalists argue are typical of Corps project planning, environmental problems were given little, if any, attention until they actually occurred or until the projects were too far along to be stopped easily.

The Smell of Pork. Conservationists believe that environmental damage from such projects is greatly compounded by the Corps' tireless promotion of projects that will maintain its Congressional favor and bureaucratic prosperity. They point out that this unceasing quest for new undertakings not only disinclines the Corps to take account of environmental values but also encourages it to seek truly massive, "big water projects" with ill-considered repercussions. Many conservationists believe the Corps has become too indiscriminate in its desire to satisfy Congress with big water construction. They cite as an example the Corps' enthusiasm for the Ramparts Dam development. In response to Congressional authorization, the Corps studied, then proposed the damming of Alaska's Yukon River, the nation's fourth largest. Estimates in 1964 suggested that the project, costing possibly $20 billion, would create a dam 530 feet high and stretching 4,700 feet across the Yukon Valley; behind it would grow a reservoir larger than Lake Erie—an inland water body two hundred miles long and eighty miles wide. The primary purpose of the project was power generation; generally considered an excellent hydroelectric site, it would have produced 34 billion kilowatts of power. While Congress initially viewed the plan favorably, conservationists and their Congressional allies stopped appropriations by arguing that the environmental damage would be massive: The U.S. Fish and Wildlife Service estimated that the *annual* wildlife loss would be 1.5 million ducks, 12,800 geese, 10,000 cranes, 20,000 grebes, 13,000 moose, 3.6 million commercial fur-bearing animals, and 400,000 salmon. Also, emphasized the opponents, by the time the electric power was available, there would be more economical means for generating what, in any case, would be energy vastly exceeding Alaska's needs for decades. Conservationists regard the dam's defeat as a major victory but hasten to point out that such proposals demonstrate the Corps' lack of restraint in its search for new undertakings. This appetite for projects, they add, is further whetted because the salaries for the Corps' civil employees, the great bulk of its personnel, are always charged against a specific project and, thus, their continuing employment depends on a steady flow of new undertakings.

The pork-barrel system has also frustrated environmentalists by making the Corps almost impervious to change. Most of the indictments leveled against the Corps by environmentalists have been made, with slight variation, for at least a half century with little effect. While the Ramparts Dam incident, among others, demonstrated that conservationists, working with sympathetic public officials, have sporadically affected Corps policy, these occasional reversals produced no fundamental change in the Corps' philosophy. Remarked a former chairman of the Corps Environmental Advisory Board: "Only when monumental, countervailing, external political pressure was used have the Corps project directions been forced to change."[16] Such pressure—"monumental, countervailing, external"—is rarely generated.

The Benefit-Cost Formula. No Corps project is authorized unless the Corps can demonstrate to Congress that it has a favorable "benefit-cost ratio." This formulation has been carefully scrutinized and often criticized by environmentalists, economists, planning experts, and even some Corps officials. To many environmentalists, the deficiencies that abound in the preparation of these cost estimates are a case of bad economics becoming the consort of poor ecology in the service of the Corps' need for political security.

Since 1936, Congress has required that any federal improvement of navigable waters should be undertaken only when "the benefits to whomsoever they may accrue are in excess of the costs."[17] The Corps, like other federal water resource agencies, prepares and presents to Congress a benefit-cost ratio for every project it studies; if, after complex calculations, the expected economic benefits over the life of the project (commonly estimated to be fifty years) exceed its total cost, the project is usually undertaken. In practice, this means that a project must have a benefit-cost ratio exceeding 1.0—that is, a return greater than one dollar for every dollar invested. Authorized projects usually have ratios of 1.05 or better. The Corps can include numerous possible benefits when assigning value to a project. In the case of a dam and reservoir, for instance, it can consider benefits in flood control, water supply, fish and wildlife enhancement, recreation, water quality, power production, transportation, irrigation, or general regional economic improvement, among many other items. Costs have traditionally included the equipment, material, and manpower for the job, the cost of land used for the undertaking, and the expense of relocating homes, communities, highways, and other structures affected by the system. Corps officials, in defense of their calculations, point out that they are sufficiently rigorous to result in the rejection of more than half the projects studied.

Environmentalists object not to the principle of a benefit-cost calculation but to the manner in which the Corps usually comes up with its figures. The Corps, they charge, will exaggerate benefits and unreasonably minimize costs to enhance projects, and it commonly manipulates the figures until it can produce a favorable ratio for a Congressionally important project. Since Congress seldom studies a favorable benefit-cost ratio carefully, the formulation too often becomes a formality to justify projects that have not been subjected to a truly rigorous economic investigation. "It's nothing but a ritual," charged a former colonel with the Engineers. "They come down the aisle swinging their incense and chanting 'benefit-cost.' You can adjust the b-c ratio to justify any project. I did it a few times myself."[18] Specifically, conservationists point to some of the following deficiencies in estimates of project benefits that economists have frequently noted:

1. *Overestimating transportation benefits.* The Corps commonly assumes a greater volume of water traffic for a project than actually develops.
2. *Misleading flood control benefits.* By a curious logic, the Corps often builds a dam in order to protect an area from flooding and then lists among its benefits the control of floods for residents who would not move into the area unless the dam were built. Flood control is often temporary, in any case, for dams frequently suffer quick siltation.
3. *Exaggerated recreational benefits.* Often, reservoirs and other impoundments that are supposed to provide extensive recreational opportunities soon silt up or develop aquatic weed and pollution problems to the point where they discourage recreational use. Also, in cases where such damage does not occur, actual use falls below anticipated levels.
4. *Overly optimistic economic gains for an area.* Too often, the Corps anticipates an influx of new business and a general rise in area prosperity that is difficult to calculate in advance or fails to develop after construction.

Among the most frequent inadequacies in figuring the costs of a project, environmentalists would put first the Corps' failure to calculate the toll of environmental damage that often accompanies a project. No estimate is provided, they note, for such effects as the destruction of game and fish habitat, the loss of timber and agricultural land, the loss of a stream's free-flowing character, or the transformation of a wilderness area into commercial and recreational development following a project's completion. Moreover, they point out that other costs are often underestimated, so that large cost overruns are frequent. Cost overruns of 30 to 100 per cent are not rare; several recent projects have cost almost 400 per cent more than estimates.

Virtually all economists familiar with water resource planning have pointed to the "discount rate" used in benefit-cost calculations as the system's greatest weakness. In simple terms, the discount rate is the return the government might expect on the money it invests in a project if it invested the same money over a comparable period in another enterprise; it is somewhat analogous to an interest rate and should generally compare to interest rates common for major types of commercial investment. The lower the discount rate applied to a project, the higher the benefit-cost ratio will be. Low discount rates thus increase the prospects for producing a favorable cost ratio; conversely, as discount rates rise, a favorable cost ratio is more difficult to obtain. Until the late 1960's, Congress permitted the Corps to use a discount rate of 3⅛ per cent, far below what economists believed to be a reasonable figure. Currently, the rate is set at 5⅛ per cent, but most economists think a realistic figure would be 9 per cent or higher. The result of this consistently low rate has been to produce a favorable benefit-cost ratio for many projects that could not have been justified with more realistic discounts; according to one estimate, the Corps would have had to reject nearly half of the 578 projects it had authorized in early 1972 if a discount rate higher than the conservative 5⅛ per cent had been used.[19]

In any case, environmentalists are correct in asserting that the Corps' benefit-cost calculations have produced numerous uneconomical, if not unnecessary, projects. After carefully studying almost 150 federal water resource projects constructed in the South after World War II, one economist concluded that almost half (63) had proved too poor an investment to have been justified; a comprehensive national study would probably reveal an equally substantial record of unwise investment elsewhere.[20] Until the 1970's, however, all these protestations availed conservationists very little, for the Corps and Congress showed little inclination to alter their approach to water resource projects and environmentalists lacked the political leverage to force a change. Then, in the early 1970's came a swift succession of events indicating that a new, environmentally sounder approach to water resource planning might be forced upon Washington.

The Reform That Might Be. The Corps of Engineers is accustomed to bad years, but 1971 was among its worst. On January 19, 1971, President Nixon surprised most Washington observers by ordering an immediate end to construction of the Cross Florida Barge Canal, then one-third completed at a cost of $50 million. In his public statement, the President told the nation that his decision "to prevent potentially serious environmental damages" had been made at the request of the Council on Environmental Quality. The President and the council were determined to protect the Oklawaha River from disfigurement by the canal. "We must assure that in the future we take not only full but timely account of the environmental impact of such projects—so that instead of merely halting the damage, we prevent it," concluded the President. The announcement inflicted a singular defeat on the Corps: A President had never before halted one of its ongoing projects in peacetime; the environmental justification added another exotic touch.[21] Before the year's end, two more Corps projects were temporarily halted on environmental grounds by federal courts (a federal court had also temporarily halted the Florida canal only days before the President's order); by mid-1972, more than fifteen Corps developments worth several billion dollars were mired in lawsuits or otherwise delayed by controversies stemming from environmental issues. This unusual turn of events marked the first time that environmentalists had been able to delay or reverse a significant number of authorized projects.

Why had ecology so abruptly intruded on the Corps' activities when before it had mattered so little? Public opinion had undoubtedly played some part. Many observers interpreted the President's order as a bid for support from environmentalists and a ploy to strengthen his appeal to a public suddenly conscious of environmental issues. A more potent explanation, however, is the National Environmental Policy Act (NEPA), which equipped environmentalists with a powerful new legal tool to force the

Corps and other water resource agencies to examine the environmental implications of projects previous to construction. The important part of the NEPA is Section 102, which, as we saw earlier, requires all federal agencies to make an impact statement for any contemplated action that might significantly affect the environment. Water resource projects, like other federal programs, were included in the scope of Section 102.

Armed with Section 102, environmentalists immediately went to the federal courts to challenge a multitude of Corps endeavors, both planned and under way, on the grounds that the Corps had failed to produce satisfactory impact statements for them. Ecologists scored some early victories in the first cases when the courts ruled that Section 102 gave private environmental groups the legal standing to challenge the adequacy of the Corps' impact statements and declared that the Corps had to file such statements on *all* incomplete projects; thus, ecologists might use Section 102 against all but finished projects. Equally important, the courts held that the Corps had to prepare a complete impact statement that fully complied with all the terms of Section 102.[22] The result was to halt three projects immediately when the Corps failed to produce the necessary impact statements; additional projects, some still on the drawing board, were also brought into the courts by environmentalists challenging the adequacy of the impact statements. By mid-1972, environmentalists had succeeded in using NEPA's Section 102 to tie up so many projects in litigation that both the Corps and Congress were unsettled, to say the least.

Environmentalists had indeed stopped numerous projects with Section 102, but the delay might only have been temporary. Federal judges had halted many early projects because the Corps had made little pretense of preparing impact statements that fully complied with the NEPA guidelines—there hadn't been time. What would happen when the Corps did have the time and experience to draft statements that seemed to follow the instructions of the NEPA? Part of the answer depended on how carefully the courts would be willing to look into the substance of these statements in judging their adequacy. Environmentalists desperately want to demonstrate to the courts that benefit-cost calculations are usually shaky, that environmental costs are not properly estimated much of the time, and that Corps research is often superficial and self-serving; in short, ecologists want to get into the substance of the impact statement and have the courts rule on that. But if the courts decide that their job is only to see that the impact statement formally complies with the NEPA—that is, if they are reluctant to get into the details of the statement beyond satisfying themselves that it *seems* proper—ecologists cannot bring many environmental issues associated with water resource projects into the courts and will lose a valuable weapon against such projects. There is ample precedent for the courts' taking a conservative approach to the impact statements, leaving it to Congress, the President, and other executives to make the final decision on project advisability.

Even should the courts retreat from in-depth evaluation of impact statements, leaving that problem to Congress or to administrators, impact statements might nevertheless alter federal water resource policy if policy-makers can be influenced by revelations of the environmental consequences that follow water resource developments. Indeed, the principal intent of the statements is to "alert" Washington's decision-makers to the environmental implications of policy so that, presumably, they will not make environmentally damaging decisions ignorantly or without reflection. But will the impact statements be carefully weighed and then lead to the modification or abandonment of environmentally undesirable undertakings? The prognosis is certainly cloudy, but it seems unpromising because Congress, after having passed the NEPA by substantial margins, now finds the early results of Section 102 an unwelcome surprise, and a movement has been spawned in both chambers to change the law.

This Congressional reaction is understandable, for many early casualties of court suits involving Section 102 have been pork-barrel projects and federally licensed power plants esteemed by Congress and at least temporarily suspended by lengthy court litigation. When a federal court halted construction of the $386 million Tennessee–Tombigbee waterway until the Corps produced a complete impact statement, one of its strongest senatorial proponents, James O. Eastland (D.-Miss.), issued a complaint now aired in many variations by other congressmen whose projects are entangled with Section 102. "Everybody is in favor of protecting the environment, but this business of yelling 'ecology' every time we get ready for a new project has got to stop," complained the senator. His argument was that the projects affected by Section 102 were frequently necessary for the public good:

> Many of these suits amount to nothing, and the result is added cost for the taxpayer . . . Many of these suits are in the vital field of public power. Any delay along these lines could mean serious consequences to an already overworked power system . . . I would urge Congress to review the operation of these laws in an effort to determine how they are working—and if they are operating in the interest of the nation as a whole.[23]

Other congressmen thundered about the "ignoramuses" in the judiciary and the "frivolous injunctions" now holding up dams, canals, and other projects. One tangible result of this Congressional ire was a number of proposals stipulating that various agencies—among them, the Corps and the Bureau of Reclamation—be exempted from requirements for an impact statement, or that exemptions for future projects be written into the legislation authorizing them. Congress was not alone in its sympathy for such measures. The Federal Power Commission, the Atomic Energy Commission, the Corps of Engineers, the Bureau of Reclamation, and some influential members of the Environmental Protection Agency and the Council on Environmental Quality have also expressed a desire to see Section 102 modified to release various agencies from the currently strict provisions.

No legislation was passed in 1972, but the forces hostile to Section 102 were gathering strength and promised to push for changes as soon as Congress reconvened in late 1972. Most environmentalists expected a fierce legislative battle over the NEPA and feared that Congress might soon weaken the act by watering down the impact statement's requirements to the point where only an ineffectual formality remained. Were this to happen, any abiding change in federal water resource policy leading to more environmentally sensitive planning would be unlikely, and the politics of water resources would revert to the *status quo ante.*

Notes

1. *Miami Herald,* October 6, 1968.
2. Grant McConnell, *Private Power and American Democracy* (New York: Vintage Books, 1970), p. 196.
3. The history of the Bureau of Reclamation is summarized in George Laycock, *The Diligent Destroyers* (New York: Ballentine Books, 1970), pp. 85–87.
4. This summary of Corps history and functions is taken from Arthur Maass, *Muddy Waters* (Cambridge, Mass.: Harvard University Press, 1951), chapter 1; and *New York Times,* November 19, 1971.
5. The pork-barrel system is well documented. Two conservationist indictments may be found in Arthur E. Morgan, *Dams and Other Disasters* (Boston: Porter Sargent Publisher, 1971), chapter 4; and Elizabeth B. Drew, "Dam Outrage: The Story of the Army Engineers," *Atlantic,* April, 1970, pp. 51–62.
6. Arthur Maass, *op. cit.,* pp. 22 ff.
7. *Ibid.,* p. 51.
8. *Ibid.,* p. 37.
9. The chronology of this battle is summarized in Arthur Maass, *op. cit.,* pp. 72–119.
10. Arthur E. Morgan, *op. cit.,* chapter 4.
11. Studies of the Corps' appeal to local economic interests, not unbiased but nonetheless illuminating, may be found in George Laycock, *op. cit.;* and in Gene Marine, *America the Raped* (New York: Simon and Schuster, 1969).
12. This relationship is explored in Grant McConnell, *op. cit.,* pp. 218 ff.
13. John McPhee, *Encounters with the Archdruid* (New York: Farrar, Straus and Giroux, 1971), p. 158.
14. William O. Douglas, "The Corps of Engineers: The Public Be Damned," *Playboy,* July, 1969, p. 19.
15. Paul Brooks, "Notes on the Conservation Revolution," in John Mitchell and Constance L. Stallings, *Ecotactics* (New York: Pocketbooks, 1970), p. 40.
16. Charles M. Stoddard, former chairman of the Corps Environmental Advisory Board, quoted in *New York Times,* July 24, 1971.
17. Flood Control Act of 1936.
18. Edwin R. Decker, formerly the Corps' St. Louis District Engineer. Quoted in *New York Times,* February 20, 1972.
19. Estimated by U.S. Office of Management and Budget and reported in *New York Times,* February 20, 1972.
20. R. H. Haveman, *Water Resource Investment and the Public Interest* (Nashville, Tenn.: Vanderbilt University Press, 1965).
21. During World War II, however, almost all public works projects had been halted by the President, and some—not Corps projects—had been stopped earlier for conservation reasons.
22. These cases are discussed in Walter A. Rosenbaum and Paul E. Roberts, "The Year of Spoiled Pork: Comments on the Court's Role as an Environmental Defender," *Law and Society Review,* Fall, 1972, pp. 33–60.
23. Quoted in *St. Petersburg Times,* October 13, 1971. Other rumblings against the bill are reported in *New York Times,* April 30, 1972.

7 *The Politics of Timber*

The nation's public forests are a sprawling, rich resource covering an area larger than all the Atlantic seaboard states and are critical to the nation's environment and economy; forest use involves public and private stakes as significant as pollution control or water resource plans. Nonetheless, national timber policy has been an esoteric business, remote from the view of the public or the media, a specialized world of governmental experts, commercial timber companies, and a handful of ecologists. Now environmentalists, aroused by Washington's administration of the public forests, are intent upon turning this public neglect into mobilized concern that will avert what many people predict is an impending devastation of the public domain in the name of the public good and economic necessity.

On one level, the controversy swirls about "clearcutting," a practice used increasingly by the commercial lumber industry, with Washington's approval, to remove mammoth batches of marketable timber from public lands by stripping large areas bare of all trees down to short stumps. Environmentalists charge that clearcutting is an environmentally vicious practice, indefensible on ecological or economic grounds, condoned because federal officials have become apostles of commercial lumbering and seek to satisfy the lumber industry's appetite for rising profits. The timber industry asserts that clearcutting is neither an ecological menace nor an economic extravagance but, rather, a responsible adjustment to the nation's growing need for wood. Caught in this crossfire is the U.S. Forest Service, an agency whose long, honorable reputation for forestry in the public interest is now jeopardized by its attempt to find a compromise between conflicting demands and incompatible philosophies of forest use. At a deeper level, however, the clearcutting controversy involves fundamental questions about public policy regarding the nation's resources still on the public lands. To whom do these resources properly belong? Which uses are justified? Which uses should come first?

Beyond these issues, the conflict also reveals some essential features of resource politics in the United States. In many respects, the struggle over timber is a microcosm of the issues, factions, and factors at work in shaping the use of other resources on public land; to understand the fight over timber is to learn, as well, something about the politics of grazing, mining, and oil. It will be helpful, in fact, to begin a description of the clearcutting issue by projecting it against the background of public policy toward all the various resources controlled by the federal government in the name of the public.

Public Lands and Public Policy

In trust for the people of the United States, the federal government holds a third of the nation's land—751 million acres of national forests, national parks, wilderness areas, wildlife refuge, and grazing land known collectively as the public domain. Many states are largely public domain: Almost 95 per cent of Alaska and 86 per cent of Nevada are federal land; so are more than half of Oregon and Utah and more than a third of California, Colorado, New Mexico, and Arizona. Within this expanse are 154 national forests, the focal point of the clearcutting controversy; these forests, distributed among forty states and consisting of 187 million acres—about a tenth of the nation's land area—are largely controlled by the Department of Agriculture's Forest Service. Unlike the national parks set aside exclusively for recreation, or wildlife sanctuaries designated for fish and game habitat, the nation's forests from their beginning were intended for "multiple use," a decision that led directly to the bitter argument over clearcutting.

The Private Use of Public Lands. Until 1891, the federal government made little effort to restrict private or commercial access to the nation's public lands beyond creating very minimal and often unenforceable conditions for the purchase and use of the land; indeed, it seemed that Washington was determined to surrender the ownership and resources of the public domain to private interests as rapidly and simply as possible. The Homestead Act of 1862, which offered 84 million acres of the public domain to buyers at $1.25 an acre—a pinchpenny price in its own time—reflected the urge of the federal government to divest itself of land throughout the nineteenth century; such policies were justified as a means of encouraging westward expansion and national economic growth.[1] No part of the public domain suffered greater degradation from this merciless exploitation of resources than the nation's forests. The nation literally cut its way across the continent. The timber industry was commonly the shock front of westward expansion, moving into sprawling stands of virgin timber, setting up mills, then depleting—or cutting bare—the forest to provide wood and fuel for the multitudes to follow. The pioneer was seldom more perceptive; when the Timber Culture Act of 1873 made a faint gesture toward forest preservation by giving 160 acres of public land to any settler who would cultivate trees on forty acres, settlers often bought 160 acres of timbered land, then cut and sold the trees on all but 40 acres. Commercial cut-and-burn timbering, practiced on a gigantic scale across the great American wilderness, made the timber industry one of the nation's most important businesses during the last part of the nineteenth century but inflicted such a toll on the forests that in 1891 President Benjamin Harrison finally obtained authority to set aside public timberlands as "reserves" from commercial exploitation. This was the beginning of the present public domain since expanded to include other types of land reserved for other uses.

The creation of federal forest reserves, soon to be augmented by other land removed from uncontrolled speculation, marked the end of unrestricted commercial exploitation of the nation's timberland, but it did not mean the new reserves were unavailable for commercial purposes. As the size of the federal land reserve expanded by progressive additions after 1891, proponents of the reserves became increasingly sensitive to the charge that they were "locking up" vital national resources; the timber industry, in concert with mining, petroleum, and grazing interests and their Congressional supporters, argued that the nation needed the resources on federal reserves and that such use was to the public benefit. Recognizing that these charges undercut support for federal land reserves and acknowledging the merit in the argument that federal resources were needed for the nation's growth, President Theodore Roosevelt and his conservation leader Gifford Pinchot proclaimed the principle of "multiple use" for much of the federal domain. Essentially, multiple use meant that federal land should be used for commercial and private purposes, as well as for public enjoyment and conservation, provided that these various uses did not permanently damage the land or otherwise harm the "public interest" in land preservation. Pinchot, first head of the Forest Service and its continuing inspiration, enthusiastically embraced the multiple-use principle for the new national forests.

> The main thing is that the land, as well as what grows on it, must be used for the purpose for which it is most valuable. On it may be built stores, hotels, residences, power plants, mills and many other things. All these are advantages to National Forests, because they help to get the fullest use out of land and its resources. Railroads, wagon roads, trails, canals, flumes, reservoirs, and telephone and power lines may be constructed . . . as long as they do not unnecessarily do damage to the forests.[2]

Beginning with the first Roosevelt, multiple use became the dominant administrative philosophy for the public domain; with the exception of the national parks and national wildlife refuges —a small portion of the present public domain—almost all federal land, including the national forests, are open to multiple use. To commercial interests, this means that grazing, timbering, petroleum exploration, and mineral prospecting and extracting are all permitted in return for fees paid to the federal government; the duration and extent of this activity are determined by law and the judgment of the agencies responsible for the land.[3] In principle, commercial use must not be carried to the point where the land is permanently damaged or other uses—such as recreational or environmental—are rendered impossible. More than 100,000 oil and mineral exploration leases and 10,000 grazing permits are currently granted on public land, turning more than 100 million acres of public domain over to some commercial utilization.

When multiple use became the federal policy for most of the public domain, it largely shaped the character of the political struggle over public resources. A great diversity of corporate concerns representing the commercial resource users immediately became interested parties to any public land policy, gradually established their access to the administrative agencies responsible for the public lands, and worked out an accommodation with such agencies that ensured their influence in policy-making and consultation between themselves and federal officials. Conservationists were equally insistent upon sharing a measure of influence in decisions affecting the public domain. The agencies responsible for administering the public lands—the Forest Service, the Bureau of Land Management, the Fish and Wildlife Service, among others—found themselves with clientele groups representing both conservationists and commercial resource users and with a responsibility to adjudicate among their often conflicting claims in a manner assuring no interest would prevail to the exclusion of others. In effect, multiple use represented a political compact, a settlement among competing claims upon public land, that did not preclude disagreement but did establish policy guidelines that were reasonably satisfactory, in principle, to the various participants in the policy struggle. However, within this compromise were the seeds of conflict, for the principle of multiple use did not settle, in practical and operational terms, which use would prevail when several inconsistent ones were advanced. Until the late 1960's, this ambiguity presented few serious problems in administering the national forests, but, with growing commercial pressure on the forests, the multiple-use formula proved too brittle to protect the Forest Service from a controversy between commercial and environmental interests over the timber reserves.

Commercial Timber on the National Forests. The volume of timber cut from the nation's forests by commercial lumber companies has grown steadily since the multiple-use doctrine was first established, but it is not the industry's major source of supply. Only a quarter of all commercial timber has come from federal lands, another quarter from forests owned by the companies themselves, and half from "timber farms" consisting of privately owned woodlands dedicated to commercial use. However, if one turns to the nation's "timber inventory"—the total woodlands available for cutting—the importance of the public domain is obvious: More than two-thirds of the nation's standing softwood (the major commercial timber source) grows on federal lands but only one-third on commercial forestland or timber farms; perhaps 80 per cent of all the virgin timber left in the nation is also on the federal reserves. With so much available timber on federal property, commercial lumber companies have regarded these reserves as the logical and most accessible place to secure most of the additional board feet they have needed in recent years. Consequently, their demand for increased cutting in federal forests has been insistent over the last two decades.

By 1960, a combination of growing commercial pressure to increase timber cuts on the federal domain and a parallel rise in conservationist apprehension over wilderness destruction led Congress to enact the Multiple Use–Sustained Yield Act, which was to guide the Forest Service in deciding how much commercial timbering to permit. According to the law, multiple forest use meant that the forests "are utilized in the combinations that will best meet the needs of the American people . . . and not necessarily the combination of uses that will give the greatest dollar return or the greatest unit output." Congress ordained that the national forests should henceforth provide the multiple benefits of watershed maintenance, recreation, wildlife preservation, timber production, grazing, and mining. In dealing with commercial timbering, the legislation instructed the Forest Service to assure that "sustained yield"—a cutting policy that guaranteed in perpetuity a high level of regular timber output—did not impair the productivity of the land, while still assuring that all basic forest uses would receive equal consideration.

The 1960 legislation was Congress's effort to dampen the growing controversy between conservationists and timbermen by designing a more formal, explicit rule to guide the Forest Service as it exercised its traditional discretion to decide how much timber was to leave the forests and in what areas. Unless given specific directives through legislation or Presidential order, the Forest Service's top echelon, in close consultation with local foresters, would still make the ultimate decisions. Such decisions, in any case, divided the forests into "commercial" timber stands available for sale to the lumber industry and residual areas, predominantly forested wilderness into which neither roads nor other artifacts of civilization intruded. By the end of the 1960's, the Forest Service had attempted to follow the Congressional guidelines by classifying almost half the land in its jurisdiction, roughly 97 million acres, as commercial woodland that could be exploited in accordance with the precepts of "multiple use" and "sustained yield." From the viewpoint of the Forest Service, Congress, and the President, one attractive aspect of this large commercial domain was that it yielded more than $300 million in annual revenue by 1970—a rare governmental profit-maker. But the uneasy accommodation between lumbermen and conservationists over timber use in the years before 1970 was collapsing. The timber industry was pressing for generous increases in the allowable "cut" and was practicing clearcutting in mounting volume; conservationists, disconcerted when any wilderness is surrendered to commercial timbering, were outraged by clearcutting and the industry's growing timber hunger. In the middle was caught the Forest Service.

The Forest Service. By any reasonable standard, the Forest Service's record is exemplary. Founded in 1905 and decisively shaped by Gifford Pinchot, one of the nation's great conservationists, the Forest Service until quite recently has enjoyed a reputation for professionalism, integrity, and dedication to conservation. The service grew out of protest against corporate abuse of the nation's resources. Pinchot intended his men not merely to preserve and protect the national forests in a highly professional manner, but to redress a century's depletion of the forests at corporate hands; henceforth, he declared, "the national resources must be developed and preserved for the benefit of the many and not merely for the few." Thus committed to forest administration in the public interest, the Forest Service with its familiar Smokey the Bear emblem has come to epitomize conservation to millions of Americans; its strong sense of mission and capable personnel have, in the past, imparted an *esprit* to the service that serves it well in dealing with Congress and the public. Despite its distinguished history, the service is now enveloped in growing controversy because it confronts the dilemmas common to governmental agencies administering public resources in the public interest; the surprise is that the controversy has taken so long to surface. Indeed, the factors leading to the Forest Service's present predicament are almost a model of the political problems confronting any agency charged with protecting the public interest.

To begin, the Forest Service was given at its inception a very nebulous mandate that subsequent legislation has done little to clarify. The concept of multiple use was itself cloudy because, while it ordained that no single use should predominate, it did not suggest how priorities among competing uses were to be determined or by whom. Pinchot's effort to provide his foresters with guidelines produced, as the following directive suggests, instructions that were often a web of vagaries.

> In the administration of the forest reserves, it must be clearly borne in mind that all land is to be devoted to its most productive use for the permanent good of the whole people, and not for the temporary benefit of individuals or companies. All the resources of the reserves are for *use* . . . the dominant industry will be considered first, but with as little restrictions to minor industries as may be possible . . . and where conflicting interests must be reconciled the question will always be decided from the standpoint of the greatest good of the greatest number in the long run.[4]

What did "the greatest good to the greatest number in the long run" mean when applied to a specific interest conflict? And how was the Forest Service to determine, as Pinchot has elsewhere urged, that the "highest good" predominate in such decisions? The Multiple Use–Sustained Yield Act of 1960 was afflicted with similar obscurities. What combination of uses would "best meet the needs of the American people" or which cutting policy would guarantee in perpetuity a high level of regular output of timber which did not impair the productivity of the land while at the same time assuring that all basic forest uses would receive equal consideration?

These uncertainties reflect, on one level, the difficulty of defining the public's interest in a particular resource use when concrete decisions must be made—the difficulty of operationalizing the "public interest" that confounds so many agencies with responsibility to defend such an interest. The ambiguity also indicates that the Forest Service was left the task of negotiating a settlement among the competing demands upon the forests; the real battle would be fought within the administrative arena. Whether by accident or design, this was certainly the result of the 1960 Multiple Use–Sustained Yield Act by which Congress displaced the battle between contending forces from itself to the Forest Service—again, a situation not uncommon in other resource areas involving other agencies.

The service also worked in a situation where the corporate groups with a stake in its work were generally more politically potent, better organized, and more persistent in advancing their claims upon the forests than were conservationists and others representing the public. Agencies charged with resource responsibilities in the name of the public must normally arrive at some accommodation with corporate interests as a matter of political survival; this accommodation almost always assures that commercial users will receive at least as much concern as any other interest in resource use. In the case of the forests, the Forest Service's receptivity to the lumber industry's demands upon forest use was greatly increased because commercial timber sales turned a profit for the service and the government, thereby investing the accommodation of the service to the industry with an aura of public benefit strongly esteemed in Congress. The result was that, over the years since the Forest Service's beginning, it had had a strong bureaucratic incentive to share the timber industry's concern for maximizing forest cutting. Given the political advantage enjoyed in resource struggles by economic interests compared to those representing the public, as well as the profitability of timber sales to both the Forest Service and the timber industry, it is not surprising that the service should be vulnerable to "capture" by the timber industry, for whose regulation it is partly responsible.

Despite these formidable problems, the Forest Service managed to administer the forests for almost a half century without facing a major political battle, largely because the industry's cutting demands had been relatively modest and conservationists did not feel the principle of multiple use gravely endangered. The clearcutting issue marks the end of this era.

Conservation and Clearcutting

The clearcutting issue has been a catalyst drawing together the major problems building for decades over multiple use of the forests and forcing them into public debate. From one perspective, clearcutting is an environmental issue because questions of forest damage are involved. Economics is also involved because the validity of the timber industry's demand for more timber is questioned. In addition, the issue raises questions of accountability and responsibility in the Forest Service's discharge of its public trust.

Clearcutting. The practice of clearcutting or even-age management, involves stripping large forest tracts, perhaps several thousand acres at once, of all trees down to the short stumps. Clearcuts have been as wide as a mile and as long as three miles, the size depending upon commercial demands and the judgment of the Forest Service. Clearcut areas resemble huge timber tracts mowed with a giant scythe. They are seldom visible to the public because clearcutting is avoided near highways or other public thoroughfares where the disfigurement would be obtrusive and objectionable. Until the mid-1960's, timber was most often harvested through an alternate method called selective cutting in which portions of timber were cut while the rest of a tract was permitted to grow until it reached marketable size; this practice meant that trees in a commercial forest area were "rotated" so that old trees were cut only in proportion to the new ones that had grown to replace them. In 1964, clearcutting became the primary harvesting procedure in the national forests. Sixty per cent of all commercial timber removed from the public domain is obtained in this manner, twice the amount taken from private reserves by the same procedure.

The timber industry and many foresters argue that clearcutting is the most scientifically sound procedure to keep the forests producing trees indefinitely. They point out that more timber per acre is produced by clearcutting than by the rotation method (an important item to the industry because it depends upon second growth and more for most of its market timber) and that many trees, such as Douglas fir, pines, and some hardwoods, regenerate best under clearcut cultivation. Company spokesmen also maintain that most wildlife prospers under clearcutting; forest animals, they assert, actually prefer the greater sunlight and broader expanse under clearcut forests than the darker, denser woodlands below virgin timber. Clearcut areas are sometimes unattractive immediately after the cutting, but the industry suggests that the regenerating forest gradually assumes an economic and environmental value equal, if not superior, to its original one.[5]

An Ecological Indictment. Conservationists generally assert that clearcutting is an environmental menace created by unjustifiable commercial timber demands and irresponsible Forest Service collaboration. The national forests, they argue, have been reduced to little more than tree farms for the timber industry.

The gravest environmental damage, say conservationists, is to the soil. Clearcutting is customarily practiced today on virgin timber, and, consequently, age-old soil conditions are radically transformed as the cover is removed and soil is exposed to the full force of rain, erosion, and weathering; the land will be gradually depleted of its essential nutrients until, within a century, its productivity is seriously impaired. Moreover, conservationists charge that the Forest Service, in its eagerness to increase timber production, has permitted commercial cutting along heavy slopes with unstable soil conditions, thereby causing heavy stream sedimentation, considerable soil erosion, and sometimes drastic alterations in the forest ecology. Logging roads are another provocation to environmentalists. They are ugly, damaging affairs that cross stream beds, follow stream paths, and meander through forests in a total disregard for aesthetics or soil damage. Not least in the environmental toll, note ecologists, is the loss of millions of acres of virgin forest whose rich ecological and aesthetic diversity can never be duplicated by second-growth timber under the best management.

A number of studies stimulated by this controversy lend weight to many of the accusations. The most widely cited by environmentalists is a 1970 report, written by a special committee of experts from the University of Montana, concerning clearcutting in Montana's Bitterroot National Forest. In a strong indictment of the Forest Service's stewardship, the report noted that "multiple use management, in fact, does not exist as a governing principle," that quality timber management and harvest practices were missing to such a degree that considerations of recreation, watershed, or wildlife appeared "as afterthoughts," and that continuing timber production was unlikely unless clearcutting was reduced.[6] The Bitterroot National Forest has become virtually a showplace for the worst ravages of clearcutting. Noted a visiting reporter, "Whole mountainsides are so skinned of centuries' growth of ponderosa pine and Douglas fir that they look more like man-made pyramids for a weird science-fiction film."[7] Evidence of substantial damage from clearcutting has also been gathered at West Virginia's Monongahela National Forest and Wyoming's Bridger National Forest, among others.

Many observers, including some officials within the Forest Service itself, have joined conservationists in tracing rampant clearcutting to the service's preoccupation with commercial timbering. The service has clearly concentrated in recent decades on increasing timber output to the point where, as the service's present chief described it, "our programs are seriously out of balance."[8] Part of the responsibility must actually be shared by Congress, which ties the level of Forest Service appropriations to the income from commercial timbering and thus goads the service to maximize timber production to keep appropriations high. Legislators have shown scant interest in encouraging the service to give greater attention to other forest uses. In fiscal 1971–72, for instance, Congress appropriated more than $500 million for timber management—commercial timber production, essentially—but only $40 million for recreation and service activity and a meager $6 million for wildlife management; generally, legislators grant better than 90 per cent of the Forest Service's request for timber management but little more than half the request for wildlife, recreation, and soil management programs. The service, however, has been an active collaborator in this enterprise. It has pushed tree cutting to the point where it appears to be chopping more timber than it is replacing, in violation of the sustained-yield concept. Edward C. Drafts, formerly second in command of the Forest Service, believes it is now "close to the brink in respect to timber management. . . . Right now it is cutting about twice as much softwood sawtimber as it is growing," he asserts.[9] Critics argue that the service chronically underbudgets its requests for reforestation funds, preferring to designate uncut wilderness for commercial logging rather than promote a sounder, but much slower, regrowth on cut lands. To prove their assertion that the Forest Service has gradually abandoned wilderness protection in favor of commercial timbering, ecologists cite the service's delay in designating areas of the national forest as "wilderness" to be protected inviolate by the Wilderness Act of 1964—a hesitation, they suggest, prompted by the service's desire to use these wild areas for commercial logging that would be forbidden once they were officially designated wilderness. Indeed, conservationists fear that much of the 97 million acres of national forest still untouched by loggers will soon fall to the timber industry unless the Forest Service is restrained from permitting it.

Finally, critics argue that the rising lumber demand cited by timbermen to justify their increased cutting is part illusion, part exaggeration. Ecologists charge that the timber industry could meet much of the rise in timber demand from its own resources but prefers to use public timber because it is more profitable. A company pays nothing for the logging roads (which may cost as much as $150,000 per mile), bears no expense for reforestation, and may purchase timber stands for future use when market prices rise. Much of the present timber "scarcity," note the critics, could easily be relieved if the industry were not allowed to ship about 7 per cent of its domestic production overseas and if it practiced better production techniques to reduce waste. In fact, the argument concludes, the economy is not as heavily dependent on timber as the industry alleges, for many other materials—steel, glass, and concrete—are available for private and commercial building needs. From this perspective, clearcutting turns out to be largely a means to assure rising industry profits rather than a necessity for the nation's economic growth.

An Industry Defense. The timber industry accepts none of these arguments. It asserts that clearcutting produces "managed forests" superior economically and ecologically to virgin ones and equally available for multiple use. According to a recent president of the National Forest Products Association, the industry's trade group, "Dynamic forests where men and nature unite their efforts to intensify growth afford multiple benefits of wood products, pure air, clear water, fish and wildlife, recreation and forage in abundance," but "forests consigned to the whimsical attentions of nature alone fall into neglect."[10] The industry argues that the motivation behind much criticism of clearcutting is a selfish desire by "preservationists" to "lock up" vital resources for the private pleasure of an elite. Taking aim at the Sierra Club, a major industry official bitterly denounced the opponents of clearcutting in terms that would excite considerable support among commercial loggers: The opposition "comes from people like the Sierra Club who pose as conservationists but really are damned, hard-core preservationists, who always want to tie up commercial timber land in wilderness, and take it out of the economy. We can't waste all these resources. Just for housing alone, we're far behind now in timber production."[11] More temperate is an industry labor leader, who voices the familiar argument among timbermen that clearcutting and other forest "management" actually open the largely inaccessible forest to most Americans:

> The inaccessible wilderness and primitive areas are off-limits to most laboring people. We must have access and campsite facilities. Otherwise, it's just a paradise for a few of the very rich. In this, it seems to me, the preservationists have cleverly misled the mass of American recreationists. They have called for a lockup which actually denies access and use to most of us.[12]

Turning to economics, timbermen assert that the public forests should be used to promote national prosperity—a legitimate use for public benefit—and that they cannot be used if they are locked up. In recent years, the industry has justified its rising demands for timber on the basis of the Housing Act of 1968 in which Congress declared its desire to create 26 million new housing units in a decade, a decision that the industry says makes rising timber supplies a national goal and removes any doubt about the reality of future timber demand. Industry spokesmen maintain that timber farms and private forest reserves are now close to the maximum output compatible with prudent forest management and that, in consequence, there is no place else except the national forests to look for increased "timber harvesting."

Ironically, while conservationists accuse the Forest Service of yielding too much land to commercial timbering, the industry criticizes the service for its reluctance to make more land available—a result of too much deference to "preservationists," in the industry's opinion. Many industry lobbyists have concluded that the best tactic for producing increased timber is to obtain legislation from Congress or a Presidential order expanding the allowable cut, thus bypassing the Forest Service's judgment entirely.

Unremitting Pressure. Even as the clearcutting controversy boiled, new pressure to expand cutting in the federal domain arose from two documents that conservationists view with extreme apprehension because, alone or in combination, they would create a new timber policy for several decades at least.

The first is the Report of the Public Land Law Review Commission, a nineteen-member panel of federal legislators appointed by the President in 1969 to study existing federal land policy and recommend revisions. Issued in 1971 at a cost of $7 million, the five-thousand-page report represented a searching review of several thousand public land laws, as well as testimony taken from nine hundred witnesses—the most comprehensive, ambitious federal study of land policy ever attempted. Conservationists suspect that many of its 137 major recommendations amount to a new raid on resources rationalized as an effort to modernize antiquated land practices. The recommendation arousing the greatest concern is the commission's proposal that federal lands be managed to favor their "dominant use" or "maximum benefit." Conservationists maintain that such a philosophy is tantamount to scrapping the multiple-use formula, for it would be possible to justify converting most federal timberlands almost exclusively to tree farming on the ground that this would be their "maximum benefit" or "dominant use"; wilderness preservation, soil conservation, recreation, and wildlife protection would be tossed out for practical purposes. The opposition includes not only such predictable hard-line preservationists as the Sierra Club but also the Audubon Society, the National Wildlife Federation, and the National Resources Council of America—a cosmopolitan sampling of the environmental movement. Like most other commercial resource users, the timber industry has generally approved the report, a sure signal, according to environmentalists, that most of the commission's blessings will flow toward private interests.

The second cause for alarm is the National Forest Timber Conservation and Management Act, a proposal introduced in Congress in 1971 by several western legislators that most conservationists regard as another onslaught upon the nation's forests. Although it failed to pass either house in 1972, some version of the legislation is expected to reappear when Congress reconvenes in 1973. Essentially, the Act asserted that the nation has a chronic housing shortage (the goal of 26 million new housing units declared in the 1968 Housing Act was used as evidence) requiring a greater timber supply that should be provided, in good measure, through more intensive timber production on federal land. Specifically, the proposed legislation would require the Forest Service to increase immediately the cut on national forests and to practice more intense forestation on all federal land capable of producing marketable timber; it also would establish a high-yield timberfund—to be financed largely from the sale of commercial timber from national forests—to hasten the reforestation of cut federal land. Conservationists argued that this was an obvious attempt to surrender the national forests to the timber industry's needs and to deprive the Forest Service of most of its authority to prevent reckless cutting.

The appearance of these two documents, regardless of their ultimate fate, is further evidence of a rapidly building pressure on the national forests that is very unlikely to lessen soon. The clearcutting controversy, in brief, marks the onset of a power struggle over federal timber that has not reached such proportions, or involved such critical decisions, since the establishment of the multiple-use formula more than a half century ago.

NOTES

1. This land policy is summarized in Grant McConnell, *Private Power and American Democracy* (New York: Vintage Books, 1970), chapter 7; and in Nancy Wood, *Clearcut* (San Francisco: The Sierra Club, 1971), chapter 2.
2. Grant McConnell, *op. cit.,* p. 35.
3. Mineral Leasing Act of February 25, 1920 (30 U.S.C., 181-263, 281-287).
4. Grant McConnell, *op. cit.,* p. 45.
5. These arguments are summarized in Nancy Wood, *op. cit.,* pp. 18 ff.
6. Nancy Wood, *op. cit.,* pp. 103 ff.
7. Gladwin Hill, "National Forests: Physical Abuse and Policy Conflicts," *New York Times,* November 14, 1971.
8. Gladwin Hill, "National Forests: Timbermen vs. Conservationists," *New York Times,* November 15, 1971.
9. Gladwin Hill, "National Forests: Physical Abuse and Policy Conflicts," *op. cit.*
10. *New York Times,* November 15, 1971.
11. Edward L. Schults, vice-president of Tree Farmers, Inc. Quoted in Nancy Wood, *op. cit.,* p. 107.
12. *Ibid.,* p. 29.

8 *Paradox One: Surface Mining*

The political status of solid waste and surface mining is paradoxical. Most Americans, ignorant of surface mining's environmental ravage and oblivious to its rapid national growth, hardly know that it is a national problem, yet it is the focus of an intensifying, bitter confrontation between conservationists and corporate power reaching from Washington to most state houses. In contrast, Americans have been avalanched with material on solid waste until the topic is a commonplace in discussions of environmental ills—this despite government's almost total inaction in dealing with the matter. The contrast between public awareness and political conflict over the two issues bears little relationship to their environmental importance, for solid waste and surface mining are both serious environmental ills likely to reach critical proportions in the 1970's.

Surface mining commanded little serious governmental concern until recently. In Appalachia, where surface mining in the guise of "stripping" became a major industry, state governments embraced strip mining fully and looked the other way when the environmental toll rose; in other states, surface mines were too economically inconsequential or too well fortified politically to occasion serious environmental regulation. Washington also seemed all but indifferent to surface mining's environmental consequences. Now, as surface mining spreads, it is apparent that the Appalachian states paternalistically promoting strip mines have paid a frightful environmental cost, as have other states where surface mines flourish. Moreover, the numerous state officials and millions of Americans now oblivous to surface mining are demonstrating an unwarranted, possibly perilous indifference. Surface mining will shortly spread across the nation in almost epidemic proportions; many states once viewing the issue as another state's problem now face prospects of a burgeoning surface-mine industry within their own borders.

The Surface-Mine Industry

No issue stirs greater passion among environmentalists than surface mining, possibly because surface-mined land is so often utterly devastated when the miners abandon it. To understand the fury in the ecologists' indictment and the political complexities in resolving the tangled problems of regulation, it is essential to understand the technological and environmental impact of surface mining.

What Surface Mining Means. Several methods of mineral extraction are known collectively as surface mining.[1] Open pits, varying from a few hundred feet to more than a mile in depth and diameter, recover minerals from earth through a series of descending terraces. Minerals are often claimed in and near water bodies by dredging moist bottomlands; huge hoses are sometimes used to wash soil from hills and mountains, which is then sifted for minerals. The most important form of surface mining economically and environmentally, however, is "strip mining" and the closely related "auger mining." On largely level ground, stripping is done by making a rectangular "box cut" that exposes mineral seams below the surface; minerals are then extracted from the exposed seams along the walls and the "spoil" (discarded earth) is thrown into the open cut as mining proceeds through the seams. In this manner, mining may proceed for a mile, leaving in the wake a deep, wide trough filled with a series of spoil deposits resembling, from the air, "the ridges of a giant washboard." On hills and mountains, "contour stripping" is used. A bench is blasted into the hillside after all topsoil and vegetation is scraped clear by bulldozers. This bench creates a "highwall," exposing mineral seams to extracting equipment, which removes the ore and commonly piles the spoil below the cut on the hillside. A bench may extend along a mountain's contour for many miles, others may be cut above and below, and mining continues until all extractable coal has been captured. Augering, the common companion to stripping, is "a method of producing coal by boring horizontally into a seam, much like a carpenter bores a hole in wood"; augers may be seven feet in diameter and drill holes two hundred feet deep and, in all cases, produce coal that is collected like shavings from a carpenter's bit.

Stripping was a negligible industry until the early 1950's because most of the nation's coal—the principal mineral recovered by stripping—was taken from deep mines. Then seams that could be mined profitably from deep shafts began to diminish at the same time the coal demand rose, sending mine operators in search of new recovery techniques that eventually led to the stripping boom. One incentive to stripping's growth was the appearance of new machines that greatly increased productivity and lowered costs. Bulldozers, leaders, scrapers, graders, and trucks of up to 100-ton capacity became available for strip mining, together with shovels of gargantuan proportions. Shovels capable of lifting 115 cubic yards of earth in one "bite" are not rare; at least one 185-cubic-yard bucket exists and a 200-yard bucket is on the drawing boards. This technology reaches its zenith in a mechanical behemoth, the Central Ohio Coal Company's "Big Muskie," operating near Cumberland, Ohio: Thirty-two stories tall, its base larger than a football field, its bucket lifting 325 tons of soil in one bite, it weighs 27 million pounds; placed in the middle of Ohio State's 81,000-seat football stadium, it would rise above the topmost seats and stretch beyond the bowl's edge.[2] With increased coal demand and this new technology, coal stripping produced far greater ore recovery than underground mining, was safer and generally cheaper on a per unit basis. The rising stripped coal output was further elevated in the late 1960's by the growing demand for electric power, the prospect of a process called "gassification" that converts coal to natural gas, and demands for low sulfur fuels to reduce air contamination.

The nation is becoming progressively more dependent upon stripping for coal and other minerals; more than 80 per cent of all ores and solid fuels used by American industry are currently produced by stripping, which also accounts for more than half the nation's coal supply. Stripped coal output has increased in great surges; between 1969 and 1970, the national output increased by almost 25 per cent, most of this originating in Appalachia, where stripped coal volume doubled between 1970 and 1971 in eastern Kentucky. By 1970, almost six thousand square miles of American earth were affected by surface mining, almost all this land the property of mining companies. Several states now depend heavily on strip mining, particularly the economically depressed states of West Virginia and Kentucky, where mining is practically the only important industry. Estimates suggest that the loss of strip mining to West Virginia would cost the state as much as $200 million yearly and idle 8,000 workers. Even now no state is unaffected by surface mining in some form. As Table 5 indicates, at least ten states have more than 100,000 acres disturbed by surface mining; since this last careful estimate of surface-mined land is now almost a decade old, newer studies will surely reveal startling increases in the extent of surface mining nationally.

This vast, growing industry is dominated by a handful of large mining companies, most of which are subsidiaries of petroleum industries or parts of vast corporate conglomerates. The corporate interlock between strip mining and the nation's great industrial enterprises is further extended by frequent "mine mouth" arrangements whereby large electric utilities generate much of their power directly from the coal-mining sites and by long-term leases upon unstripped coal reserves owned by major utilities throughout the nation.

The Vulnerable West. The American land now surrendered to surface mining will pale to insignificance beside the projected future toll, for the United States is expected to witness an explosive growth of surface mining—stripping especially—west of the Mississippi River. According to a government geologist, "We are on the brink of, not years, but generations of strip mining for coal that will make the evacuation of the Panama Canal look like a furrow in my backyard vegetable garden."[3] Stimulated by the constant escalation in coal demand, the mining industry is now turning west, where more than 70 per cent of the nation's strippable coal reserves lie, capable of profitable, intensive mining for the first time.

TABLE 5
Land Disturbed by Strip and Surface Mining in the United States as of January 1, 1965, by Commodity and State
(Acres)

State	Clay	Coal (bituminous, lignite and anthracite)	Stone	Sand and Gravel	Gold	Phosphate Rock	Iron Ore	All Other	Total
Alabama [1]	4,000	50,600	3,900	21,200	100	—	52,600	1,500	133,900
Alaska [2]	—	500	—	2,000	8,600	—	—	—	11,100
Arizona [1]	2,700	—	1,000	7,200	1,200	—	—	20,300	32,400
Arkansas [2]	600	10,100	900	2,600	—	—	100	8,100	22,400
California [2]	2,700	20	8,000	19,900	134,000	—	900	8,500	174,020
Colorado [1]	2,000	2,800	6,200	15,500	17,100	—	25	11,400	55,025
Connecticut [1]	—	—	100	16,100	—	—	—	100	16,300
Delaware [2]	200	—	200	5,200	—	—	100	10	5,710
Florida [1]	13,200	—	25,300	3,900	—	143,600	—	2,800	188,800
Georgia	[3] 1,300	[3] 300	[3] 6,800	[3] 1,200	—	—	[3] 100	[3] 12,000	[1] 21,700
Hawaii [2]	—	—	—	—	—	—	—	10	10
Idaho [3]	500	—	700	11,200	21,200	3,100	35	4,200	40,935
Illinois [2]	1,400	127,000	5,700	9,000	—	—	—	—	143,100
Indiana [2]	1,500	95,200	10,200	18,000	—	—	—	400	125,300
Iowa [1]	1,300	11,000	12,200	17,600	—	—	6	2,300	44,406
Kansas	[1] 1,100	[2] 45,600	[1] 7,500	[1] 5,100	—	—	—	[1] 200	59,500
Kentucky	[1,2] 2,400	[1,2] 119,200	[1] 3,900	[1] 1,700	—	—	—	[1] 500	127,700
Louisiana [1]	900	—	100	29,700	—	—	50	—	30,750
Maine [1]	400	—	4,400	28,200	12	—	100	1,700	34,812
Maryland	[1,2] 1,200	[2] 2,200	[1] 2,200	[1] 18,800	—	—	[2] 20	[1] 800	25,220
Massachusetts [1]	700	—	1,200	36,400	—	—	1,100	900	40,300
Michigan [2]	600	—	7,700	25,200	—	—	2,200	1,200	36,900
Minnesota [1]	600	—	3,900	41,600	3	—	67,700	1,600	115,403
Mississippi [2]	2,700	—	400	26,500	—	—	30	—	29,630
Missouri [2]	6,600	31,800	8,400	3,800	—	—	200	8,300	59,100

Montana [2]	—	1,500	10	[3] 13,500	5,600	100	10	6,200	26,920
Nebraska [2]	900	—	4,300	23,700	—	—	—	—	28,900
Nevada [1]	100	—	1,600	5,500	5,600	—	600	19,500	32,900
New Hampshire [2]	—	—	100	8,000	—	—	—	200	8,300
New Jersey [2]	1,400	—	2,000	27,600	—	—	1,000	1,800	33,800
New Mexico [2]	13	1,200	100	400	40	—	100	4,600	6,453
New York [1]	1,700	—	12,500	42,200	5	—	700	600	57,705
North Carolina [1]	5,800	10	6,000	18,400	2,200	300	100	4,000	36,810
North Dakota	[1] 800	[2] 7,700	[2] 300	[1] 26,100	—	—	—	[1] 2,000	36,900
Ohio	[1] 10,200	[2] 212,800	[1] 21,000	[1] 28,100	—	—	[1] 4,000	[1] 600	276,700
Oklahoma [2]	—	23,500	—	[3] 2,500	—	—	—	1,400	27,400
Oregon [2]	100	—	300	1,300	6,300	—	10	1,400	9,410
Pennsylvania	[1] 10,400	[2] 302,400	[1] 24,400	[1] 23,800	[1] 2	—	[1] 8,800	[1] 400	370,202
Rhode Island [1]	—	—	20	3,600	—	—	—	—	3,620
South Carolina [1]	10,900	—	1,400	10,400	200	8,100	100	1,600	32,700
South Dakota	[2] 2,000	[2] 900	—	[3] 28,000	—	—	—	[3] 3,300	34,200
Tennessee [2]	2,700	29,300	4,400	18,400	—	27,000	5,300	13,800	100,900
Texas [1]	6,800	2,900	21,900	122,300	—	—	9,600	2,800	166,300
Utah [2]	600	—	200	2,200	—	10	500	2,000	5,510
Vermont	—	—	[2] 2,300	[1] 4,000	—	—	—	[2] 400	6,700
Virginia	[1,2] 1,100	[2] 29,800	[1] 4,300	[1] 13,100	[1] 600	[1] 100	[1,2] 7,700	[1,2] 4,100	60,800
Washington [2]	500	100	1,300	5,700	400	—	20	800	8,820
West Virginia [2]	300	192,000	2,800	300	—	—	100	—	195,500
Wisconsin [2]	100	—	9,000	26,400	5	—	49	—	35,554
Wyoming	[1,2] 3,500	[2] 1,000	[1,2] 300	[1,2] 200	—	[2] 800	[1,2] 300	[2] 4,300	10,400
Total	108,513	1,301,430	241,430	823,300	203,167	183,110	164,255	162,620	3,187,825

[1] Data obtained from Soil Conservation Service, U.S. Department of Agriculture.

[2] Data compiled from reports submitted by the States on U.S. Department of the Interior form 6-1385X.

[3] Estimate.

SOURCE: U.S. Department of the Interior, *Surface Mining and Our Environment: A Special Report to the Nation.*

The Department of the Interior has already issued permits for private interests to explore more than 2,390 square miles of federal land in search of coal—a small area, nonetheless, alongside the private lands scheduled for mining. The Washington Waterpower Company expects to strip mine 5,000 acres containing 135 million tons of coal near Centralia, Washington. Pacific Power and Light owns mineral rights to 1.6 billion tons of strip-mine reserves in Wyoming. Three Texas utilities will soon begin stripping 17,500 acres of coal seams near Waco, a job expected to take thirty-five years. Expanded surface mining is already under way. In Belmont County, near the eastern Ohio border, Consolidated Coal's Hanna Division, which currently owns almost a third of all the county's land, is already stripping part of the 95,000 acres it plans to mine there; using its huge earth-moving machine night and day, Hanna Coal will soon add another behemoth for the task. In Missouri, the mammoth Peabody Coal Company, having consumed 200 square miles of the state in surface mines, expects to increase land consumption shortly. All this seems modest, however, next to the surface mining rapidly expanding to feed the generators of the Central Arizona Project. When all six power-generating plants in the project are complete, they will consume 2,000 railroad cars of stripped coal daily; the single generating plant now in existence—the Four Corners installation in Farmington, New Mexico—alone consumes so much coal that the sacred Hopi Indian lands now being worked will soon be exhausted.[4]

It is difficult to anticipate the final extent of this stripping, but early estimates by environmentalists indicate it will massively transform the land in many western states. According to one study, if the mining industry were permitted to reclaim all the coal reserves now available for stripping, it would affect an area more than twice the size of Connecticut. Stripped land would increase three-fold in Iowa, four-fold in Oklahoma, fifty-two times in Wyoming, 125 times in Montana, and 136 times its present area in New Mexico.[5] Even when practiced under strict supervision by public agencies requiring land restoration and other environmental safeguards, stripping of this magnitude will affect state ecologies profoundly; unregulated, it can fashion an environmental devastation that will take generations to heal. Yet few western states or their eastern counterparts have any explicit surface-mine regulations designed to prevent gross environmental degradation. The nation's public officials have barely awakened to the consequences.

"An Imminent and Inordinate Peril." Surface mining produces an immediate, violent, pervasive metamorphosis in the land it affects. "Surface mining frequently shocks the sensibilities," declares the Department of the Interior. "Some of the surface evacuations are so vast as to resemble craters of the moon. . . . Square miles of land may be turned over to a depth of 100 feet or more and valleys rimmed by mile after mile of contour benches."[6] It is a minor irony of environmentalism that the Kentucky legislature, so often the indulgent and protective guardian of mining, should have written one of the most brutally accurate, concise descriptions of stripping's impact in the preamble to a bill requiring the "restoration" of stripped land:

> The General Assembly finds that the unregulated strip mining of coal causes soil erosion, stream pollution, the accumulation of stagnant water and the seepage of contaminated water, increases the likelihood of floods, destroys the value of land for agricultural purposes, counteracts efforts for conservation of soil, water and other natural resources, destroys or impairs the property rights of citizens, creates fire hazards dangerous to life and property, so as to constitute an imminent and inordinate peril to the welfare of the Commonwealth.[7]

Much of this ruination is common to most surface mines, but stripping's environmental viciousness arises quite often from the distinctive "spoil" banks along the side of steep hills; the spoil quickly becomes a danger to wildlife and man alike. More than 3.5 million acres of land have been affected by all surface mining, and half of this is stripped on hilly surfaces. Only a third of this surface-mined land has been "reclaimed" in any manner, leaving the greater portion a ravaged waste.

Appalachia is the national showcase for strip mining's environmental impact, particularly West Virginia and Kentucky, where stripping is most intensive. Across the Appalachian region spread 18,000 miles of spoil, 20,000 miles of highwalls that isolate mountaintops from their lower levels, and 4,000 miles of streams polluted by mine drainage. Throughout the area are more than 20,000 surface acres of impoundments and reservoirs affected by mine drainage and siltation. Impoundments laid across the region's numerous hollows to control spoil erosion and mine drainage are a menacing presence to people in the valleys. Impoundments sometimes collapse, breached by heavy rains or the pressure of accumulated wastes, sending a cascade of destruction through the hollows. Such a catastrophe occurred on February 26, 1972, when a waste impoundment broke at Buffalo Creek, West Virginia, unleashing 5 million cubic feet of water that killed 117 persons and erased several small hamlets in its path. At least 70 per cent of all the land stripped in Kentucky and West Virginia has received little, if any, reclamation work; all the nation's surface-mined land needing reclamation would now reach across the United States in a swatch more than a mile wide, extending from New York well beyond San Francisco.

Against this backdrop of devastation, conservationists have mounted a campaign for governmental regulation of surface mines that mounts in scope and intensity as surface mining ceases to be a unique Appalachian agony and becomes a national issue.

The Politics of Regulation

The nation has almost no public policy to control the ecological damage of surface mining, despite the industry's growing size and geographic reach. Washington is still officially silent. The few states with environmental regulations have, in the past, produced largely a sham. Official silence, however, masks a political battle of mounting severity between ecologists, determined to force government into a tough surface-mine regulatory policy, and the mining industry, which, in consort with its allies in the fuel industry, has been a powerful opponent to most regulatory proposals.

The Environmental Attack. The political opposition to surface mining began first in Appalachia, where stripping's profound ecological damage was most fully and massively revealed. It started shortly after stripping began its expansion in the mid-

1950's. In the beginning there were only isolated, futile protests, such as those of widow Ollie Combs, a stoic little woman who, by lying down in front of bulldozers about to strip her land in 1954, caused practically the first stir of national attention to stripping. Isolated opposition throughout Kentucky and West Virginia coalesced to form "Save Our Kentucky" in the early 1960's, the first alliance of citizens, conservationists, and public officials dedicated to controlling strip mines. As stripping's ruin marched across the Appalachian hills, the protest was swelled by the Sierra Club, Wilderness Society, Audubon Society, Izaak Walton League, and other groups with a national constituency. In the late 1960's, the legal talents of the Environmental Defense Fund and the Natural Resources Defense Council were added to this alliance in an effort to sharpen the legal attack upon surface mines. As environmentalists publicized their indictments, an effort was made to create a national environmental coalition capable of pushing regulatory legislation through Congress. This resulted in the Coalition Against Strip Mining, formed in 1971 with Washington headquarters, which drew together a multitude of regional and national conservation groups in the legislative struggle. At the same time, the number of national organizations and meetings to protest unregulated surface mining is growing; in 1972, for instance, the National Conference on Strip Mining—held, appropriately, in Kentucky—brought together citizens, public officials, and scientists to study and publicize the ecological consequences of surface mines.

There is little disagreement among environmentalists about what regulation is necessary. Many, distrusting state government and weary of all governmental compromise with the mining industry, want the federal government to ban stripping immediately and totally. One of these is West Virginia's Congressman Kenneth Hechler, who has repeatedly introduced federal legislation to eliminate strip mines. No national political figure is identified more closely with the battle against stripping than is Hechler, whose rage against the mine operators reflects the feelings of many citizens throughout Appalachia. He told his Congressional colleagues during a fiery floor speech:

> I have seen what havoc and obliteration is left in the wake of strip mining. It has ripped the guts out of our mountains, polluted our streams with acid and silt, uprooted our trees and forests, devastated the land, seriously disturbed or destroyed wildlife habitat, left miles of ugly highwalls, ruined the water supply in many areas and left a trail of utter despair for many honest and hard working people.[8]

The wrath of the Ken Hechlers will drive neither Congress nor the states into banning stripping wholly, for the mining industry's own political and economic importance lies firmly across that path. Many ecologists reluctantly concede this and urge instead that Washington issue stringent environmental regulations upon the industry and that the states be compelled to enforce them. Conservationists want at least four provisions in the law:

1. *Federal supervision must extend to all surface mining, whether on public or private land.* This would extend federal authority across the vast majority of strip mines currently excluded from governmental regulation because they lie on private property. It would also assure some consistency of regulation in place of fifty different schemes that could emerge if the states were left to enact regulations.

2. *Spoil banks, and perhaps strip mining itself, should be forbidden on slopes too steep and vulnerable to water erosion to be adequately restored.* Many environmentalists want all stripping banned on slopes with gradients more than fourteen degrees; others would settle for a twenty-degree limit. In either case, the effect would be to eliminate strip mines throughout most of Appalachia and prevent it in most hilly regions elsewhere. Environmentalists contend that if stripping is not wholly prevented on slopes, at least the spoil banks must be removed by the strippers to prevent dangerous erosion, landslides, and visual ugliness.

3. *Mining companies must post performance bonds in advance of their operations to ensure that they restore—not simply "reclaim"—the disturbed land.* Environmentalists insist that the mining companies must carefully restore their disturbed land to ecological usefulness and that they should not be allowed to mine any land they cannot restore. Not only should the restoration

standards be strict and strictly enforced, but government should have the authority to order a cease-and-desist order to stop all mining operations where promises of land restoration are violated.

4. *A public notice and public hearing must occur before any mining permits are issued by federal or state agencies.* One objective of this provision would be to assure that administrators charged with responsibility for mine supervision do not deliberately or inadvertently permit stripping or other surface mines where environmental restoration is too difficult. Another purpose is to put administrators under pressure to consider environmental interests before granting permits. Not least important, public notice and hearing give environmental groups a chance to mobilize and educate public opinion on their behalf in permit controversies.

Even were such provisions to be written into a federal law, the effectiveness of the regulation would depend, as we have already seen, on the skill and dedication of administrators charged with their enforcement. The administrative record of states with some form of mine regulations has been generally dismal, suggesting that this problem will be prominent in any future federal regulations. The administrative problems, in turn, have been compounded by the mining industry's past attitude. Although the industry has now professed a new willingness to accept some regulation, environmentalists are very skeptical about its good faith.

The Mining Industry. The surface-mine industry, especially strip mining, is dominated by a handful of corporations. Most strip mines are controlled by eleven companies; in order of their coal production, these are Peabody Coal (subsidiary of Kennecott Copper), Consolidation Coal (subsidiary of Continental Oil and known in the trade as Consol), Island Creek Coal (part of Occidental Petroleum), Pittston, U.S. Steel, Amax Coal (part of American Metals Climax), Bethlehem Mines (a facet of Bethlehem Steel), Eastern Associated Coal, General Dynamics, and Old Ben Coal (part of the Standard Oil complex).[9] In their confrontation with ecologists, these companies commonly speak through representatives of their trade associations, particularly through the National Coal Association—which led the public debate over recent federal regulatory proposals—the National Association of Coal Lessors, and the American Metals Congress. Even this list of politically powerful groups fails to portray fully the industry's political strength. The industry commonly enlists the economic and political support of the parent corporations and many other major industries that depend on coal and other surface-mined minerals as a primary fuel. In short, ecologists face the mining companies, as well as the political power of the whole "fuel complex," when they enter the political arena against the surface miners.

Until very recently, the strip miners and their allies fought savagely and effectively against governmental regulation. In Appalachia, the story of stripping's progress across the Cumberlands was a bleak chronicle of the land's dismemberment almost unrelieved by any government restraint or corporate environmental responsibility; in their eagerness to strip the hills, the mining industry often appeared so callous that they finally provoked a movement in West Virginia and Kentucky to require some "restoration" of the wrecked sites. The mining companies' arguments against stringent regulation in Appalachia were similar to those put forth when the matter was raised elsewhere. The industry's principal assertions were that restrictions on surface mines would impose an "undue burden on the industry," would force operators out of business and thus create an economic depression in the region, and would drive industry from the state or earn the state an anti-business reputation.

Since strip mining flourished in Appalachia, the mining companies' warning of the economic damage from stringent regulation struck a responsive cord among many Appalachian businessmen, public officials, and citizens. Without mining, most of Appalachia's already depressed areas would be further impoverished for many years: Many impartial, competent studies indicate that sharp cutbacks in stripping would indeed be serious. But without tough environmental controls, the land might be ruined. It is this cruel dilemma—or at least a belief in it—that the region's public officials often cite in explaining their reluctance to force stringent cutbacks in strip coal production. Appalachia and its leaders are confronted with perhaps the starkest conflict between environmental protection and economic costs of any region in the United States and, consequently, are less indifferent to the industry's mood than state officials elsewhere.

Given its great economic importance throughout the Cumberlands, the industry might have weathered the assault of environmentalists and deflated the national campaign for its regulation if it had shown more restraint. However, mining companies provoked a growing outrage among numerous residents of Appalachia—many of whom fully realize the industry's economic importance—by their characteristic insistence upon access to coal at any cost. More than anything else, the miners' use of "broadform deeds" and other legal devices has brought a citizen uprising against the industry. Kentucky has seen this tactic used most conspicuously. Between 1880 and 1900, mining-company lawyers ranged the hills, purchasing mineral rights to thousands of acres of land through broadform deeds running to many pages of fine print. These deeds customarily declared that the mineral rights so obtained could be assigned to new owners forever, that the companies and their successors could do "any and all things necessary, or by him deemed necessary or convenient in mining and removing the coal," and that the new owner was immune from lawsuits for damage arising out of the extractive process. These documents were often signed by people who were illiterate; their "X" on the deed brought many as little as 50 cents for each acre they surrendered. Neither they nor the coal companies could have foreseen the impending coal boom or the physical damage that might follow; stripping was wholly unanticipated.

Citing the broadform deeds, the mining companies now insist on their right to extract coal, even when the total destruction of the land follows—this despite their legal claim to only the minerals. Kentucky's high court proved a sympathetic ally. It has consistently upheld the legality of the broadform deeds to the extent that the mining companies have been permitted to ruin almost any land upon which they hold the mineral rights.[10] The court has interpreted the deeds to mean that a coal company engaged in deep-shaft mining on land where it owned only mineral rights could nonetheless cut as many trees as was necessary for underground props. In another ruling, the court declared the right of a mining company to "divert or pollute" all water "in or near" the land on which it was operating. When stripping began, the high court held that all environmental damage was a permissible result conveyed by the broadform deeds, even though lawyers for the landowners argued that the deeds were written when stripping could not have been imagined and other state courts recognized no right to coal at the cost of the property owner's land. In many western states, as in Appalachia, stripping has often resulted in the total destruction of land upon which only mineral rights were sold; while state courts have sometimes insisted on compensation to the landowners (as sometimes occurred in Appalachia), they have done little to restrain the destruction of the land itself.

In addition, the miners commonly failed to restore the lands they had mined, even when they were publicly pledged to restoration or forced by law to make the effort. Through such indifference, the mining companies alienated much of the Appalachian public that had been its political ally; a new climate of opinion materialized, and protest movements gathered momentum. The companies had also forced growing national attention upon themselves and had fashioned an image that often seemed an amalgam of avarice, ruthlessness, and environmental recklessness. Its spokesmen seldom seemed concerned. As late as 1969, a vice-president of giant Consolidation Coal felt it appropriate when addressing the American Minerals Congress to call those demanding a restoration of mined lands "stupid idiots, socialists and Commies who don't know what they're talking about. . . . I think it is our bounden duty to knock them down and subject them to the ridicule they deserve."[11]

By the early 1970's, however, the industry could ill afford its image. As the miles of highwalls and spoil banks mounted together with the environmental damage in Appalachia and elsewhere, the need for environmental regulation seemed ever more obvious to many observers. The environmental movement had gathered force. The companies' past behavior was an easy target of criticism to which public officials, increasingly interested in a positive environmental image, were more receptive. Beginning in 1972, therefore, spokesmen for the National Coal Association and other mine groups dropped the harsh, unyielding attitude toward regulation and, instead, appeared more enlightened by admitting that "reasonable regulation" might be needed. While they have continued to decry the "national hysteria" over surface mining, leaders of the mining industry have expressed general agreement that reasonable regulations might include a uniform federal strip-mine law to prevent fifty different state laws, a requirement that stripped lands be "restored," and that the mining companies be subject to performance bonds and, perhaps, to cease-and-desist orders for noncompliance. But the industry has fought tenaciously against the prohibition of strip mining on slopes over twenty degrees, arguing that this would virtually wipe out strip mines in Appalachia and severely curtail stripping elsewhere. Moreover, it has contended that the "restoration" standards that environmentalists hope to impose upon the industry are unduly harsh and economically dangerous to many companies.

Serious, effective land restoration, when possible, is often a costly business indeed. In Britain, where restoration is uniformly required, as it is in most other nations, the cost often runs to $1.15 for every ton of extracted coal, a ratio that might well consume the profit margins of many stripping operations and materially reduce the profitability of others. In Japan, the cost of restoration and the environmental damage of stripping has led to the virtual abolition of strip mines; the Japanese purchase stripped coal from the United States instead.

Critics of surface mining commonly have little patience with the industry's warning about the consequences of severe regulation; they believe the companies exaggerate the prospective economic impact, can absorb it with only a modest profit loss, or should be forced out of business (stripping especially). Nonetheless, the nation is currently unprepared for a drastic cutback in the availability of surface-mined fuels and other minerals. If regulation were to significantly reduce coal supplies, for instance, in all probability a drastic, perhaps unacceptable, dislocation of the economy might occur—an issue that militant conservationists often dismiss too readily and frequently fail to discuss adequately. Thus, when industry spokesmen talk about the economic consequences of regulation, they are by no means dealing in irrelevant matters. At least in part, public officials have been cautious in weighing surface-mine regulations because of the nation's dependence on mined resources.

In any case, regulation at the moment rests entirely with the states. Their experience, while limited, provides a useful perspective on some of the problems associated with any regulation of the surface miners.

The States and Mining. To speak of the state's role in surface-mine regulation is mostly to confront a vast silence. Though every state is disturbed by surface mining, only a few have regulations dealing with environmental impact, and these confine themselves largely to requirements, or exhortations, that the surface miners "restore" their damaged land. Until 1970, only three states permitted or ordered their officials to require restoration as a condition of mining on public lands; nine states did attempt to regulate stripping and other surface mines on private property by ordering, or encouraging, "restoration." In the early 1970's, six additional states enacted laws requiring strippers to restore mined lands on public property, private land, or both.[12] This modest increase in states requiring land restoration was significant, but only one state lies west of the Mississippi, where stripping is expected to boom. Moreover, a critical question remained: Would the restoration laws be adequately enforced? Past experience is not heartening. Although the states with restoration laws before 1970 have estimated that half the private land affected by stripping was "reclaimed" according to the law, this was a dubious estimate, calculated by understaffed agencies with pinched budgets. In truth, restoration laws were widely ignored, for their administration lay in the hands of agencies with slight legislative support and powerful political opposition.

Even states that did make an effort to require land restoration were in the past waging largely a paper war on environmental degradation. This restoration was seldom more than a gesture, rarely returning the land to a condition remotely resembling the original. Harry M. Caudill, who etches a haunting portrait of Appalachia's social and physical disintegration, describes in his sad chronicle what "restoration" often meant in Kentucky:

> Under the law strippers are required to replant their wrecked and ravaged acres. The State Department of Conservation recommends short leaf or loblolly pines for spoil banks. Conservationists insist that a full year must pass before the young trees are planted. This delay permits the freshly piled soil to settle enough so the trees can take root. The seedlings are approximately five inches long when planted, supposedly at intervals of six feet. Some ten years must elapse before trees growing in such impoverished earth will reach the height of a man's head. In the meantime, the rains have clawed the earth about their roots into deep gullies and there is little left for their foliage to protect. Few operators seriously attempt to comply with the reclamation regulations; most are permitted virtually to ignore them.[13]

Reclamation was sometimes attempted elsewhere by treating the spoil with nothing more than huge hoses spraying water mixed with the plant nutrients, grass and tree seeds; even when careful restoration was attempted, hard rains and acid soil conspired to kill much of the new trees and grass, often sparing only a few scrubs and patches of vegetation to eke out a precarious existence. There were, to be sure, more successful efforts by private companies, which testified to the impressive capacity of the miners and their technicians to salvage the land when money and will were present. Nonetheless, restoration has been largely a fiction or a failure; two of every three acres touched by stripping remain almost totally abandoned.

The growth of surface mining simultaneously with the rise of the environmental movement appeared to reinvigorate some state interest in regulation during the early 1970's. The Kentucky legislature toughened its lackadaisical restoration law. West Virginia, which wrote the nation's earliest restoration act but produced largely a vague, unenforced memorial to good intentions, suddenly renewed its attack. In 1971, the state legislature created a tough new law banning stripping in twenty-two counties for several years and permitting it in productive coal seams only after performance bonds and restoration plans were produced by the mining companies and carefully supervised by the state. One immediate result was a rise in state prosecution of mining companies for environmental damage and a sizable drop in coal production and new mining starts, partly traceable to the economic pinch some operators were experiencing from restoration costs. Many companies had tolerated the law (if only because it quieted the clamor to ban stripping entirely), but the industry's sudden, if modest, economic retreat sent ripples of unease through many sectors of the state.

Both Ohio and Illinois have recently enacted similar new laws imposing stringent standards on strip mining. In 1972, Ohio's legislature passed what may be the toughest control law in the nation, a considerable achievement in light of the coal industry's great political and economic stature there and its frequent opposition to many of the law's provisions. Essentially, the law requires strippers to restore all mined land to its original contour in almost all circumstances and empowers state officials to deny permits to mining operators who cannot guarantee protection against major forms of environmental damage. A number of the large coal companies, including giant Consolidated Coal, have expressed guarded approval of the measure, reflecting the industry's changing attitude toward restoration laws.

Despite these glimmerings of concern, stripping proceeds westward, mounting in volume and environmental impact, against a backdrop of general state indifference. As stripping leaves its previously circumscribed boundaries in Appalachia to become truly national, many observers have concluded that surface mining must now be regulated largely by Washington or, at a minimum, Washington must provide strong support for state regulations. However, until recently, Washington has seemed hardly more concerned than most states.

Awakening on the Potomac. Washington today exercises no authority over strip mining on private lands, a situation that drastically reduces the federal government's influence on surface mining because nine out of every ten strip-mined acres rest in private hands. Nonetheless, Washington has been in a position to strongly affect the course of strip mining through its control of the public domain, a mineral-rich expanse equal to more than a third of the nation's land, and through its administration of the Tennessee Valley Authority (TVA), the largest electric power complex in the country. Until the late 1960's, federal officials demonstrated scant interest in controlling environmental degradation from stripping in the public domain or from the activities of the TVA. Reclamation of stripped land controlled directly or indirectly by Washington was insignificant. As late as 1965, "research" was the greatest contribution that the Department of the Interior could claim for Washington in the fight against stripping's environmental damage.

For more than a half century, federal officials have possessed a potentially strong weapon to control strip mining on the public domain in the Mineral Leasing Act of 1920. This act confers upon the Secretary of the Interior the authority to grant prospecting and mining permits for minerals on public land, gives him the right to deny permits if mining "would impair other important land uses," and allows him to impose standards for land restoration following mining. The wording of this authority is sufficiently broad to enable the Secretary or his subordinates to promulgate strict restoration standards for stripping on the federal domain or to forbid it whenever satisfactory restoration is deemed impossible; with the current growth of stripping and its westward expansion, this authority assumes great importance, for most of the public domain lies in the West, where extensive mineral deposits constitute an important foundation for the industry.

Until 1969, well after stripping was familiar on federal land, virtually no environmental restraint on surface mining or restoration of stripped land was evident on the public domain; as far as stripping was concerned, the 1920 law had been largely an arrangement for mining's growth but not its control. In early 1969, the Department of the Interior at last seemed willing to draw upon the dormant power of the 1920 legislation to regulate stripping on public lands. Specifically, the department promulgated new regulations that, among other provisions, required (1) that the Bureau of Land Management and the Bureau of Indian Affairs conduct a "technical examination" to determine the environmental impact of a mining operation before issuing a permit; (2) that these agencies establish requirements for reclaiming the mined land in advance of mining; (3) that a performance bond equal to the cost of land reclamation be posted by mining companies; and (4) that periodic reports on environmental damage and reclamation be submitted to the agencies by companies subject to the regulations.[14] Environmentalists were cautiously optimistic about this, encouraged by the intent yet apprehensive lest such "restoration" measures suffer the same haphazard enforcement found in similar state measures.

In late 1972, a careful review of the administration of these regulations, prepared for Congress by the Comptroller General, seemed to confirm these misgivings; enforcement was indifferent, sometimes negligent, prompting some critics to charge that the Department of the Interior was incapable of regulating its own clients. Based on a sampling of leases and permits issued by the department since 1969, the study revealed that in almost half the cases, no technical examination of environmental impact had been conducted prior to issuing mining permits, that the required performance bonds were often unposted, and that periodic reports on mining activity required of the companies were sometimes unprepared.[15] The controversy was further stirred by western conservationists, joined by the governor of Montana, protesting pervasive environmental damage on public lands near Yellowstone National Park caused by mining exploration and operations. Environmental spokesmen, joined by some influential Congressional leaders, argued that control of stripping on public land would have to be removed from the Department of the Interior and vested in the Environmental Protection Agency or a new superagency responsible for all resource matters.

This controversy boiled up simultaneously with growing concern over the environmental damage caused by the giant TVA complex. Built in the early days of Franklin Roosevelt's New Deal, the Tennessee Valley Authority was once primarily a hydroelectric facility symbolizing for millions of Americans the finest achievement of governmental conservation, a monument to wise environmental use bringing economic and physical regeneration to the whole Tennessee River Valley. In the decades since its beginning, however, the TVA gradually shifted to generating 80 per cent of its electric power from coal and, in the process, became the largest single consumer of coal for electric power in the nation, today burning more than 5 per cent of the nation's yearly coal output in huge drafts of 1,600 carloads daily. The focus of the environmental controversy is the TVA's massive demand for strip-mined coal. The facility yearly negotiates thirty to forty strip-mine contracts from which it obtains more than 16 million tons of coal, thus becoming a major stimulus to the growth of surface mining throughout all Appalachia. Conservationists argue that the TVA has been negligent in seeking alternative fuel supplies or production methods that do not wreak such environmental damage. They assert that the TVA could, at the very least, use its enormous purchasing power as leverage to force strip miners to practice environmental restoration on mined lands if they want government contracts. Further, many conservationists charge that the TVA has become so consumed with obtaining cheap coal that it drives down the market price, thus denying many coal companies the extra income that might be allocated to environmental restoration. If Washington wants to diminish the environmental degradation of strip mining, say many conservationists, the TVA is a logical place to begin.

In response to this criticism, the TVA's directors announced a new coal-purchase policy in 1972, which, they asserted, would greatly encourage environmental protection from strip mining and diminish their own contribution to environmental negligence. In the future, the TVA would purchase no coal from strippers operating on slopes so steep that the spoil would constitute an environmental hazard, nor would coal be bought from companies operating in scenic and wilderness areas; mines creating water pollution or endangering streams or public water supplies would be similarly excluded from future contracts. Additionally, a portion of the coal supplier's payment would be withheld until he had satisfactorily reclaimed the land disturbed by stripping; failure to meet new restoration standards established by the TVA would result in the loss of a portion of the supplier's usual bonus. These regulations are too newly minted to have proved themselves yet, but conservationists suspect that the results will be no less dismal than those commonly witnessed in other state and federal restoration laws.

Modest as they are, these actions represent the first evidence that Washington has become concerned enough about strip mining's environmental consequences to take preventive action. Even if the federal government should achieve some environmental protection through regulations regarding the public domain and the TVA, most observers believe that surface mining's ravages will be contained only when the federal government enacts a national surface-mine policy applicable to all the states. Some national legislation seems very likely before the end of President Nixon's second term, and the general outlines seem reasonably clear.

A National Policy. The Congress came very close to enacting the nation's first federal strip-mine legislation in 1972—a beginning toward the environmental control of the whole surface-mine industry; the legislation passed the House but died in the Senate. The Coalition Against Strip Mining had fought hard for the legislation, but its defeat was not considered irreversible. With the mining industry's apparent willingness to accept some regulation and a demonstration of political power by environmentalists that overthrew several veteran Congressmen with bad ecology records, conditions seemed congenial for legislation to emerge within the next Congressional session.

In general, the legislation would have required the states to establish restoration standards for all stripped land, to order performance bonds from the mining companies, and to issue cease-and-desist orders for violators. Additionally, public hearings prior to the issuance of permits for strip mining would have been required of all state and federal administrators with authority to issue such permits. Some major issues remained contentious. Congress could not agree upon the prohibition of stripping on hills with a gradient greater than twenty degrees. The exact requirements for restoration that the states were expected to enforce as minimum standards were hotly and inconclusively debated. Finally, environmentalists were largely cold to the prospect that the new law would be enforced by the Department of the Interior, whose sympathies are regarded as too closely aligned with the mining industry.

In short, large and important questions were unresolved by the 1972 legislation, and its defeat was, in good measure, tied to the failure of environmentalists, the mining industry, and their Congressional allies to reach a compromise. All that is certain in the future is that Washington is likely to move, belatedly and lumberingly, toward the first national public policy on surface mining. Whether it will prove to be an effective, immediate control on stripping's ravages or merely another example of Washington's going to war against environmental degradation armed largely with pens remains to be seen.

Notes

1. This description is adapted from U.S. Department of the Interior, *Surface Mining and Our Environment* (Washington, D.C., 1967), pp. 33 ff. Quotes, unless otherwise noted, are from this source.
2. Described in Harry M. Caudill, *My Land Is Dying* (New York: E. P. Dutton and Co., 1971), p. 23.
3. *New York Times,* August 22, 1971.
4. Caudill, *op. cit.,* chapter 7.
5. The study, prepared by Friends of the Earth, is reported in *New York Times,* January 30, 1972.
6. U.S. Department of the Interior, *op. cit.,* p. 51.
7. Cited in Caudill, *op. cit.,* p. 85. Quoted from the dissenting opinion in *Martin* vs. *Kentucky Oak Mining Co.,* 429 S.W. 2d (Ky.) 395.
8. *New York Times,* October 15, 1972.
9. According to National Coal Association figures published in the *New York Times,* October 15, 1972.
10. These deeds and court opinions are extensively discussed in Harry M. Caudill, *Night Comes to the Cumberlands* (Boston: Little, Brown and Co., 1963), chapter 19.
11. Quoted in Harry M. Caudill, "Are Capitalism and the Conservation of a Decent Environment Compatible?" in Harold W. Helfrich, Jr. (ed.), *Agenda For Survival* (New Haven: Yale University Press, 1971), p. 177.
12. State performance prior to 1970 is summarized in U.S. Department of the Interior, *op. cit.,* pp. 98–99. Information on state laws since 1970 is taken from Council on Environmental Quality, *Environmental Quality, 1972,* pp. 188–89.
13. Caudill, *Night Comes to the Cumberlands, op. cit.,* p. 316.
14. Summarized in U.S. General Accounting Office, *Administration of Regulations for Surface Exploration, Mining and Reclamation of Public and Indian Coal Lands* (Washington, D.C., August, 1972), chapter 1.
15. *Ibid.,* chapter 2.

9 *Paradox Two: Solid Waste*

Standing in splendid isolation atop Mt. Rainier, a companion to wind and perpetual snow more than 14,000 feet above sea level, may soon appear the nation's highest privy. Officials of the National Park Service have been forced to ponder such a possibility because the volume of waste left by climbers on the popular peak has become an acute problem. Such a grotesque monument to human carelessness would be one sign of the rising volume of wastes on the nation's mountains; it would, in turn, testify to the fact that some portion of the continent undefiled by solid waste no longer exists. Trash dumps have been found at the 17,200-foot level on Mt. McKinley; recently, conservationists removed more than four hundred pounds of junk from its upper slope alone. In one national park, the debris found at high altitudes included cans, bottles, paper, tools, aluminum chairs, tents, medicine, food waste, and even a pornographic library. In the White Mountains National Forest, campers are discouraged from pitching tents above the timberline, for campsite litter and other human damage have seriously impaired the fragile plant and animal life at high altitudes. "People will drop almost anything if they figure they don't have to carry it out," concluded one Park Service official in explaining the mountain litter.[1] As more than 250,000 Americans yearly climb the nation's major mountains, the last barrier to human litter has been conquered; solid waste marches upward.

Below the mountaintops, solid waste has been skyrocketing into a national problem over many decades. Little has actually been done to reduce the volume or to discover new methods for its disposal. Solid waste is accumulating at a rate that many public officials predict will create a disposal crisis within a decade. Public expenditures for solid-waste collection and disposal, almost all financed by the average taxpayer, is currently $4.5 billion, yearly and likely to triple by the century's end. Solid waste is synonymous with visual ugliness, health problems, impaired property value, and general environmental degradation. Yet the technology of solid-waste collection has been almost static for fifty years; disposal methods are only slightly better and still largely experimental. So recently has concern arisen that basic data about solid-waste production is almost unavailable for the years before 1965. The reasons for the flagging attack on disposal are complex, related to the behavior of consumers, the nation's economic structure, technology, and other matters. The nature of the problem and the broad outline of its solution nonetheless are quite clear.

The Making and Unmaking of Solid Waste

Most Americans associate solid waste with the contents of the garbage dump: glass, plastic and metal containers, food remnants, paper products, toothpaste tubes, perhaps the rusting hulks of mattresses, cars, and metal appliances. This refuse, despite public attention, is only a small portion of all solid waste produced annually in the United States. More than half the nation's solid waste is produced by agriculture, mostly from animals (farm animals alone produce ten times the metabolic waste of the whole U.S. population); an additional quarter of the nation's solid waste comes from mining, principally fossil fuel extraction. Compared to this massive load, the solid materials produced by residential, commercial, and institutional sources—about 250 million tons annually—might seem trivial; this debris, which we shall call "consumer waste," is nonetheless troublesome, expensive, and dangerous. It is often the most difficult to destroy satisfactorily; it commonly accumulates near communities, where it may pose grave health hazards; it almost always insults sight and smell. And this waste, feeding upon our affluence, continues to multiply.

The dimensions of the solid-waste problem are writ large in a few statistics. In 1920, the average American threw away 2.75

pounds of garbage daily; in 1970, it had jumped to 5 pounds daily. By 1980, we will each produce about 8 pounds of garbage every day with no slackening of growth anticipated. In national terms, this means that the nation's urban communities must daily dispose of more than 800 million pounds of solid waste and can expect this volume to increase three-fold by 1980. Many of the collection and disposal problems can be understood by examining briefly the content of this consumer waste.

Consumer Waste. Consumer waste is extremely troublesome because of its many elements as well as its growing volume.[2] One large component is *packaging material,* which accounts for more than half of all consumer garbage. The most familiar of these packaging materials is the disposable container, primarily metal, glass, and plastic; we now use and discard more than 30 billion glass and plastic bottles and 60 billion cans annually. Another 30 million tons of paper products, much of it wrapping material, ends on the trash heap. To this massive debris is added uncounted tons of foil trays, flashlight batteries, cosmetic sprays, film cartridges, pesticides, and aerosol containers of every sort. This packaging has grown in volume phenomenally over a very short time, increasing at a rate far faster than the gross national product—from 400 pounds per person in 1958, to 578 pounds in 1970, to a predicted 661 pounds by 1976 with no terminal point anticipated; Americans spend more than 3 per cent of the gross national product in producing these materials. This packaging caters to the consumer's affluence and demand for convenience, especially in the food industry, where, for instance, packaging single units or a small volume of items previously sold in bulk has significantly increased the demand for wrapping material.

Another large portion of consumer waste is *organic products* of all kinds, mostly food garbage. Food wastes are biodegradable, creating a less difficult disposal problem than other consumer wastes; however, organic wastes usually attract scavengers and vermin, breed many pathogenic organisms, and rapidly become a menace to public health if they accumulate in large volume and are left to stand for long periods.

Having conquered the road, the American automobile is rapidly claiming the land; *abandoned and junked auto bodies* today constitute a growing solid-waste problem. No one knows exactly how many junked or abandoned autos exist in the United States. Estimates of abandoned auto bodies along the highways reach as high as 20 million. In Philadelphia, 21,700 cars were deserted in 1971; in New York, 82,000. Altogether, perhaps 7 million autos are abandoned every year. All estimates indicate that abandoned and junked autos will increase for decades, adding millions of metal corpses to the automobile litter already decorating the highways and roadsides. Part of the explanation for mounting auto bodies is the decreasing life of cars, which averaged more than fourteen years between purchase and disposal prior to 1950 but now averages about eight years. Then, too, with growing affluence, the average American buys a car more often; even the relatively poor have little trouble finding the credit to purchase a car of some type. Population expansion alone would greatly increase the demand for new cars and, ultimately, the proliferation of junked ones.

Beyond the consumer waste that can be readily identified are tons of miscellany, still more of our culture's discard pile. During one recent year, Americans tossed away more than 7 million television sets, presumably because they no longer worked. Other appliances—toasters, washers, refrigerators, small motors of all kinds, and ovens—are common fare on any city dump. Grass cuttings, wood shavings, leaves, even animal bodies are also collected and must somehow be destroyed.

What Must Be Done. Among those who have studied consumer waste, there is surprisingly little disagreement about the remedies or the urgency of taking action. Although environmentalists might debate the proper order in which these policies should be initiated, they have generally discovered that the principal problem is to convince public officials that solid waste is now a grave ecological ill that requires the creation of politically difficult but environmentally imperative remedies.

The key to managing consumer waste lies in three policies: source reduction, recycling, and sanitary waste disposal. Taken together—and experts commonly insist that they should be combined—these policies could form the framework of a combined local, state, and federal government attack. Source reduction aims at deflating the volume of consumer wastes generated in the nation by discouraging the production and consumption of materials commonly ending in the garbage dump or salvage yard: disposable containers, packaging materials, and large metal items (including auto bodies) are among the most important. Any proposal for source reduction encounters formidable opposition because it requires government to intervene in the economic marketplace and to obstruct the smooth flow of disposable goods that American industry produces in such extravagant amounts. Yet environmentalists maintain that both American industry and the consumer share a responsibility for generating consumer waste, and both must somehow be discouraged from this enterprise if the nation's waste problems are to be solved. Industry too often creates planned obsolescence and caters too diligently to the consumer's convenience—both producing unnecessary waste. "Planned obsolescence . . . is a way of life," remarks one solid-waste expert. "The consumer is urged to buy the new and trade in or throw away the old. The rise of the nonreturnable container despite the fact that it costs the user more is another example of the close relationship between market strategy and the generation of solid waste."[3] Essentially, both producers and purchasers of disposable products must be discouraged from their accustomed behavior if source reduction is ever to work.

Even a generous reduction in the volume of materials would still leave an enormous load of consumer waste as a continuing responsibility for government. Today, government seldom does more than carelessly bury this debris on a constantly shrinking volume of available land—an unimaginative, environmentally damaging practice that fails to exploit the constructive possibilities for waste use. "The ideal of solid waste management," declares one ecologist, "would be the disposal of wastes by reuse or recycling, and the disposition of the irreducible residue without insult and perhaps even with enhancement to the environment."[4] No tenet in the environmental movement has been more widely advertised than recycling, currently a glamour concept among ecologists. While there are many economic, technological, and political problems in recycling, which we shall soon examine, there are also many persuasive arguments in favor of recycling refuse as a means of reducing solid waste. Organic materials can be converted into compost and used for fertilizer and soil enrichment, a common European practice. Most of the metal in automobile frames, appliances, and disposable containers can be collected, sorted, melted, and reabsorbed into a great variety of industrial processes. Paper refuse can be sorted, shredded, and treated to make new paper products. Recycling can, moreover, diminish the pressure on rapidly diminishing raw resources; each ton of recycled paper, for instance, can be a substitute for seventeen trees otherwise cut, while reprocessed organic wastes such as garbage, waste paper, and animal manure might, according to an experimental study by the U.S. Bureau of Mines, yield large quantities of oil when converted in large volume. The nation has clearly made little effort to use recycled materials; thus, a potentially large market might be available. Less than 3 per cent of glass containers are currently reused, less than 4 per cent of aluminum ones are recycled, and only 2.3 per cent of metal cans are ever used again. Against such a background of apparently neglected opportunities and with the prospect of a solid-waste crisis approaching, it is hardly surprising that many environmentalists have concluded that recycling must be a major strategy of the future. "This is," according to one representative viewpoint, "the only ecologically sensible long-term solution to the solid-waste problem."

Under the most favorable conditions, however, recycling would still leave a very large amount of waste to be eliminated. There are few ways in which this residual waste can be treated: It can be dumped in landfills, hauled out to sea and then dumped, or incinerated. In the past, a number of seaboard communities, including New York and Boston, did haul part of their sewage out to sea and sink it, creating ocean contamination of such magnitude that the federal government prohibited the practice. Today, most communities simply purchase landfills and use them until overflowing; seldom, however, do these dumps meet the standards of a "sanitary landfill" that environmentalists regard as an essential ingredient in any sound waste-disposal program. A sanitary landfill, according to the American Society of Civil Engineers, is one where refuse is confined to the smallest practical area, is reduced to the smallest practical volume, and then is covered with a layer of earth at the conclusion of each day's operation or more frequently if necessary; it is also an expensive, labor-demanding form of disposal. Because sanitary landfills are costly, most communities only use open dumps; seldom carefully managed, they are commonly rat-infested areas of visual and ecological devastation stretching over many square miles, much of the debris burning or smoking from deliberate and spontaneous combustion. Although large incinerators can be a very efficient, environmentally safe method of waste disposal when properly constructed and supervised, very few communities have such facilities; instead, the ubiquitous open landfill prevails. In short, environmentalists have considerable justification for asserting that the government has yet to invest time or interest in truly sanitary, efficient waste-disposal methods.

Even recycling, source reduction, and sanitary waste disposal will not prove effective in restraining solid-waste growth unless solid-waste management is viewed as "a problem of the whole system." Waste management requires concern for economics, public health, engineering, law, urban planning, geography, and a host of other matters; these, in turn, must be brought together by governmental planners at many levels who are themselves working within the framework of a comprehensive policy design. If such planning and integration of many governmental units is possible, it is likely to occur only when the federal government assumes the leadership in the planning process. Thus, the quest for an effective solid-waste policy leads, as do most other governmental problems, to a search for comprehensive, coordinated national governmental planning. Given Washington's erratic and often disappointing record in past efforts at environmental management, conservationists are by no means convinced that such an attack on solid waste will occur; they are almost unanimous, however, in asserting that, without Washington's participation, solid waste will soon overwhelm the nation's capacity to handle it.

Government and Solid Waste

If the nation can be said to have any solid-waste policy at all, it is little more than the assumption that solid waste is only refuse, the disposal of which should be left to local government, while the volume cannot really be affected by governmental controls. There is no national planning of solid-waste management. Attempts to reduce the volume of solid waste are largely confined to futile appeals for voluntary restraint on waste—"Don't be a litterbug," for example. A few collaborative efforts between industry and private groups to recycle some waste materials have produced indifferent results, not unexpectedly, since industry has little enthusiasm for the job and national policy actually discourages the use of recycled materials in industry. The nation's local governments continue to bury ever mounting quantities of debris with growing apprehension as landfills become scarcer. Within the last few years, the first glimmering of public concern and governmental initiative to reverse this official apathy has appeared. Still, the nation's public officials largely behave as if the earth can accommodate our garbage indefinitely.

State and Local Approaches: "Bury and Forget It." The nation does not lack a large volume of state and local waste laws. It is evident from Table 6 that a great many states have written legislation dealing with solid waste in their jurisdiction; according to this compilation, thirty-two states have at least some general waste management plans or guidelines, forty-two have some specific solid-waste regulations, and twenty-five have gone so far as to require permits before landfills and other dumping can be done by municipalities. Unfortunately, these laws are often vague; they frequently lack detailed, operational provisions and are often erratically enforced, largely because enforcement customarily depends on the uncertain will of local governments. Many states have been reluctant to enact provisions that might be enforceable (note that only half the states even require disposal permits from municipalities). In any case, state regulations generally deal with solid-waste collection and disposal but not with the management of solid-waste volume. The states have so far made little effort to control the volume of solid wastes entering or leaving their borders, or to encourage a significant recycling of materials. But it is doubtful that the states, acting individually or in concert, can contribute much to managing the nation's growing volume of solid waste, for problems of coordi-

TABLE 6
Status of State Solid Waste Regulation

	Solid Waste Laws	Rules and Regulations	Disposal Permit Required	Political Subdivisions: Technical Assistance	Political Subdivisions: Financial Assistance
Alabama	×	×			
Alaska					
Arizona	×	×			
Arkansas	×				
California					
Colorado	×	×	×	×	
Connecticut	×	×	×	×	×
Delaware		×	×	×	
District of Columbia		×			
Florida		×			
Georgia		×			
Hawaii	×				
Idaho		×			
Illinois	×	×	×	×	
Indiana	×				
Iowa	×	×	×		
Kansas	×	×	×	×	×
Kentucky	×	×	×	×	
Louisiana		×			
Maine				×	
Maryland	×	×	×	×	×
Massachusetts	×	×	×	×	×
Michigan	×	×	×		
Minnesota	×	×	×	×	
Mississippi		×			
Missouri		×			
Montana	×	×	×	×	
Nebraska					
Nevada	×				
New Hampshire	×	×	×	×	
New Jersey	×	×	×	×	
New Mexico		×	×		
New York	×	×		×	×
North Carolina	×	×			
North Dakota		×		×	
Ohio	×	×	×		
Oklahoma	×	×			
Oregon	×	×	×	×	
Pennsylvania	×	×	×	×	×
Rhode Island	×	×		×	×
South Carolina		×	×		
South Dakota	×	×		×	

TABLE 6 (*Continued*)

	Solid Waste Laws	Rules and Regulations	Disposal Permit Required	Political Subdivisions	
				Technical Assistance	Financial Assistance
Tennessee	×	×	×		
Texas	×	×	×	×	×
Utah		×		×	
Vermont		×	×	×	×
Virginia		×	×	×	×
Washington	×	×	×	×	×
West Virginia		×		×	
Wisconsin	×	×	×	×	
Wyoming	×			×	
American Samoa					
Guam					
Puerto Rico					
Trust Territory					
Virgin Islands					

SOURCE: U.S. Environmental Protection Agency.

nation and political obstacles are formidable impediments to a state-by-state effort at waste management; it may well be that any significant regulation of solid-waste production must rest with the federal government, which has the necessary power to regulate interstate commerce.

Such state regulations as do exist are commonly administered at the local level, together with any additional laws that municipalities and counties may enact. Governmental waste management on this basis becomes extremely decentralized and fragmented among thousands of municipalities, counties, and special waste management districts. Local officials, customarily strapped with tight revenue sources, concerned with other high-priority programs, and facing very limited technical resources and labor problems, have rarely been innovators in solid-waste management. "Local governments," explains the Council on Environmental Quality, "have only limited funds, and municipal officials are timorous about interfering with refuse collection routines for fear of upsetting labor relations and public relations. . . . Even when the evidence is clear that new methods result in improvements, jealousies and fear of adverse employee relations sometimes prevent implementation."[5] In recent years, a handful of local governments, reversing this trend, have attacked solid waste by prohibiting or taxing the sale of disposable containers within their jurisdictions (the city of Oberlin, Ohio, has even banned the *possession* of nonreturnable beer and soft drink containers), but state courts often strike down these ordinances or public opinion rises to smite them; at best, such measures are a piecemeal, minor contribution to waste management on a national basis. A great many municipal governments have almost abandoned the management of solid wastes entirely, turning the responsibility over to private companies operating by governmental franchises.

The majority of local governments are still managing their own solid wastes in the face of growing problems. Collection is one nettlesome task. Cities spend several billion dollars annually simply to haul the garbage to disposal sites—the average community spends about 6 per cent of its total revenues on this alone. Solid-waste collection, moreover, is a very labor-intensive activity, requiring much manpower and capital expenditure for equipment; both are sure to rise with growing labor costs and mounting waste volume. Collection technology is largely undeveloped—the compactor truck is practically the only significant innovation in the last half century. Still, many municipalities could greatly improve the quality of their collection by purchasing better equipment, hiring more manpower, and arranging more frequent pickups; all this, of course, would mean a major increase in collection costs to be passed on to consumers. The high cost of collection could be somewhat reduced and better service almost assured if consumers were willing to take several modest steps to simplify collection tasks. Unfortunately, Americans seldom cooperate in such situations. Few consumers, for example, will voluntarily sort organic and inorganic materials into separate containers, a simple act that could vastly simplify municipal garbage disposal and increase its efficiency; few municipalities have the courage to force such action.

Collection seems a simple matter, nonetheless, compared to disposal problems. The essence of the crisis is that land for dumping is rapidly disappearing. Blessed with a seemingly inexhaustible bounty of cheap land, the United States has tradi-

TABLE 7
Disposal of Residential, Commercial, and Institutional Solid Wastes, 1969

	Million Tons	Percentage of All Solid Waste
Open dumps	146	58
Sanitary landfills	25	10
Incinerators	15	6
Uncollected	60	24
Salvaged, composted, dumped at sea	4	2
Total	250	101*

* Estimate exceeds 100% because of errors in rounding.
SOURCE: Council on Environmental Quality, *Environmental Quality, 1971,* p. 111.

tionally depended on land disposal of solid wastes; we are still largely burying our refuse. In Table 7 is an estimate of how consumer waste was handled in 1969, the last year for which accurate estimates are available. Clearly, about 60 per cent of all this solid waste ended in the ground, most often in open, unsanitary landfills. While small or impoverished communities are most likely to purchase cheap land for unsanitary dumps, even large cities are sometimes careless about dump siting; the San Francisco Metropolitan Region annually unloads more than 3 million tons of refuse in seventy-seven sites, more than two-thirds of which are along the shoreline of San Francisco Bay, where dump drainage poses a constant aesthetic and health problem. Many large cities, currently pressing the available dumping sites to the limit, may soon face a land scarcity. Estimates suggest that New York City may exhaust its available dumping space before 1980. Other cities, accustomed to using neighboring counties and municipalities for dumps, are now encountering greater resistance to this refuse exportation. San Francisco, already transporting some of its refuse more than a hundred miles for disposal in thinly populated adjacent counties, is finding its neighbors increasingly reluctant to accept additional loads.

Ultimately, the amount of land that large communities can use for landfills is finite. Unless a major technological or economic innovation reduces drastically the volume of solid waste now accumulating in American communities, there will be some future point, perhaps not many years hence, when the land is gone. But short-range planning and limited objectives still dominate municipal planning; because dumping is the cheapest form of disposal for most communities, this economic appeal alone often perpetuates it.

Despite its promising potential as an alternative to land dumping, the nation has given relatively slight attention to incineration as a major disposal method. It is technically possible to create incinerators capable of destroying most solid waste without undesirable air emission; incinerators can handle a great volume of solid waste daily, operating almost constantly. In Europe and Asia, where scarce land has made dumps prohibitively expensive, incinerators have been imaginatively planned and built for a wide range of uses. The city of Düsseldorf, West Germany, besides incinerating most of its solid refuse, uses the energy generated to manufacture steam that is then sold to other city agencies; scrap iron and other useful salvage products are sold from the incinerator remains. Paris and Osaka, Japan, also rely on huge municipal burners for solid-waste elimination and steam generation. Our nation's lagging concern with incineration undoubtedly reflects the easy access to landfills in the past, but an additional explanation is the plastics problem. Many experts have asserted that burning chloride plastics—the common ingredient in most plastic containers—releases hydrochloric gas and acid that corrode incinerators and reduce their efficiency. This problem has not been acute elsewhere because few other nations use such a glut of plastic items. However, some experts have recently asserted that plastics can safely be incinerated and that the nation ought to proceed immediately toward greater incineration research to relieve the pressure on open land for refuse deposit.

Despite all the evidence indicating that solid waste is now a major problem, ecologists do not expect policy innovations to come from state and local governments. There is little public outcry for reform at the local level and much resistance to the increased taxes that would almost surely accompany new disposal technologies. Moreover, such innovations as local government might undertake would be piecemeal and uncoordinated unless a national waste policy first existed to serve as a guide for state and local action. Equally important, solid-waste management will not prove effective unless there is some reduction in the volume of the nation's solid wastes, an accomplishment that requires recycling of materials and points to Washington, where any effective recycling policy must originate. Today, therefore, environmentalists are putting increased emphasis on action that will persuade federal officials to encourage greater recycling of solid waste and to develop a national waste management plan.

Washington and Recycling. If the recycling of used materials is to reduce the nation's solid waste significantly, a major alteration in the economics of use must occur in the United States. This would require important changes in the way industry uses and prices raw materials, in the present government regulations concerning transportation rates for raw and used materials, and in the pricing of consumer goods. These are by no means the only economic transformations required to make significant recycling a reality, but they are sufficient to suggest how complex and controversial such a policy is likely to be. Ecologists have, unfortunately, often advertised recycling as a panacea to solid-waste problems without enough regard for the harsh economic, technical, and political problems that stubbornly stand between the idea of recycling and its realization. To appreciate the formidable task facing federal policy-makers in creating a recycling policy, let us examine briefly some of the major aspects of a recycling system.

Massive recycling is practical only when recycled materials can be profitably used; today the economy discriminates against recycled materials. It is very expensive to separate the organic and inorganic materials in solid waste prior to recycling, a necessary measure often adding enough extra expense to recycled materials to render them uncompetitive with unused materials. Shipping costs are another factor. According to the National Association of Secondary Industries, a trade group representing producers of recycled materials, almost two-thirds of the nation's recyclable copper is not reused because, among other reasons, it costs at least 50 per cent less to ship virgin copper; recycled paper often costs twice as much to ship as unused paper. The demand for recycled materials fluctuates widely, often dipping so low that producers of secondary materials cannot sell at a profit sufficient to stay in business for long. In fact, many of the recycling programs currently in operation for disposable containers show a profit only because they are heavily subsidized. One ecology center in San Diego, begun in late 1971, collected more than 130 tons of glass in less than a year, but ended in the black only because a disposal company donated collection containers and trucks for transportation at cost while a glass company paid a five-dollar premium over market price for the recycled material. In short, proponents of recycling are often guilty of exaggerating the real demand for secondary materials under present market conditions. Industrial technology can also be troublesome. In the metals industry, for instance, new, more efficient furnaces often appear that require a higher grade of pure scrap than recycled materials may achieve.

Many of these general difficulties can be illustrated by examining the problem of processing auto bodies. Auto bodies are now desirable for their parts, which, once stripped from the frame, leave a metal hulk of highly variable market value. If a junk dealer is to sell the auto body, it will ordinarily be as scrap to mills using it for low-quality steel. A dealer might make a modest profit—if the demand for such scrap is currently high and if his collection and disposal costs for the hulk are manageable. In early 1972, one Virginia junk dealer itemized his costs; excluding his expense in collecting an auto body (which can be high if it must be rescued from rough terrain), it cost him four dollars to crush one car in a Mobile Auto Crusher, seven to eight dollars a ton to truck it to a shredder, and seven dollars a ton to shred it. For every ton of car he had shredded, he would get about eighteen dollars for the iron—barely enough to break even; if the demand for scrap diminished slightly, of course, there would be no profit and no incentive to salvage further bodies. The demand for scrap iron has sometimes risen to the point where a profit could be turned by selling auto bodies to the steel industry, yet the long-run outlook for scrap metal sales is very cloudy because many steel companies are introducing new technologies, particularly giant new basic-oxygen furnaces, which require a higher grade of scrap than many secondary metals dealers can now supply. The scrap supplier can also anticipate a continuing rise in labor costs that could cut significantly into his thin profit margin for auto body sales.

As this discussion suggests, the seller of scrap auto metals is, to a great extent, dependent upon market forces and industrial technology to set the price and demand for recycled auto materials. His prospects are not necessarily bleak. There is a promise of new electric furnaces that will accept lesser quality scrap than present ones, thereby increasing the salability of current scrap to the steel industry. New, more efficient automobile shredders and compactors are being developed that might lower the unit cost of auto salvage and even produce a higher grade of scrap; shredders are now available, though still limited in quantity, which can chew up more than one thousand autos a day—about equal to the number of autos that an equally new giant hammer mill has reduced to fist-sized fragments of clean steel scrap at several operation sites in the United States. The prospect of these new salvage technologies might be encouraging if they reduce the cost of auto salvage and increase the appeal of scrap to the metals industry. At the moment, however, the future of scrap metal recycling still rests almost entirely in the care of the economy's private sector, with little important participation by government in the recycling process. In this respect, the auto salvage business is typical of the recycling mechanism of the nation generally. Almost all the fundamental processes associated with solid-waste generation and disposal, particularly the economic factors controlling the nation's volume of solid waste, are touched by government only indirectly, if at all.

In 1970, Washington gave the first faint indication that it realized something officially might be done about recycling. The federal government passed the Resource Recovery Act of 1970, which emphasized programs to encourage greater resource recycling, thereby very tentatively touching the problem for the first time.[6] This legislation authorized funds to a variety of federal agencies to create demonstration programs in recycling technology; guidelines for the construction and operation of solid-waste systems were also to be propounded by the federal government through the Environmental Protection Agency and then enforced upon all federal agencies. The federal government also began wielding its massive purchasing power in the cause of recycling by ordering studies leading to a new federal policy for purchasing recycled products. By late 1972, the modest result of this legislation was some tax incentive for private firms to create recycling facilities for their material, a new federal directive that Washington agencies use recycled paper in most of its purchases, and some new experimental programs in resource reuse. Beyond this, Washington was indisposed to go. In his 1972 Environmental Message, the President gave only brief, oblique mention to solid-waste problems and indicated in other ways that he hoped industry would take greater voluntary steps toward new recycling systems without strong federal prodding.

In fact, industry has not been indifferent to recycling, but it has had little incentive to press beyond a few experimental programs in materials reuse. Corporations currently spend more than $1 billion annually in solid-waste management, much of this in attempts to recycle materials economically. There is, for instance, more than $1 billion in usable metal in abandoned autos that industry would scrap if its salvage could be made profitable. There are also many production changes that industry could make to increase the feasibility of recycling. Automobiles might be designed to be more easily cannibalized through greater interchangeability of parts and greater sensitivity to recycling problems in the planning of new models. For example, steel mills currently encounter difficulty in melting auto bodies because cars contain a very small amount of copper wiring (about four pounds per car) that is too inaccessible to be removed economically; this copper forms an alloy with steel when melted, greatly reducing the metal's quality. If aluminum were substituted for the copper wiring, it would form a slag that could easily be skimmed from the molten bodies. One well-publicized industrial response to the recycling problem has been the formation of the National Center for Resource Recovery, Inc., a cooperative enterprise among container manufacturers to collect and reuse disposable containers. However, the center has made it clear that it intends to operate its program only until local governments take over the disposal responsibility, an attitude that annoys many public officials, who assert that the industry is refusing to accept its own responsibility for better recycling procedures.

So the situation remains today with neither government nor American industry committed to more than experimental, timid efforts at solid-waste management. Economists and environmentalists generally believe that the federal government must end this impasse, for only Washington's vast resources and authority are likely to prove adequate for the task of national economic planning that any effective recycling policy entails. Yet a national recycling policy, however imperative, will prove most beneficial when it is created as part of a broader national solid-waste policy, because the attack on recycling also involves other problems, such as the reduction of national waste volume and the development of better waste disposal technologies.

Toward a National Waste Program. Ecologists have a rather clear concept of what a national solid-waste policy should be. It should originate from Washington and begin with a federal determination to create a comprehensive attack on solid waste in which federal officials draw up the broad policy guidelines for state and local governments to follow. The funding of such a program, like many other programs aimed at environmental improvement, can be shared among governmental units, with Washington taking the major funding responsibilities. Other important provisions would include:

1. *A reduction or stabilization of solid-waste volume by a national tax on disposable containers to decrease their marketability, while raising revenue to be pledged to national refuse management.* Aside from the ire this might generate among consumers, the most formidable political obstacle to such a proposal is the intense opposition it raises from container manufacturers and beverage producers. Such tax proposals were introduced in most state legislatures between 1970 and 1972 but encountered such stiff opposition from the container interests that only Oregon succeeded in creating a state disposable tax. Container manufacturers customarily argue that the tax is no solution to solid-

waste problems because most customers will pay the additional premium for the throw-away container or buy a returnable bottle and later discard it. "The consumer has been less and less willing to return bottles over the years," observes one large beverage bottler. "In many large cities, which usually set the pace in these matters, the average returnable bottle sees only 5 round trips. Since the people who buy returnable bottles today are doing so by choice (and hence are more likely to return them), we can safely assume the number of round trips would drop even further if people had no other choice but to buy them."[7] Interests partial to disposable containers also assert that throw-away containers are but a small portion of the solid-waste problem. Proponents of the container tax argue that the industry's real motivation for opposing the tax is a fear of losing the lucrative profits for container manufacture and sale; conservationists assert that the tax would, in fact, stimulate greater use of returnable bottles and that it might even be desirable to ban all disposable containers.

Since state and local governments have an especially difficult time passing such tax legislation in the face of massive industry opposition, ecologists assert that Washington should take such measures and leave the states with no option but to comply.

2. *Increasing the economic attractiveness of recycled materials.* Here the federal government can take a number of immediate measures. One would be to eliminate the discriminatory freight rates for recycled materials enforced by federal agencies. Another step would be to eliminate or reduce the 15 per cent depletion allowance granted corporations for using virgin material and to combine this with tax incentives for using recycled materials. Washington might also subsidize the salvage of auto bodies and disposable metal containers to assure salvage companies at least a small profit on the work. Perhaps a "burial fee" might be paid to the automobile owner who turns in his auto to a scrap dealer rather than abandoning it; alternatively, a premium might be added to the price of a new car to defray the public expense involved when local governments must haul away abandoned automobiles. Citizens might be required to separate organic and inorganic garbage prior to collection, or the separation might be subsidized if local government takes the responsibility; in

either case, the cost of separation could be reduced, thereby cutting the price of recycled goods.

3. *Greatly increased funding for research in new disposal technologies.* To date, the only comprehensive federal policy that deals with disposal research is the Solid Waste Disposal Act of 1965. It instructed the departments of HEW, Agriculture, and the Interior to develop and demonstrate new collection and disposal techniques by increased research in refuse management problems.[8] Unfortunately, most of the responsibility for this research fell to the Bureau of Solid Waste Management, then in HEW; the bureau was underfunded and undervalued, shuttled about within the hierarchy of HEW and beset with morale and manpower problems. Now part of the new Environmental Protection Agency, the bureau has been somewhat reinvigorated by an anticipation of greater status and more appropriations.

What is the likelihood of any of these measures becoming law in the next few years? Environmentalists usually reply that the chances are almost zero. However obnoxious and urgent the solid-waste problem may be, it does not yet appear sufficiently life-threatening and therefore fails to arouse public concern on the scale pollution does. Public officials, always beset with the claims of many competing groups, have already given many environmental issues considerable attention and do not seem disposed to make yet another environmental matter a major issue when so many other conflicts have to be settled. And there is still land available to be filled. So the solid-waste problem is likely to languish, probably until the nation is literally buried in its own refuse.

Notes

1. *New York Times,* September 5, 1972.
2. This discussion is largely drawn from William E. Small, *Third Pollution* (New York: Praeger Publishers, 1971).
3. Rolf Eliassen, "Solid Waste Management," in Huey D. Johnson, ed., *No Deposit–No Return* (Reading, Mass.: Addison-Wesley, 1970), p. 57.
4. *Ibid.,* p. 63.
5. Council on Environmental Quality, *Environmental Quality, 1970* (Washington, D.C., 1970), pp. 118–19. See similar comments in the council's third annual report, *Environmental Quality, 1972,* pp. 204–6.
6. P.L. 91-512.
7. "A Pledge and a Promise" (Anheuser-Busch, Inc., 1972).
8. P.L. 89-272.

10 *The Future Fight for Environmental Planning*

No goal is more central to the environmental movement or more politically contentious than comprehensive environmental planning. If one looks upon current environmental policy struggles for a sign or portent of the future direction of environmental politics, the quest for planning appears constantly, albeit in different guises, as a common objective.

Environmentalists are forcing a major struggle, ranging across the whole scope of government, for environmental planning on a scale and with an authority never previously witnessed in American life; planning is becoming the central axis about which evolve the multitude of individual conflicts over particular environmental difficulties. This preoccupation is reflected in Lynton Caldwell's summary of the movement's objectives. "Unless the present course of human society is reversed by causes now unforeseen," he asserts, "the ultimate establishment of environmental administration as a major function of society seems inevitable."[1] This "environmental administration," he notes, must begin with a "national policy for the total environment."

Despite the welter of differing viewpoints over the details, environmentalists reach considerable accord on the broad requirements for such a national administration. First, the federal government must become the nation's comprehensive environmental planner. Washington must establish priorities for environmental protection, must calculate and create the "trade-offs" to be made between environmental protection and other national goals, and must plan resource use and protection over several generations. Indeed, as Donald Michael notes, whenever broad social problems must be met with complex, sophisticated technology, such as that required for environmental control, government is the institution most often involved in planning the national effort:

> One way or another, indeed in most ways, it will be government that promotes and implements specific technologies for specific social ends. . . . Only government is obligated and organized to serve the public interest and only it will have the enormous coordinating resources and funds required to carry out such plans even when private enterprise is the government's chosen vehicle for implementing specific programs.[2]

Among the difficulties it poses to public officials, planning forces them to grasp the nettle by abandoning the more politically expedient piecemeal decision-making common in the past, and to aggressively assert governmental power in vast areas of the economy that have been left largely free to private interests.

More than comprehensive planning is necessary. Environmentalists also believe that the national government itself must become more sensitive to the environmental impact of its own policies and more willing to sacrifice other objectives to environmental protection when good ecology dictates. In the past, the nation's governments—national, state, and local—have been potent environmental degraders because their planners usually treated the environmental consequence of policy as a "secondary effect"—unnoticed, unplanned, and seldom emphasized. Thus, officials viewed highway construction as an engineering and economic problem, licensed power-generating plants with meager attention to long-range resource planning, and promoted suburban growth without sensitivity for prudent land use. Whether through indifference, ignorance, or political expediency, public officials, by disregarding ecological values, established a highly stable formal and informal policy process that circumvented the environmental problems they were generating. To ecologists, any effort to create a new system of governmental environmental planning would be inadequate unless public officials charged with the nation's environmental management developed an ecological conscience themselves.

Not least important, to ecologists this must be coordinated planning within government. The common lack of such coordination has been so amply demonstrated that the evidence is almost a ritual in administrative reports. Part of this problem, notes the Council on Environmental Quality, is that environmental problems are not seen in their entirety, hence responsibility for their management is fragmented among federal agencies and among federal, state, and local governments. Fragmented authority, in turn, frustrates a wholistic view of environmental ills. The council describes the consequences:

> In the past, as problems have been perceived to be distinct issues rather than subparts of other problems, new departments and agencies have been created to deal with them. . . . Air pollution control problems historically have been the stepchild of health agencies and water pollution control programs the wards either of the same health agencies or of water resource agencies. Solid waste management was considered only an agricultural concern while environmental radiation was dealt with in the overall context of atomic energy.[3]

In the end, Washington works at cross-purposes. The Interior Department campaigns for solid-waste recycling while the Interstate Commerce Commission discriminates against the shipment of recycled materials. The Environmental Protection Agency urges state and local governments to discourage auto use, but Congress and the Department of Transportation expand the nation's highways through the multibillion-dollar Highway Trust Fund and thereby enhance motoring's appeal. It would be fanciful to expect contradictions in public policy to disappear entirely from any governmental system, regardless of administrative reforms. Environmentalists, however, believe that better coordination of federal environmental activity would greatly reduce the inconsistencies and produce better allocation of manpower and material for environmental management. The creation of the Environmental Protection Agency is regarded as a step in the right direction, pulling pollution control activities together within a single administrative unit. But a more comprehensive agency with still broader authority for total environmental planning is considered almost essential. The EPA and even a new National Resources Department such as that proposed by President Nixon for managing all government resource programs are both interim measures. What most environmentalists prefer is a "superagency" for all environmental planning.

National environmental planning that is comprehensive, coordinated, and sensitive to government's own environmental impact constitutes the framework of the ecologist's most sweeping political objectives. Environmentalists are often quick to emphasize that the nation will bear not only severe environmental costs for delaying such planning but will incur steep political economic costs as well. Generally, the longer the nation waits to create prudent environmental management, the fewer options will be available, the more authority government will have to possess, the higher will be the economic costs, and the more severe the solutions: Delay, in brief, leads to a situation increasingly close to crisis and requires the social costs of crisis management.[4] Following this logic, the long-range political consequence of failing to plan for electric power use today is likely to be the necessity to cut back power demand severely within a few decades; industrial development may have to be radically abated, unemployment might be severe, control measures might be extremely costly, and only a radical cutback is likely to work. Today, however, none of these social costs might be imposed if planning is started. Such projections about the future course of environmental affairs are always open to challenge, but they do emphasize that, in the absence of comprehensive planning, there might well be mounting social costs that have yet to be realistically calculated.

Viewed purely in the perspective of ecology or sound administration, these arguments might be persuasive. But there are massive practical impediments to implementing them. Quite apart from the technical problems involved in creating a proper administrative design for this planning, there are the political difficulties. We have already noted the heavy "sunk costs" that governmental agencies have invested in existing arrangements for environmental management. We have observed that the White

House and Congress view any proposal for environmental planning as a major political issue—a multitude of private interests involved in such planning must be weighed, their stake in present and future policy carefully assessed. The electoral costs of supporting or failing to support comprehensive plans must be pondered. State and local governments are bound to be affected in new ways by comprehensive planning and will make their influence felt in any quest for better environmental management. And comprehensive environmental planning is impossible without a collaboration among nations for environmental protection; the search for planning ultimately leads into the perilous domain of international politics and rivalries.

In spite of these obstacles, pressure for planning is growing. In political terms, the quest for planning has become not a single, decisive battle fought on one front but a series of engagements in different governmental theaters that aim at planned ecology as the final objective. Let us examine several of the planning conflicts likely to intensify in this decade.

Rich Nation's Ecology, Poor Nation's Ecology

The earth is one vast, interdependent ecosphere whose guardianship rests in the hands of over 120 more or less sovereign nations, each intensely suspicious of the other and jealous of its own power and privilege. Yet environmental protection does not respect political boundaries. Each nation has become both creator and victim of another's pollution, so that it is impossible for nations to protect their own environment without collaboration with the other; in the end, all nations are bound together by the interdependence of their ecological fate. Though some effective means of international collaboration for environmental control is imperative, it is a hard and tedious task. Not only are there the normal international rivalries and tensions to obstruct such collaboration. Overlaying all discussions of international environmental planning is the great social and economic disparity between the world's rich and poor nations, a cleavage that is the most fundamental political element in all discussions of international environmental protection. National planning for environmental protection cannot alone succeed in arresting the planet's environmental degradation, and so the quest for an international approach continues despite the obstacles.

International Degradation. No aspect of the world's environment better illustrates the need for global environmental collaboration than the problem of contaminated international waters. Ocean pollution is a multinational accomplishment. Inland water bodies such as the Baltic, Black, Mediterranean, and North seas are collectively degraded by many nations using their rivers as sewer pipes into international waters. More than twenty-one nations pour tons of pollutants daily into the Mediterranean; the Po and Rhone rivers, once the "lungs of the Mediterranean," whose generous flows were practically the only important source of the sea's renewal, now fill it largely with filth. The Atlantic and Pacific oceans are major global pollution problems. Almost all the petroleum polluting these seas is emitted from nations along their shores; the Rhine River alone empties 60 million tons of solids into the ocean yearly. The international pollution pouring into the Atlantic and Pacific is especially serious because the contamination is concentrated along the continental shelf. The ocean's shallow rim accounts for only one-tenth of the sea's area but produces almost all its food fish; experts suggest that if the shelf is not soon protected, the whole ocean will be gravely damaged.

Major rivers flowing through several nations are almost always contaminated collectively, so only collective measures are likely to solve the problem. Holland, for instance, receives most of the Rhine's considerable pollution from upstream nations; Rumania and Hungary, each heavily dependent on the murky Danube for almost all their water, are both victims of upstream pollution to which they make an additional contribution. This collective national degradation of the world's major rivers has reached the point where the United Nations Food and Agricultural Organization warns that river pollution is now "the greatest danger to humanity." There is, it concluded, "a widespread expectation of an inevitable exhaustion of rivers, and an awareness of the necessity to substitute new sources of water supply."[5]

Perhaps the need for international water protection is most strikingly illustrated by the building of Egypt's Aswan Dam, a monumental structure designed and constructed within the last two decades, when, one might suppose, technicians and public officials could be expected to demonstrate a sophisticated environmental understanding. The dam has become an ecological disaster. It drastically altered the Nile's flood plain and the flow of vital organic debris along its whole downstream course; sardine stocks in the eastern Mediterranean have been reduced, agricultural output has dropped along the entire Nile Valley, and the chronic parasite disease, schistosomiasis, is spreading in nations along the river. Americans have ample examples of internal water pollution close to home. Virtually all the Great Lakes have been polluted; the national boundary between the United States and Canada passes through four of the five lakes, so that not only the cause of the pollution but also its cure must involve both nations.

Water pollution is only one symptom of international environmental damage; there is also air pollution, pesticide dangers, surface-mine damage, forest abuse, and other ills whose creation and cure must depend upon multinational collaboration. Ultimately, many environmentalists assert, international population growth will bring the earth to desperate straits long before these other problems become mortal global threats. Pointing to studies such as the Club of Rome's *Limits of Growth,* which predicts a major world crisis in resource supply unless global population growth is diminished, many ecologists argue that population should be considered the world's first-order environmental problem. In the end, it matters little which problem is emphasized; they all point toward a need for international means to protect the environment if any nation is to enjoy environmental protection.

Against this ominous backdrop, it is understandable that American environmentalists have been anxious to launch the nation into a broad range of international efforts for environmental protection. However, this has proved to be an extremely demanding and often disappointing endeavor, for the quest runs hard against the deep, often bitter cleavage between the world's developed and underdeveloped nations over the means and ends of environmental control.

"A Growing Fear." Underdeveloped countries are customarily

poor in industry, pressed to feed burgeoning populations with lagging agricultural output, beset with widespread illiteracy, and afflicted with inadequate public health care; much of the population lives near subsistence level, and the nations generally suffer low economic productivity with their low capital production. Disparities between rich and poor nations are starkly emphasized in comparisons of gross national product (GNP), a measure of national prosperity. The eighty-seven underdeveloped nations of the world, with more than half the globe's 3 billion people, have an average GNP of only $174 per capita, while the world's twenty-five developed nations average $2,461 per capita.[6] For the majority of the world's nations, therefore, a major preoccupation has been to increase economic growth and production, thus creating circumstances congenial to growing education, better health care, shelter, and food production.

The advanced nations, having reaped the plentiful benefits of intensive industrialization, have now reckoned the environmental cost and decided that global industrialization is a major ecological threat. They press for limitations on world economic growth, for restrictions on further world resource depletion, and for population control. To the underdeveloped nations, industrialization is the *cure* for their environmental problems—illiteracy, hunger, poverty, and the rest; they consider ecological controls as a serious enemy of their national welfare. "The rich countries may look upon development as the cause of environmental destruction," explained India's Prime Minister Indira Gandhi recently, "but to us it is one of the primary means of improving the environment for living, of providing food, water, sanitation and shelter, of making the deserts green and the mountains habitable."[7] Most poorer nations fear that the richer ones will increasingly write restrictions into economic and technical assistance; underdeveloped countries, urgently needing this assistance, might then be forced to curtail industrial output and to engage in other practices satisfying to the ecological outlook of aid donors but detrimental to their own needs. Concluded a recent international conference: "There are growing fears in the developing world that the current environmental concern in the developed countries will affect them adversely in the fields of trade, aid, and transfer of ecology." This apprehension takes several forms:

Fear of "neoprotectionism." The affluent nations may discriminate in international trade against the productions of nations without acceptable environmental protection measures.

Fear that ecology may divert foreign aid funds. Many underdeveloped countries suspect that the growth of environmentalism among the developed nations will lead to greater diversion of funds from foreign aid to domestic environmental protection programs.

Fear of environmental chauvinism in conditions for aid. The nations donating economic and technical assistance may impose *their* environmental standards upon recipients when deciding what projects to underwrite. In the end, donors would prevent the poorer nations from deciding how best to use aid and what priority to assign ecology among many social needs.

Fear of undesirable technologies for exportation. As richer nations increasingly develop more nonpolluting technologies, there is a fear that these will be forced upon aid recipients, regardless of expense or suitability to the recipient nation.

This apprehension appeared almost paranoid at the first U.N. Conference on the Human Environment at Stockholm in 1972, a conference that displayed the manifold conflicts over ecology between the rich and poor nations. The underdeveloped nations controlled most formal conference deliberations with their numerical majority and stamped almost all discussions and reports with their suspicion of the environmental movement. The Conference's "Declaration on the Human Environment" was practically a catalogue of the underdeveloped countries' fears and a remarkably clear revelation of the rich-poor nation cleavage underlying world ecological discussions. At least eight of the twenty-six "principles" written into the Declaration were dictated by the underdeveloped countries to ensure that ecology would not become a restraint upon them. Among these eight principles were ones endorsing continued global economic development, encouraging economic and technical aid to the less developed countries, and condemning discrimination in world trade against less developed nations; the eleventh principle, however, best captured the essence of the poorer nation's ecological outlook:

> The environmental policies of all states should enhance and not adversely affect the present or future development potential of developing countries, nor should they hamper the attainment of better living conditions for all, and appropriate steps should be taken by states and international organizations with a view to reaching agreement on meeting the possible national and international economic consequences resulting from the application of environmental measures.

Many underdeveloped countries, notably those with prospects for immediate industrial growth, have made scant pretense of collaborating in any serious international pollution abatement schemes. None have been more candid than resource-rich Brazil. The Brazilian Government's position is that the industrialized nations are creating the world's current pollution and should attend to the problem of stopping it; Brazil, in any event, does not intend to slow its economic growth by restraining environmentally damaging industries. "Brazil can become the importer of pollution," states the nation's planning minister. "Why not? We have a lot left to pollute." Noting that Brazil recently welcomed a huge wood pulp processing plant in spite of its pollution potential, he concluded, "If we don't do it, some other country will."[8] Other countries are less pugnacious about their anti-environmentalism, but Mexico, Argentina, and numerous Afro-Asian nations are currently promoting heavy industrialization with full recognition of the ecological consequences. Other disadvantaged nations will be powerfully disposed to follow if they can. For these nations, apparently, the choice between economic growth and environmental protection is no choice at all.

The Developed Nations' Ecology. The United States, a leader among industrialized nations in their campaign for global environmental protection, reflects the ecological attitudes common to these countries. The irony of the affluent nations' late environmental consciousness is quite commonly the butt of criticism by their less endowed neighbors and places the United States and its allies in a compromising position. The United States, as we have often observed, had few environmental sensibilities when industrializing and, one suspects, would have found good reason to avoid an ecological conscience if the issue had been forced upon it in the manner it is now forced upon newer nations. The other industrial nations were little different. The Soviet Union, loath until recently to admit environmental ills, was so consumed with its own industrialization that it wreaked fearful damage upon land and resources. The infatuation with electrification, for instance, was so intense that Lenin minted a slogan: "Communism equals Soviet power plus electrification of the whole country," The attitude of Russia's economic planners is still a major problem, for they are heirs and disciples of this growth mania and resent restraints imposed in the name of environmental protection. Nonetheless, industrialized nations have been forced to invest increasing capital in environmental protection because their own mounting environmental degradation has forced their hand. It is the cost of this control and its trade implications, as much as an altruistic concern for ecology, that has shaped the affluent nations' interest in worldwide ecology.

In its quest for global environmental protection, the United States has pressed for uniform pollution standards among nations and has tried to restrict the development of environmentally damaging projects financed through aid to underdeveloped countries; it has encouraged greater international collaboration in combating pollution of international resources and has sought restrictions upon world resource use and population growth. None of these objectives are easily or quickly attained. World pollution standards are very difficult to establish because nations disagree about the proper standards for protecting life and property and about the importance of these ends in comparison to economic growth; further, nations disagree about what use is to be assigned to given resources, and this affects definitions of "pollution." Not least important, nations are jealous of their own sovereignty and fiercely resist schemes that seem to impose the authority of outside agencies upon them. Efforts to limit resource use—and to control population especially—often generate intense resentment among the disadvantaged nations. When the developed nations speak of population control, remarked a spokesman for a Latin American government, it almost seems as if the developed nations believe they "have demonstrated, by their development, a special right to salvation and perpetuation, thus passing on to the more numerous underdeveloped peoples the responsibility for creating the necessary space on earth."[9]

There are very pragmatic economic calculations behind developed nations' attitude toward pollution control. The United States has repeatedly expressed a fear that the less developed nations may become "pollution havens" where major industries will flock in preference to the countries that impose costly pollution controls upon them. This might mean that firms operating in the United States, or other nations with pollution controls, would suffer competitively in international trade; firms operating in environmentally minded nations would have to add the cost of pollution controls to their goods, which would then be overpriced in comparison to goods from nations where no pollution control costs are imposed. The United States and other industrialized nations have urged all countries to follow a "polluter pays" rule in which the cost of pollution control must be reflected in the price of products. This would prevent a nation from subsidizing its industry for pollution control expenses and then dumping goods on the international market that were underpriced in comparison to those from countries where pollution control costs were largely borne by industry. Although the United States and its allies were unsuccessful in keeping many objectionable resolutions from inclusion in the final "Statement of Principles" of the 1972 Stockholm Conference, there is no doubt that the industrial nations will still attempt to tie their economic and technical assistance to the developing nations to environmental controls that will prevent the newer states from becoming "pollution havens."

The Impasse of Global Ecology. The Stockholm Conference is an object lesson in the impediments to international environmental protection. Only slightly less glaring than the conflict between rich and poor nations over environmentalism was the reluctance of most nations to sacrifice any national interest to world environmental protection. Japan, notwithstanding its official representative's assurance that his people "have for centuries loved nature and lived in harmony with nature," could not bring itself to endorse an international ban on whale killing because it is the last major whaling-nation. While Mainland China thundered against the reckless environmental exploitation in the industrialized countries, it would not vote to ban atmospheric nuclear testing for ecological protection. The United States did not consider its deliberate ecological devastation in Vietnam to be a suitable topic for the conference. Against such a background, it is obvious that only modest, tentative advances toward a global strategy of environmental management are possible.

Some limited progress has been made. One promising start is the recommendation of the Stockholm Conference, likely to be acted opon favorably by the United Nations, that a small, permanent U.N. agency concerned with environmental problems be created. Significantly, the agency's purpose would be confined to directing financial and technical help to countries seeking aid and to coordinating the U.N.'s own scattered environmental programs; it would in no sense be an "action" agency with broad powers to accomplish environmental management anywhere. More noteworthy is the effort of several international lending agencies, which channel economic and technical assistance from developed to underdeveloped countries, to impose modest environmental standards upon projects—a procedure easier to achieve because these agencies represent developed nations and operate outside direct U.N. supervision. Recently, the World Bank, U.S. Agency for International Development, and other lending institutions in Sweden and Great Britain have formulated guidelines requiring recipients to meet some pollution control standards for most projects. The most impressive international accomplishment to date, however, has been the ninety-one-nation agreement to limit the dumping of poisonous wastes in the ocean, the first operational accord for environmental protection with massive support. These events, though helpful, represent only tentative beginnings toward international environmental management.

Despite such occasional evidence of international cooperation, most of the collaboration between developed and underdeveloped nations still consists of the exchange of technical data and statements of broad, largely unimplemented principles. Collaboration beyond this point has been largely confined to the developed countries; indeed, almost all international agreements negotiated by the United States and aimed at operational programs have involved other industrialized countries. In 1972, for instance, the United States signed an agreement with the Canadian Government committing both nations to a heavy technical and financial investment in cleaning up the Great Lakes; shortly afterward, another treaty was signed with the Soviet Union to exchange technical and financial information about eleven common environmental problems.

Thus, global environmental planning is barely beyond the talking stage. Even without the participation of the underdeveloped nations, the world's major industrial powers can advance far in a short-term reduction of world environmental devastation, since they create much of the present problem. But as industrialization spreads and the world's entire ecosystem becomes increasingly degraded through the inevitable spread of pollution everywhere, the need for global environmental management enlisting all nations will intensify. Ultimately, a scheme for world environmental management will become as urgent as the present imperative for national measures among the developed countries.

The Battle over the NEPA

Although a global system of environmental planning is only a vision buoyed by a battered hope, a crude framework for national environmental planning is beginning to emerge in the United States. With the passage of the National Environmental Policy Act of 1969 (NEPA), Washington appeared to move, albeit slowly, toward a comprehensive design for environmental policy-making. It is intended to force upon federal officials a greater sensitivity to the environmental impact of their work, to commit them to environmental protection, and to make them liable to citizen action to enforce this responsibility. This falls short of comprehensive environmental planning—it does not, for instance, establish any national planning agency or ordain priorities and goals for environmental usage—but, if faithfully executed, it would be one foundation upon which a comprehensive national planning system could be erected.

The NEPA, however, cuts deeply across the bias in much Presidential behavior, Congressional interest, and administrative habit. If enforced, it compels administrations to rethink programs, reorganize decision-making, and, in some instances, abandon or severely modify past agency policies and established understandings with Congress and clientele interests. Congress, traditionally demonstrating low environmental sensibilities, would have to examine legislation with an eye to environmental consequences and, perhaps, to change its policy priorities and, with them, the balance of interests indulged by legislators. The President would also be affected for, like Congress, his room for political maneuver would be constricted as environmental values intruded on past understandings and commitments to interests and programs. Understandably, the NEPA has generated numerous efforts to undercut its effectiveness; this pressure is both open and covert, blatant and subtle, at many points within government and among interests affected by it. The proponents and opponents of the NEPA are currently engaged in a conflict to determine how potent the NEPA will be. This is a critical struggle; the outcome may largely determine whether the NEPA is truly a first step toward national environmental planning or an abortive reform.

"A National Policy for the Environment." It is one of the curiosities of the legislative process that the NEPA exists. Despite the enormous criticism and discomfort it has generated among many legislators and administrators and notwithstanding its unprecedented substance and scope, it passed Congress with extraordinary swiftness, stirring scarcely a ripple of debate. Congress, it appears, only dimly perceived the consequences of this legislation, even though it wrote a bill that, on its face, fashioned a new environmental policy in broad, vigorous language. Congress declared its intention to do nothing less than encourage harmony between man and nature, promoting efforts to eliminate or prevent environmental damage and "to enrich the understanding of the ecological system and natural resources im-

portant to man." This, declared Congress, would henceforth govern all federal actions. This might have been only a statement of eloquent and airy intentions had not Congress also written into the NEPA its Section 102, requiring that all federal agencies henceforth must write an "impact statement" assessing in detail the environmental consequences of any "major federal action significantly affecting the environment." By writing this requirement, Congress created an "action-forcing" mechanism that could virtually compel administrators to examine the environmental consequences of their actions and to see that they were consistent with the intentions of the bill. Since other provisions of the NEPA created a procedure for reviewing these statements not only within agencies but also at the Congressional and White House level, the impact statements might lead to a revision or cancellation of programs not only by the agencies themselves but by Presidential or Congressional action.

To better appreciate the potentially great importance of the NEPA, one needs to examine briefly what specific changes it promises in federal policy-making. To begin, it issues a categorical directive that all federal policy—whether Congressional, Presidential, or administrative in origin—must now "to the fullest extent possible" be made and interpreted in such a way that it is consistent with the broad purpose of the NEPA; federal decisions might now be challenged in the courts by citizens, environmental groups, or others on grounds that they do not meet this requirement. The language of the NEPA also insists that federal agencies which in the past have not been required to consider the environmental impact of their policies must now do so. Further, agencies whose mandates previously required a rather narrow consideration of environmental consequences—such as agencies expected only to consider how their actions affected human health—must now consider all important environmental impacts. Also, this extensive reflection on environmental matters must not only extend to programs directly implemented by federal agencies but also include an environmental study of activities licensed or otherwise indirectly affected by agency policy. Finally, agencies are expected to create *new* policies to further the purpose of the act.

For most federal administrators, the most important effect of the NEPA was to require their creation of "impact statements" for all "major federal action significantly affecting the environment." As we saw earlier, this must contain (1) an assessment of the environmental impact of the proposed action, (2) a clear statement of unavoidable environmental impacts, (3) alternatives to the proposed action, (4) a judgment of the short-term impact of the policy weighed against the long-term use of the environment, and (5) an inventory of irreversible and irretrievable resource commitments involved in the action. The act requires that such statements be prepared in time for careful public review, for inspection by other agencies affected by the policy, and, finally, for review by the Council on Environmental Quality.

The significance of these impact statements rests not solely in their influence upon individual administrators who may alter their own policies (or be forced to change them by superiors) after a review of the statements. The statements force an operational procedure for considering environmental consequences of policy upon the one branch of the federal government that is likely to have the greatest continuing responsibility for creating, implementing, and refining environmental policy in the future: As we have seen, environmental policy is increasingly becoming administrative policy. Moreover, the courts have interpreted the NEPA to mean that citizens are permitted to challenge administrative decisions judicially if they believe federal officials did not properly discover and weigh the environmental consequences of their decisions; this does provide a means by which environmentalists can force administrative decisions affecting the environment into the open for public scrutiny. Not least important, challenging administrative decisions in this manner is a powerful weapon for obstructing and delaying the administrative process. Administrators can be forced to bargain and compromise with ecologists if they are to proceed quickly with administrative matters. In brief, the NEPA's impact statement gives environmentalists new access to the bureaucracy and new weapons for political in-fighting.

The counterattack against the NEPA, aimed primarily at its impact-statement requirement, has been provoked because the

NEPA has proved in the few years since its enactment to be an action-forcing mechanism. More than two hundred suits in federal court have already challenged, and in some cases overturned, administrative decisions on grounds of improper impact statements. In particular, a number of water resource projects sponsored by the Corps of Engineers and federal licenses for airports, power generating plants, and housing projects have been delayed or suspended, hitting Congress directly in the pork barrel and evoking protestations from the groups promoting such undertakings. Many more projects have been permanently stopped when administrators did reflect upon their environmental impact. A highway bridge across San Francisco Bay was shelved by the Coast Guard after an impact statement had been evaluated; the Corps of Engineers stopped a channelization of a bayou near Houston when its undesirable aesthetic effects were known. No accurate tabulation of federal projects suspended, canceled, or revised as a result of impact statement requirements is available, but the Council on Environmental Quality, estimating that impact statements have probably affected "thousands of decisions," has already concluded that the NEPA "has gone far toward fulfilling its promise as one of the major pieces of governmental reform legislation in decades."[10] Understandably, the legislators and private groups partisan to projects and programs adversely affected by the NEPA have often been critical of the legislation and forceful in demanding its revision or repeal—in which demand they are often joined by administrative agencies and bureaucrats whose own programs are jeopardized as well. Arrayed in varying combinations, this phalanx of hostile forces is currently working vigorously to diminish the NEPA's authority. Considered alongside the many other factors that might undercut the NEPA's strength, this attack makes the legislation vulnerable to severe emasculation.

The Unmaking of the NEPA. The most forthright campaign against the NEPA has been the effort to cripple or eliminate Section 102 emanating from Congress and principally involving legislators with pork-barrel projects delayed or scuttled by the act. One hotbed of dissatisfaction with Section 102 is the House Public Works Committee, a frequent promoter of water resource developments and the authorizing committee for all such undertakings. Several committee members, incensed by citizen suits using the NEPA to suspend federal projects (those "insipid and multitudinous suits," fumed one member), have proposed several strategies for circumventing the legislation. One proposal is to exempt each Congressionally authorized public works project from Section 102 individually; another is to exclude whole programs, such as the highway program or all rivers and harbors projects, from Section 102's ambit. More ingenious was a suggestion that the committee flood administrative agencies with requests for impact statements on each project proposed to the committee, creating such a bureaucratic backlash that administrators would readily join Congress in demanding a change in Section 102.

Among the many strategies that might relax Section 102's stringent provisions, those designed to exempt individual projects or whole programs from Section 102 have good prospects for success. There is considerable support for such proposals, not merely from aggrieved Congressmen but from influential Administration spokesmen urging revision of the NEPA for other reasons. Both the chairman of the Council on Environmental Quality, Russell E. Train, and the Environmental Protection Agency's administrator, William D. Ruckelshaus, have noted that the federal courts are interpreting Section 102 so rigorously that many vital federal programs, including the licensing of power generating plants and the issuance of industrial permits for pollution in navigable waters, have been almost immobilized while the long procedure for preparing impact statements is completed; they argue that such essential programs cannot be delayed and ought to be implemented, if necessary, by excluding them from Section 102. Environmental lobbyists have resolutely fought efforts to exclude any federal program from Section 102, even though they recognize that some crucial federal projects might be delayed while impact statements are being prepared. Environmentalists assert that a delay in essential programs, though troublesome, is preferable to creating a precedent for excluding programs from the NEPA; the exclusion, they believe, would quickly provoke such a host of further exclusions as to render Section 102 impotent in short order.

Within the administrative branch, many agencies unsympathetic to Section 102 have blunted its impact. Undercompliance and overcompliance have both been used as weapons. With the exception of the Department of Transportation and the Corps of Engineers, most federal agencies have been tardy in filing impact statements; the Corps and the Transportation Department together accounted for almost all the impact statements filed with the CEQ during the first three years of the NEPA's existence, leaving all the remaining federal agencies to account for only a fourth of all impact statements—a meager eight hundred documents. In a great many agencies, concludes the Council on Environmental Quality, "the question is not whether the goals of NEPA are being implemented effectively but whether they are being implemented at all."[11] The Department of Transportation, according to one member of the Council on Environmental Quality, has frustrated the purpose of Section 102 by "snowing us under with mountains of paper on every six-block paving project in the country." Such overcompliance has thus far been unique to that agency, but it represents a tactic that might be employed to good effect by other agencies.

There are other ways through which the intent of the NEPA can be defeated or badly compromised. One potentially great impediment to the NEPA can be the administrative discretion in interpreting it. We have often noted that great discretion must be delegated to administrators in implementing most legislation, and the NEPA is no exception. Indeed, discretion plays a particularly great part in determining NEPA's effectiveness, for the law is quite vague and the legislative record that might shed light on the intent of its drafters is unusually spare. All federal agencies, for example, have been left with considerable freedom in deciding which of their actions are "major federal actions significantly affecting the environment," to which Section 102 statements apply. The CEQ is supposed to advise agencies concerning when statements are required and how to prepare them, but it has a small staff and a huge workload; it must often rely on the good faith and judgment of agency officials to assure that environmentally important programs do indeed receive impact statements. The CEQ must also depend on administrators to see that impact statements are circulated to concerned parties early enough in the decision-making process to be a significant factor in the outcome. Administrators charged with implementing the NEPA must often be the final judges in assuring that their agencies have considered opposing views on proposed undertakings, have carefully weighed the alternatives to a proposed policy, and have "balanced" opposing interests in reaching a decision on environmentally related policies.

The administrator's importance in all this is heightened by the courts' attitude toward impact statements. The courts have taken a very cautious view of their role when environmentalists have challenged the preparation of impact statements because they allegedly failed to conform to the requirements of Section 102. Generally, federal jurists have been reluctant to investigate deeply into the substance of an impact statement so long as they are convinced that a reasonable effort to include important information has been made. Also, federal judges—demonstrating the courts' traditional aversion to substituting its judgment for that of an administrator on a "policy" question—have declared that they will not overturn administrative decisions to which impact statements apply unless an administrator's misinterpretation of the law can be demonstrated; this means, in effect, that environmentalists cannot use judicial means to counteract an administrative judgment simply because they believe an administrator made an environmentally unwise policy.

Congressional hostility, lukewarm administrative support, the vagaries of the administrative process, and judicial problems—these by no means exhaust the factors that can collectively sap the NEPA of its vigor, but they do indicate how uncertain is the future course of this potentially vital environmental legislation. When it was first enacted, many environmentalists spoke of the NEPA grandly as "An Environmental Bill of Rights." Clearly, such praise was premature, for the NEPA's full promise will be realized, if ever, only after a long, arduous struggle over many years and against many foes.

Putting the Reins on Growth

In their quest for environmental planning, ecologists have taken dead aim on the growth psychology deeply imbedded in American character and culture. "Each increment of the gross national product has gone hand in hand with a decrease in the livability of our cities and the cleanliness of the overall environment," asserts former Secretary of the Interior Stewart L. Udall. "It is little wonder that we are beginning to call into question the assumption that the present pattern of economic expansion can continue indefinitely."[12] The movement's reservations about unrestrained economic growth, arising from a recognition that most environmental problems are created or intensified by such activity, are beginning to be echoed in other quarters. Many public officials, as a rule extraordinarily circumspect about utterances that seem to oppose a healthy economy, have nonetheless made cautious references to the need for future restraints upon the nation's economic growth. "The American economy is now increasingly faced with changing values which call for changes in resource commitments," notes the Council on Environmental Quality. "Greater attention to the environment will result in taking more of the increase in productivity in the form of enhanced environmental quality."[13]

President Nixon, while carefully avoiding a direct reference to inhibitions on economic growth in the 1972 Message on the Environment, nonetheless advised Congress to look into the relationship between the nation's economy and its environmental problems. The "incentives and disincentives built into our economic system," he noted, should be considered when attempting to remedy environmental destruction. Even some parts of the American business community appear willing to recognize that unbridled economic growth and environmental protection are incompatible. "Isn't it time to examine the growth syndrome that we have had in our country?" asked the president of the nation's largest electric utility recently. Environmentalists might consider such a sentiment from this source to be suspect indeed, yet newborn concern with unbridled economic growth among government officials and business leaders cannot be dismissed entirely as a passing fancy or pretense.

Environmentalists can agree upon the needs for economic restraints but not upon the formula. Some impassioned ecologists have opted for a "no-growth" gospel, vehemently pressing upon businessmen, government officials, and the public their exhortations that the American economy be held at a steady state with little if any future expansion. Whatever its theoretical appeals—and they are highly debatable—such a proposal has virtually no prospect of success and diverts many conservationists from the task of finding a more practical formula compatible with political and economic possibilities in the nation. Many leaders concerned with environmental preservation have advocated a more realistic strategy of "controlled" growth. Rather than advocating untenable proposals to arrest all economic expansion, they suggest selective governmental planning by which public planners would slow growth in some economic sectors, perhaps arrest growth in others, while imposing few restrictions in still other sectors; which sectors would be subject to varying restraint would, according to this logic, be determined with reference to future environmental needs. Controlled growth is a sufficiently ample and vague concept to permit considerable disagreement among its advocates over the proper economic sectors for regulation, the proper timing and degree of constraints. Nonetheless, some governmentally directed, selective inhibition upon economic expansion is advocated in principle by almost all leaders concerned with environmental safety.

Even modest restraints upon future economic growth, imposed in the name of ecology, will be difficult. Clearly, economic expansion has been the orthodoxy of American economists, the unquestioned premise of business and political leaders, the alpha and omega of community developers; it will not be easy to engineer a sudden reorientation. Moreover, American business often overreacts to most proposals for economic restraint, tending to treat them all indiscriminately as a portent of impending national economic disaster. ("All in favor of unemployment, please rise," began a recent oil company advertisement in major national newspapers and magazines. "It's impossible to get many people to stand up and be counted in favor of breadlines. But it's just as difficult to get some people to see the connection between economic growth and full employment.") Public officials, often convinced that uninhibited growth is a sovereign cure for social ills and very reluctant to advocate policies without substantial public support, will often repeat such dire warnings about economic controls. "Never has growth been more important," argued the Secretary of the Treasury in a recent paean to expansion. "You can never feed the poor or ease the lives of the wage earning families, ameliorate the problems of race or solve the problems of pollution without real growth."[14] There may well be, moreover, tangible costs to the consumer in economic restraints; these might vary from mild inconvenience to temporary unemployment or economic dislocations in a community—all certain to increase public reluctance to embrace controlled growth as a national policy.

The task of creating controls can be appreciated by examining several areas of the economy where the ecological reasons for restraint are compelling and the struggle for economic restraints will be waged in the 1970's; the outcome is likely to determine the ability of environmentalists to press further restraints upon growth. Many general problems in growth limitation can be seen by turning to current efforts to limit the growth of the electric power industry and to control community land development, both of which present problems typical of the battle for bridling the nation's economy.

Pulling the Plug. Those concerned with limited economic growth turn naturally to electric utilities as one American industry ripe for controls. The power producers are a strong stimulant to expansion of the whole fossil fuel complex and an important determinant of the growth in most other sectors of the American economy that depend on electricity. Unless the mounting demand for electric power is somehow abated, a severe depletion of fuel resources seems likely in the future, together with grave environmental damage. According to a recent Rand Corporation study, unless California decreases its projected power demands by 60 per cent between now and the year 2000, severe environmental damage will result; if the plants needed to meet this uncontrolled power demand were built where they are customarily planned, California would have a major power-generating site every eight miles down its coast from the Oregon border to Mexico. With present national demands for electricity expected to grow by three or four times by the turn of the century, California's future, according to most experts, would be no worse than that facing most other heavily populated states.

Despite a compelling case for some restraint, it will be difficult. To begin, the industry has a jaundiced view of governmental restrictions upon its growth and works through its major trade associations, including particularly the American Power Association, to thwart growth limitations. The industry is not insensitive to its environmental impact but advocates more effort to develop pollution control, more efficient fuel conversion, and better transmission techniques as a cure for its ecological problems instead of constraints upon its expansion. It prefers, additionally, that the capital to finance this massive research undertaking come directly or indirectly from government (in the form of tax incentives or subsidies) or from the electricity consumer (in the form of a premium on his bill) rather than from its own capital. The industry's aversion to controlled growth is made even more politically potent by the support it receives from the whole fuel complex—the gas, oil, and petroleum industries—whose economic fortunes are bound together with the power industry's. Since a change in the power industry's growth rate would have profound implications for the fuel complex, this vast aggregation of huge corporations tends to support the power companies' desire for uninterrupted expansion.

Changing the growth pattern of the electric power companies would mean, as well, a major alteration in present federal power policy to which many governmental agencies and Congressmen are deeply committed. The Federal Power Commission, responsible for enforcing federal controls on electric utilities, has been charged by the Federal Power Act to ensure that "an abundant supply of electric energy throughout the U.S." is always available, a responsibility that admirably suits the growth bias of the power companies and has long motivated the commission to encourage the industry's expansion. The commission will not even discourage promotional advertising among power companies, though it recognizes that many utilities have almost reached the limits of their generating capacities. Other federal regulations encourage the industry's growth. A public utility's permissible earnings are set by federal law as a fixed percentage of its invested capital; further growth means more invested capital and higher permitted earnings. Federal law generally endorses a policy of the most power for the least money, providing an incentive for power companies to offer lower rates for large power users; when the power industry's growth appears to outrun its fuel supplies, federal policy has been to increase the sources of fuel rather than to restrain the industry's demands for it. Given the present governmental commitment to promoting electric power and the powerful alliance of private interests that joins public officials in the endeavor, it is hardly surprising that one recent governmental study concluded that any significant change in federal power policy was unlikely "until a very sizable constituency favoring decisive action" emerges. Such a "sizable constituency"—composed, presumably, of environmentalists and their allies—will not be any easier to create when the public becomes aware that restraints on the power industry are likely to mean not only restraints upon corporate use of electricity but upon per capita electric consumption as well.

These impediments to regulating power consumption might be insurmountable if the demand for electric power and the environmental degradation from generating sites were not rising so steeply that the control issue is being forced upon even reluctant public officials and business leaders. Public officials, in short, are being crowded into confronting the power issue and will have to deal with it within this decade. They will be faced with a number of proposals, several of which have already been made by environmentalists at many governmental levels. One such proposal is that the federal government compel electric utilities to charge higher rates for higher power consumption; this might deflate private and industrial power demands in the future and would certainly reverse the tendency of most communities to encourage industrialization by offering preferential utility rates to large power consumers. Another frequent proposal is that utilities charge premiums upon power used during the peak-load periods, when power capacities are strained; this would encourage a more even power demand over long time periods and reduce the pressure to expand generating plants to meet increasing peak-load requirements. Most experts concerned with power regulation also believe that the cost of pollution control equipment and the cost of environmental damage attributable to electric power generation should be passed to the consumer in the form of higher electric rates; this higher electric bill, which would more realistically reflect the social costs of power generation, might decrease electricity's present appeal to consumers.

Almost all environmentalists would like to see some shackles upon the largely unregulated promotional advertising common to the electric utilities; they argue that the utilities incessantly, persuasively promote their product, create high demand for their services, and then use the demand as a justification for their continuing expansion to meet "consumer needs." Why not, suggest these critics, end the advertising for "all-electric living," with all the glamorous embellishments, that the industry has so long relied upon to escalate its sales. Finally, proposals have been made that governmental bodies set limits on the permissible power consumption in American homes.

Since the power industry is largely unreceptive to these proposals—it favors present federal policy encouraging growth through expanding fuel supplies and more efficient pollution controls—the stage is set within this decade for a prolonged, politically intense conflict between environmentalists and the electric utilities, with profound implications for the nation's future. If some restraints on the present rate of the industry's growth cannot be engineered through political means, we may face an extremely grave environmental crisis attributable to our insatiable appetite for power before the turn of the century.

Controlling Land Use

In 1971 and again in 1972, President Nixon proposed to an unresponsive Congress that the federal government create a National Land Use Act that, for the first time, would bring heavy federal pressure upon state and local governments to protect environmentally important land and to control unbridled land development. "We have come to view our land as a limited and irreplaceable resource. No longer do we imagine that there will always be more of it over the horizon," noted the President. Then he came to the nub of the forthcoming political struggle: "We must create the administrative and regulatory mechanism necessary to assure wise land use and to stop haphazard, wasteful or environmentally damaging development."

What the President clearly envisioned was a strong federal presence in future land-use decisions at all the nation's governmental levels, an "administrative and regulatory mechanism," which meant an unprecedented federal intrusion into areas of environmental policy-making heretofore reserved largely to state and local government. Such a proposal, coming from a Chief Executive normally reluctant to assert vast federal powers in the domain of state and local government and generating enormous resistance from a multitude of private and public sources, testifies to the gravity of the nation's land-use problems. That Congress did not respond is understandable, given the complexity of the political struggle and the hostile forces aligned against a strong federal role in land use. But Congressional passivity has done nothing to abate the pressure from environmentalists for greater governmental regulation of land use, especially from Washington. Not only has imprudent land use created many major environmental problems, but the commercial and residential development of land has been a major component in the nation's whole growth surge.

The scope of land-use problems in the nation is vast indeed. As we have seen, it includes questions about the proper uses of the public domain, the development of wetlands, the planning of core cities, the growth of suburbs, the disappearance of open spaces, and much else. Those concerned with land-use planning believe that several of these issues are especially acute; they are likely to be the focus of land-use controversies in the immediate future.

What Must Be Controlled. Environmentalists are increasingly advocating comprehensive community planning. To numerous ecologists, many of the most injurious land-use practices in the nation are attributable to thoughtless, random community development in which decisions about the use of land are left largely to the autonomous power of industry, commercial and residential developers, and private citizens, with only minimal and often ineffective governmental intervention. In essence, environmentalists maintain that too many communities have been planned by default, their "design" being the composite of the haphazard, ecologically insensitive decisions of private groups and public agencies working without a comprehensive concept of how communities should develop and when they should stop.

Specifically, ecologically minded planners point to several characteristic failures in community design. The core city is often permitted to become an aging, decaying example of bad economic and environmental planning. Noise, visual pollution, loss of amenities, the intrusion of environmentally contaminating industry, and the all but sovereign control of open space by automobiles are compounded by the changing socio-economic composition of the core city's population—producing a depressed (and depressing) deterioration of once attractive inner-city environments. The suburbs, doubling in population during the last twenty years and consuming a half-million additional acres each year, have absorbed most of the massive middle-class migration from the city, with comparatively little attention paid to the environmental consequences. Often, suburbs simply followed the radiation of highways without any anticipatory planning for their growth or consideration about the desirability of growth in this manner.

As suburbs expand, their incorporation usually produced only minimal zoning practices and other local government controls on land use. Most communities, for example, have few governmental restraints upon the size, location, or composition of commercial signs and other advertising; ordinances that impose some landscaping requirements upon commercial and private land developers are often absent or weak. Many communities, anxious for economic development, permitted undesirable juxtaposition of commercial and industrial activities next to residential housing;

often, service industries have been permitted to locate in such concentration that many suburban traffic lanes are throughways between curb-to-curb franchises in garish array.

While the absence of controls upon advertising, landscaping, and commercial development detracts severely from the amenities of suburban living, more profound environmental consequences have also followed suburban growth. Developers are often permitted to strip land of trees and other cover, to build upon scenic and irreplaceable land sites, to dredge and fill streams and wetlands with little restraint. Building upon flood plains—common in many communities when the pressure for residential development becomes massive—has exposed many homeowners to flooding and other water hazards that inevitably cause considerable expense to local government when the damage must somehow be controlled. Equally important is the mounting loss of open space and the disappearance of "green belts" around many communities, a loss explained by local government's reluctance to limit further suburban growth and by the fact that agricultural land and other open space is often taxed in a manner that makes its owners anxious to sell to developers when attractive offers are made.

This brief survey is only a partial inventory of the environmental problems created or aggravated by unplanned community development, but it does suggest why community design occupies such a prominent place in the ecologist's vision of controlled growth. Since many of these ills concerned urban specialists long before ecologists looked upon them as an environmental problem, a great many proposals for their cure have already been made. Let us examine several general proposals for community management, taken from a vast array, which help to explain the political divisions that commonly appear when community growth is discussed.

What Might Be Done. Among the many ways in which environmental degradation from community growth might be reduced, several are proposed with great frequency; indeed, some have already been successfully tried in many communities. These include:

1. *Ordinances against "visual pollution," excessive noise, and other loss of amenities.* Community governments have the right, as an exercise of their police powers, to regulate the size and placement of signs and other advertising. They can set standards for permissible noise levels within their jurisdiction, providing the laws are not arbitrary, too vague, or unenforceable. Local government can, as well, require a great variety of landscaping practices in order to permit building or renovation of land within their control. Restrictions upon the use of automobiles and other transportation within cities is equally permissible.

2. *Strict zoning codes built around a comprehensive land-use plan.* The power to zone is the power to specify how land will be used—in effect, to determine when and how a community will develop. While most communities now have zoning plans, they are often made without attention to good environmental planning, are too often susceptible to compromise when they offend local economic powers, and are seldom made *after* a master plan for community development is created. Zoning plans are too often made in response to immediate community needs, too seldom after long-range designs for community development have been considered and chosen.

3. *Control of obvious environmental degradation.* Communities can pass "flood plain ordinances," which prevent or restrict the residential and commercial development of flood plains. Builders and homeowners can be compelled to hook into sewers and to practice other anti-pollution measures as a condition for obtaining and using land. Trees can be protected by law from uncontrolled cutting on residential or commercial property. Scenic areas can be declared off limits for any development.

4. *Tax incentives to keep land undeveloped.* The tax practices of state and local government, however unintentionally, are usually discriminatory against open land; most often, owners of agricultural land or open space near communities have incentives to sell to commercial developers. Methods for land valuation and taxation can be, and have been, created to give owners of open space an economic incentive to keep the land out of development.

5. *Discouragement of growth.* This is the least palatable suggestion for most communities and undoubtedly the most difficult to

implement politically; it is not, however, difficult to find the means to implement such a scheme. Growth can be inhibited through deliberate community efforts to discourage new industry, through limitations on the provision of utilities and other governmental services, through strict zoning laws that discourage high-density housing and prevent large increases in residential or commercial development of existing lands.

These proposals, any of which has countless variations, fall into a rough order from the least to most difficult politically; relatively many communities have been able to control amenities through sign ordinances, landscape controls, and the like; almost none have embarked upon a deliberate plan to discourage growth. None, however, is easily attained. The reason why uncontrolled and uncoordinated community development is still prevalent in the United States can be discovered in the political problems posed by this kind of community management.

The Politics of Land Use. Except for the public domain controlled by Washington, land use is determined primarily by state and local government with some federal participation. Local governments often exercise almost unrestricted freedom to ordain how land within their jurisdictions will be used. Many land-use problems arise, or worsen, from the multiplicity of governmental units with land-use powers; more than 81,000 local governmental bodies, uncounted special districts, and fifty state governments claim some of this authority. Prudent land planning often requires the cooperation and coordination of an enormous number of these units; especially when planning is considered on a community or regional basis—often a sensible procedure ecologically—the task of bringing together the many local governments that divide the area jurisdictionally is enough to discourage the enterprise. Moreover, local governments are often unenthusiastic about collaborative planning. They may be competitors for tax dollars and public support, extremely suspicious that land planning may benefit other governments at their expense; they may be inspired by inconsistent or contradictory land-use philosophies—a frequent occurrence when one government represents a growth-minded constituency while another does not. Inner-city governments and the suburban governments surrounding them often have differing priorities for land use. In many ways, therefore, the extreme decentralization of land-use power in the United States represents a case of fragmented governmental powers and inadequate governmental organization in the face of a pervasive environmental problem.

Local governments, however, are commonly slow to use the powers they do possess when it seems to delay community expansion. Part of this behavior is motivated by the constant pressure upon local government to increase its tax base to generate the revenues for numerous local services increasing in demand and expense. Then, too, the elective policy-making bodies of many local governments are dominated by men and women whose businesses prosper with community expansion—bankers, savings and loan officials, real estate people, small businessmen, land developers, and others from service industries. Often, even conservation-minded public officials have difficulty resisting large industries whose bid to move into their communities is almost always accompanied with projections of new "growth." Once growth industries become established within communities—particularly when they are the foundation of the local economy or dominate local politics—it becomes extremely difficult to create land-use practices and other policies inhospitable to further growth. In the end, no doubt, putting checks on community growth is also difficult because the benefits of growth seem tangible, immediate, and pervasive in a community, while the benefits of environmental protection seem more diffuse, indirect, and problematical. For all these reasons and more, the U.S. Conference of Mayors recently concluded, "Local officials tend to think of growth as being virtually the sole criterion of economic health and their economic programs are dedicated almost exclusively to growth."[15]

Given the high esteem in which "growthmanship" is held at the local level, many advocates of strict land-use management believe the most satisfactory method of obtaining rapid land control is to vest the authority and responsibility in the hands of state and federal officials—in effect, to end the nation's traditionally great decentralization in land management and commitment to land-use decisions at the local level. President Nixon's proposed National Land Use Policy moves decisively in this new direction, and, while it is not likely to represent the final shape of federal policy, it suggests the broad direction such a policy will undoubtedly take.

A National Land-Use Policy. The purpose of the President's 1971 and 1972 proposals was to compel state governments to establish minimum land-use controls upon local governments by making these controls a condition of federal aid to the states. Using the federal dollar as the incentive, the President proposed that the states assume the responsibility for land-use decisions "having an impact beyond the local jurisdiction where the development decision is made." This would mean that coastal wetlands, historic sites, public facilities such as airports and recreation areas, and other environmentally significant areas would no longer be subject to local land-use practices. Further, the states would be expected to develop statewide land-use programs that identified critical land areas, established the priorities for use, and accomplished the division of responsibility for land use between state and local governments in a manner most consistent with good environmental practices. States failing to implement this comprehensive policy would be penalized by progressive cutbacks in federal moneys (reaching a 21 per cent reduction of funds at the maximum), which would be redistributed to other states cooperating in the program.

Neither the President's proposals nor the variations developed among several Congressional committees would have reduced local powers over land use so greatly as to remove most control from local governments. But the proposals all superimposed higher authorities and more comprehensive land-use perspectives upon local governments in making many environmentally critical decisions; the effect would have been to force local planners to abandon many policies that previously were equated with growth and produced undesirable environmental consequences.

In any event, the President's proposals are the beginning of what is sure to be a protracted, bitterly intense conflict over land-use policy. Since the whole growth psychology is involved in the conflict, it is understandable that the battle will take many years to resolve, if it can be resolved at all. For ecologists, there is at least hope in the fact that the battle has even been initiated.

A Dream Dying or Aborning?

"For each age is a dream that is dying/ or one that is coming to birth" insists the poet with his permitted license. If such be our age, do we sit closer to Year One of an environmental era or the end of a brief stirring, soon to lapse into insignificance?

Despite the grand Presidential proclamations of an "environmental era" and the flurry of new laws and agencies designed to make it a reality, the environmental movement remains fragile and vulnerable, so close to its inception and so unproved in its endurance as to remain an enigma. One has only to look at what environmentalists hope to accomplish, their "national environmental administration," to realize how difficult, costly, and formidable will be the struggle to bring the environmental movement into full political potency and to ensure its continuing power. What the environmental movement has produced in the political arena is a beginning—and hope. Perhaps, as one environmentalist has commented, we will need a major environmental tragedy every five years to awaken the public and its officials to their environmental responsibilities. Perhaps, on the other hand, we have actually begun a new era of environmental consciousness.

We may not again have the opportunity to begin with so many possibilities for environmental protection still open to us. If not to ourselves, we owe it to generations unborn, whose only voice and power are our own, to protect this Spaceship Earth, upon which, so far as we know, the only human life in the universe exists.

NOTES

1. Lynton K. Caldwell, *Environment* (Garden City, N.Y.: Anchor Books, 1971), p. 203.
2. Donald N. Michael, *The Unprepared Society* (New York: Harper & Row, 1968), p. 81.
3. Council on Environmental Quality, *Environmental Quality, 1972* (Washington, D.C.: Government Printing Office, 1972), p. 341.
4. Robert Rienow and Leona Train Rienow, *Moment in the Sun* (New York: Ballantine Books, 1967).

5. *New York Times,* September 23, 1971.
6. Miguel A. Ozerio de Almeida, "The Confrontation Between Problems of Development and Environment," *International Conciliation,* January, 1972, p. 40.
7. Quoted in *Bulletin of the Atomic Scientists,* September, 1972, p. 37.
8. *New York Times,* February 13, 1972.
9. Ozerio de Almeida, *op. cit.,* p. 54.
10. Council on Environmental Quality, *op. cit.,* p. 255.
11. *Ibid.,* p. 247.
12. Stewart L. Udall, "Limits: The Environmental Imperative of the 1970s," in Harold W. Helfrich, Jr., ed., *Agenda for Survival* (New Haven, Conn.: Yale University Press, 1971), p. 227.
13. Council on Environmental Quality, *op. cit.,* p. 265.
14. *New York Times,* February 9, 1972.
15. *New York Times,* September 31, 1972.

Index